New Revised
Gardening Indoors

I would like to express my sincere thanks to all of the wonderful gardeners that helped to make this book a reality. Many individuals, garden center employees and owners contributed information, photos an drawings. Thank you all for your help in making all *New Revised Gardening Indoors* the best book possible .

A special thanks toTom Alexander and *Growing Edge Magazine* for supplying us with much information, numerous drawings and photographs.

Published by Van Patten Publishing
Artwork: D. B. Turner, Connie Cohen, Hart James & *Growing Edge Magazine*
Book Design: G. F. Van Patten
Cover Photo: Courtesy American Hydroponics, Arcata, California
Back Cover Photo Courtesy Brew & Grow, Chicago, Illinois
Copyright 1995, George F. Van Patten
First Printing
9 8 7 6 5 4 3 2 1

This book is written for the purpose of supplying gardening information to the public. It is sold with the agreement that it does not offer any guarantee of plant growth or well-being. Readers of this book are responsible for all plants cultivated. You are encouraged to read any and all information available about indoor gardening and gardening in general to develop a complete background on the subjects so you can tailor this information to your individual needs. This book should be used as a general guide to gardening indoors and not the ultimate source.

The author and Van Patten Publishing have tried to the best of their ability to describe all of the most current methods to garden successfully indoors. However, there may be some mistakes in the text that the author and publisher were unable to detect. This book contains current information up to the date of publication.

The publisher nor the author endorse any products or brand names that are mentioned or pictured in the text. Products are pictured or mentioned for illustration only.

Table of Contents

Introduction

This book provides a simple, complete, how to description of basic gardening techniques used to grow foliage and pot plants, flowers and vegetables indoors today. Horticulture is the art and science of growing plants. High Intensity Discharge (HID) lamps have made indoor gardening grow by leaps and bounds. Today it is possible to grow large quantities of fresh tomatoes, cucumbers, succulents and all kinds of flowers in your own home all year round.

Many factors should be considered when gardening indoors. To have the best garden possible, you will need to monitor and control all environmental factors and understand the needs of your plants.

Rules of Thumb are given for a quick, easy reference. They are an easy-to-remember guide that is somewhere between an educated guess and a scientific formula. The Rules of Thumb give everyone a feel for the task or subject.

This book deals mainly with annual flowers and vegetables. We refer to these plants as annuals throughout the text. If the plants you are growing do not fit in this category, look up the specific growing conditions (temperature, humidity, light etc.) requirements in the "Plant Selection Guide" in Chapter Eleven.

Publications such as *Growing Edge, Practical Hydroponics, Houseplant, Organic Gardening, 21st Century Gardener, National Gardening, Horticulture, Fine Gardening, Flower & Garden, Sunset* and Harrowsmith Magazines and the gardening section of the local newspaper offer valuable background information on gardening. Reading such publications regularly will keep you updated on the newest trends in gardening.

SECTION I

The Indoor Environment

Chapter One
Indoor Gardening

The key to successful gardening is to understand how a plant produces food and grows. Plants have the same requirements for growth regardless of whether they are cultivated indoors or outdoors. Plants need six simple things to grow and flourish: light, air, water, nutrients, a growing medium and heat to manufacture food and to grow. Without any one of these essentials, the plant will die. Of course, the light must be of the proper spectrum and intensity, air must be warm and rich in carbon dioxide, water must be abundant and the growing medium must be warm and contain the proper levels of nutrients. When all these needs are met consistently, at the proper levels, optimum growth results.

Many flowers and vegetables are normally grown as annual plants, completing their life cycle in one year. A seed planted in the spring will grow strong and tall through the summer and flower in the fall, producing more seeds. The annual cycle starts all over again with the new seeds. Marigolds, zinnias, tomatoes and lettuce are just a few examples of annual plants.

Biennials are plants that normally complete their life cycle in two years. They bloom the year after seeds are planted and die after flow-ering and producing seed the second year. Examples of biennials include delphiniums, foxglove, parsley, Brussels sprouts and beets. If some biennials are planted early enough in the growing season, they are fooled into believing that two years have passed; will bloom and go to seed the same year.

Perennial plants live for more than two years. Many of the most common houseplants are leafy perennials that are valued more for their lush and interesting foliage than for their flowers. Examples of indoor foliage plants include fiddle leaf and Benjamin figs, false aralea, sansiveria, pothos, philodendrons and peperomias.

Flowering perennials that grow well indoors generally have interesting foliage, but may be a little more difficult to cultivate than indoor foliage plants. Examples of common flowering indoor plants include Christmas cactus, African violets, joya and many varieties of orchids.

Except for a few exceptions, plants all start their life from seed. Some seeds are very small such as the lettuce, tomato or celery seed while others are quite large such as pumpkin, corn or nut tree seeds. Many plants will reproduce by cuttings or pieces of their roots such as pota-

toes. We will not deal with many types of
propagation in this book, since the subject can
become so complex. We'll only look at starting
seeds and taking cuttings, the propagation
methods most common when gardening
indoors. See pages 167-171 "Starting Cuttings"
for more information.

Seeds are magic. Inside each seed are the
complete genetic instructions for a lifetime.
Plant breeding has blossomed in the past 50
years. In the last 20 years we have seen an
dynamic increase in the amount of seeds that
are available to the home gardener. Many small
seed companies have started, providing seed
from domestic breeders as well as Japanese and
European breeders. Many of the seed varieties
are acclimated to different geographic areas or
specifically designed to grow indoors and in
greenhouses. Before these seed companies, the
only seeds available commercially to home gardeners were the same seeds that domestic farm-
ers grew. Many companies offer vegetable,
flower and exotic seeds. Check with advertisers
in the back of the book or in garden magazines.

The seed has an outside coating to protect
the embryo plant and a supply of stored food
within. Given favorable conditions, including
moisture, heat and air, a healthy seed will usually germinate. The seed's coating splits, a
rootlet grows downward and a sprout with seed
leaves pushes upward in search of light. A
seedling is born!

The single root from the seed grows down
and branches out, similar to the way the stem
branches out above ground. Tiny rootlets draw
in water and nutrients (chemical substances
needed for life). Roots also serve to anchor a
plant in the ground. As the plant matures, the
roots take on specialized functions. The center
and old, mature portions contain a water transport system and may also store food. The tips
of the roots produce elongating cells that continue to push farther and farther into the soil in
quest of more water and food. The single-
celled root hairs are the parts of the root that
actually absorb water and nutrients, but must

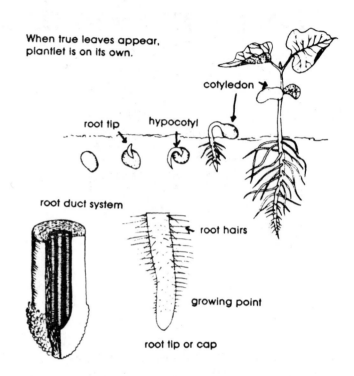

When true leaves appear plantlet is on its own.

be in the presence of oxygen. Without water
and oxygen these frail root hairs dry up and
die. They are very delicate and may easily be
damaged by light, air or careless hands if
moved or exposed. Extreme care must be exercised during transplanting to ensure success.

Like the roots, the stem grows through
elongation, also producing new buds along the
stem. The central or terminal bud carries
growth upward; side or lateral buds turn into
branches or leaves. The stem functions by
transmitting water and nutrients from the delicate root hairs to the growing buds leaves and
flowers. Sugars and starches manufactured in
the leaves are distributed through the plant via
the stem. This fluid flow takes place near the
surface of the stem. If the stem is bound too
tightly by string or other tie-downs, it will cut
the flow of life-giving fluids, thereby strangling
and killing the plant. The stem also supports

Stomata on leaf underside

the plant with stiff cellulose, located in the inner walls. Outdoors, rain and wind push a plant around, causing production of much stiff cellulose to keep the plant supported upright. Indoors, with no natural wind or rain present, stiff cellulose is minimal and plants may need to be staked up, especially during flowering.

Once the leaves expand, they start to manufacture food. Chlorophyll, the substance that gives plants their green color, converts carbon dioxide (CO_2) from the air, water, containing nutrients and light energy into carbohydrates and oxygen. This process is called photosynthesis. It requires water drawn up from the roots through the stem into the leaves where it encounters carbon dioxide. Tiny pores located on the underside of the leaf, called stomata (stomata can also be spelled: stomatae or stoma) funnel carbon dioxide into contact with the water. In order for photosynthesis to occur, the leaf's interior tissue must be kept moist. The stomata open and close to regulate the flow of moisture, preventing dehydration. Plant leaves are also protected from drying out by an outer skin. The stomata also permit the

outflow of water vapor and waste oxygen. The stomata are very important to the plant's well-being and must be kept clean at all times to promote vigorous growth. Dirty, clogged stomata breathe about as well as you would with a sack over your head!

Flowers and vegetables flower when conditions are right. Flowering is triggered by different stimulus in different plants. One of the main variables that triggers flowering is the length of nighttime or dark hours plants receive. Short-day plants will flower when daylight diminishes and nights grow longer. Plants in this category include poinsettias, Christmas cactus and chrysanthemums. In the fall, the days become shorter and plants are signaled that the annual life cycle is coming to an end. The plant's functions change. Leafy growth slows and flowers start to form.

The majority of long-day plants bloom according to chronological age. That is, when they are two or three months old they start to bloom. Flowers such as marigolds, petunias, pansies, cosmos, California poppies, zinnias etc. will continue to bloom once flowering starts. Long-day vegetables will set blossoms that soon drop when fruit forms in the wake of the flower. Many common vegetables such as tomatoes, peppers, egg plants, squash etc. fall into this category. Vegetables grown for their roots (carrots, potatoes, onions) generally bloom before the final underground produce is ripe. Leaf crops such as lettuce, spinach, parsley etc. are very productive indoors. The bulk of these crops are consumed and little concern about maturity is needed.

Blooming is triggered in other plants by temperature. Cilantro (coriander) for example will flower if the temperature raises above 85 degrees F. for a few days.

Many plants are hermaphroditic, dawning plants or flowers with both male and female parts.

Some plants have both male and female flowers. When both female and male flowers are in bloom, pollen from the male flower lands on the female flower, thereby fertilizing it. The male dies after producing and shedding as much pollen as possible. Seeds form and grow within the female flowers. As the seeds are maturing, the female plant slowly dies. The mature seeds then fall to the ground and germinate naturally or are collected for planting the next spring.

Indoor vs. Outdoor Gardening

Gardening indoors is very different from outdoor cultivation, even though all plants have standard requirements for growth. The critical factors of the outdoor environment must be totally recreated indoors if a plant is to grow well. Outdoors, a gardener can expend a minimum of effort and Mother Nature will control many of the growth-influencing factors. Indoors, the horticulturist assumes the cherished role of Mother Nature. The horticulturist is able to wield control over many factors influencing growth. Since few people have ever played Mother Nature before, they usually do not fathom the scope of the job. We must realize that Mother Nature constantly provides the many things plants require to grow. The indoor gardener must manufacture the most important elements of the outdoor environment. This requires a general knowledge of the environment about to be created as well as specific guidelines to follow.

Outdoor cultivation is normally limited to one growing season. However, two or more growing seasons are possible in semitropical and tropical climates. Outdoors, light can be inadequate, especially if it is midwinter and you live in a city or an apartment or both. Outdoor air is usually fresh, but can become uncontrollably humid, arid, cold or windy. Water and nutrients are usually easy to supply, but acid salts could keep the nutrients unavailable to the plants.

With indoor horticulture, light, air, temper-

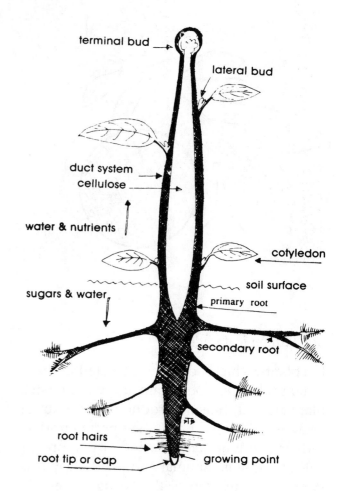

Workings of a plant

ature, humidity, ventilation, carbon dioxide, soil, water and nutrients may be precisely controlled to yield a perfect environment for plant growth.

Not long ago, with fluorescent tubes, this was not true. An inexpensive, easy-to-manage artificial light source, providing adequate intensity, was the main factor that limited growing many varieties of plants indoors.

Technological breakthroughs and scientific research have shed bright light on indoor horticulture, by producing the metal halide and high pressure (HP) sodium, High Intensity Discharge (HID) lamps. Now a reasonably priced artificial light source, providing the color

Healthy cauliflower is just forming under a super metal halide.

spectrum and intensity necessary to grow any plant imaginable, is on the market. With the HID lamp, a gardener can totally control the indoor environment. The high pressure sodium lamp can be used in conjunction with a halide or in a greenhouse to augment the sun. Conversion bulbs that burn a HP sodium arc tube in a metal halide system are also available. The HP sodium emits a light spectrum similar to the autumn or harvest sun, providing the intense yellows oranges and reds necessary for forming large flowers. When an HP sodium lamp is used, flowers grow 20 to 100 percent larger than if only a single metal halide were used. By using a timer, a regular day-night schedule (photoperiod) can be set up. The HID, with a timer, may be even better than the sun! Exact control can be exercised over the hours of light per day. This control of day length lets the horticulturist create his or her own seasons. Spring and summer and fall are recreated over and over, winter is forgotten and virtually non-existent to the indoor horticulturist!

In climates where the season is "long" (eight or nine months) a much larger selection of flowers and vegetables can be cultivated.

Gardeners living in northern climates can grow tomatoes in containers outdoors until the weather cools, then move them under the halide in the basement for a complete winter crop.

Halides are also used very effectively to get an early start on annuals and vegetables. Since HID's are so bright, the little plantlets get a very strong start in life. This strong, early start is carried on throughout life.

Flowers and vegetables can also be grown in a greenhouse. The HP sodium lamp works extremely well to provide supplemental light to natural sunlight. Young seedlings get an early start with more hours of light per day. Fruit and flowers that mature late can be forced to produce sooner. All of the extra hours of intense light will make them think it is midsummer!

Outdoors, seeds are normally sown in the spring, mature and bear fruit and flowers in the summer.

Indoors, all growth factors may be individually controlled to give the plant exactly what it needs to promote any stage of growth.

The air outdoors is usually fresh and contains 03. to .04 percent carbon dioxide. Ventilation is usually adequate, but the wind sometimes howls, burning leaves or even blowing plants over. Humidity and temperature are almost impossible to control.

Indoors, air may easily be controlled to promote growth and create an unfriendly environment for bugs and fungus. The carbon dioxide content may be enriched to double or triple plant growth. An open door and forced-air ventilation system will provide circulation and ventilation necessary to keep air fresh. Humidity is raised by misting the air with water or letting water evaporate from a bucket. Humidity is lowered by drying the air with heat from the HID system, heater, furnace or dehumidifier. Circulation, ventilation, humidity and temperature regulation are also fundamental to insect and fungus control. Cuttings root much faster in a warm, humid indoor environment. Temperature is easy to keep constant. Usually heat from the HID system provides ample heat for the garden room. An indoor garden will flourish between 70 and 75⁰ F (21 and 24⁰ C), but most cuttings root best at 80 to 85⁰ F (27 to 30⁰ C). Air temperature may be raised with extra heat and lowered by means of an exhaust fan attached to a thermostat, if outside air is cooler.

Outdoor soil may vary greatly. It could be too acidic or alkaline, have toxic qualities, drain poorly, be full of harmful insects, fungus and bad micro-organisms.

Indoor growing mediums can be purchased from a nursery in the form of potting soil or soilless mix. These growing mediums are generally certified free of fungus, insects and weeds. The mediums normally have the proper acid-to-alkaline or pH balance. Potting soils usually contain complete, balanced nutrients, while soilless mixes may or may not be fortified with nutrients. Nutrient levels may easily be checked in these growing mediums. Nutrients may then be added or leached (washed) out of containers, providing total soil control. The moisture content of the growing medium can be precisely monitored with a moisture meter and controlled. Potting soil and soilless mixes are blended to retain water evenly, provide good aeration and consistent root growth.

Outdoors, insects and fungi are usually kept in check by Mother Nature. Indoors, the gardener must take over in Mother Nature's absence. Keep the insects out of the garden room by simple sanitary precautions. It is easy to wash your hands, use clean tools and sweep the floor regularly. If insects and fungus do get started, they are easy to control in an enclosed room, since the gardener controls the factors that inhibit their well-being. Organic or chemical sprays are used in conjunction with humidity, ventilation and temperature regulation to control the pests.

In summary, indoor gardening can be far superior to outdoor cultivation for many gar-

deners, especially in northern climates. It provides exacting control of all growth-inducing factors. The indoor garden yields vine ripened produce, beautiful fragrant flowers and exotic plants the year round!

About Garden Rooms

The best location for a garden room is an unused corner of the basement. The basement is probably the best room in most homes for indoor gardens, since the temperature is easy to keep constant the year round. Humidity that would destroy the rest of the house can be easily managed in the plant room. The unsightly pots, soil and flats do not have to be shared with the public. The room is well insulated by concrete walls and soil. Basements also remain cool, which helps prevent heat build up.

The size of the garden room and the light intensity required by plants grown determine the wattage of lamp used. A 400-watt lamp are just fine for smaller rooms, spaces from 10 to 40 square feet of floor space. A 1000-watt bulb should be employed for a garden room of 40 to 100 square feet.

The drawings on page 18 show several common garden room floor plans. As the drawings of rooms demonstrate, there are several basic approaches to garden room production. The climate you create in the garden room depends on the plants that are grown.

A second method is very similar to the first, but utilizes two rooms. The first room is for vegetative growth, rooting cuttings and growing seedlings. Since plants are small, the room is about a third to half the size of the flowering room. The flowering room is harvested and the vegetative crop is moved into the flowering room. A crop of cuttings is transplanted into large pots to start the vegetative cycle.

A third method provides a perpetual crop.

Several clones are taken each day or two. An equal same amount of plants are moved from the vegetative room to the flowering room. Of course the harvest is essentially perpetual!

About Greenhouses

Greenhouses or growing environments using natural and artificial lighting are very productive. The same principles can be applied to both the indoor garden room and the greenhouse. However the heat and light intensity might be substantially different.

When combined with natural sunlight, artificial light is most optimally used during non-daylight hours. Greenhouse growers turn the HID lights on when sunlight diminishes and off when sunlight strengthens.

Turn the HID on when the daylight intensity is less than two times the intensity of the HID. Measure this point with a light meter.

Turn the HID off when the daylight intensity is greater than two times the intensity of the HID.

Rule of Thumb: Turn the HID "on" in the greenhouse at sunset and "off" at sunrise.

Supplementary lighting has greatest effect when applied to the youngest plants. It is least expensive to light plants when they are small. This should be considered when budgets are concerned.

One greenhouse is double-glazed on the south, east and west walls and insulated with a reflective interior on the north side.

Developed in England, this cool-weather structure is called the Northern Light Greenhouse. Available from Gardeners Supply, 128 Intervale Road, Burlington, VT 05401.

Setting Up The Garden Room

Before any plants are introduced, the garden room should be set up. Construction requires space and planning. There are a few things that need to be accomplished before the room is ready for plants.

Step One: Choose an out-of-the-way space with little or no traffic. A dark corner in the basement is perfect. Make sure the room is the right size. A 1000-watt HID, properly set up, will efficiently illuminate up to a 10-by-10-foot room if a "light mover" is used. The ceiling should be at least 5 feet high. Remember, plants are set up about one foot off the ground in containers and the lamp needs about a foot of space to hang from the ceiling. This leaves only three feet of space for plants to grow. However, if forced to grow in an area with a low 4-foot ceiling, much can be done to compensate for the loss of height, including, bending and pruning.

Step Two: Enclose the room, if it's not already enclosed. Remove everything not having to do with the garden. Furniture and especially drapes or curtains harbor many a fine fungus. Having the room totally enclosed will permit easy, precise control of everything and everyone that enters and exits and who and what goes on inside. For most gardeners, enclosing the garden room is simply a matter of tacking up some sheet rock in the basement or attic and painting it flat white.

Step Three: See: "Setting Up the Vent Fan" pages: 124-126. Constant circulation and a supply of fresh air are essential. There should be at least one fresh-air vent in a 10-by-10-foot room, preferably two. The fresh air vent may be an open door, window or heat vent. Most gardeners have found that a small exhaust fan, vented outdoors, pulling new fresh air through an open door will create an ideal air flow. A small oscillating fan works well for circulation. When installing such a fan, make sure it is not set in a fixed position, blowing too hard on tender plants. It could cause windburn or in the case if young seedlings and clones, dry them out. If the room contains a heat vent, it may be opened to supply extra heat or air circulation.

Step Four: The larger your garden gets, the more water it will need. A 10-by-10-foot garden may need as much as 30 gallons a week. You may carry water in, one container at a time. One gallon of water weighs 8 pounds. It is much easier to install a hose with an on/off valve or install a hose bib in the room. A 3 to 4-foot watering wand can be attached to the hose on/off valve. The wand will save many broken branches when watering in dense foliage. Hook the hose up to a hot and cold water source, so the water temperature can be regulated easily.

Step Five: Cover walls, ceiling, floor, everything, with a highly reflective material such as flat white paint (pages 42-47). The more reflection, the more light energy that is available to plants. Good reflective light will allow effective coverage of a 1000-watt HID lamp to increase from 36 square feet, with no reflective material, to a maximum of 100 square feet, just by putting $10 to $20 worth of paint on the walls.

Step Six: A concrete floor or a smooth surface that can be swept and washed down is ideal. A floor drain is also very handy. In garden rooms with carpet or wood floors, a large, white, painter's dropcloth or thick white visqueen plastic, will save floors from moisture drainage. A tray can also be placed beneath each container for added protection and convenience.

A vent fan and an oscillating circulation fan are necessary for adequate ventilation and circulation in a garden room.

Step Seven: Mount a hook, strong enough to support 30 pounds, in the center of the growing area to be serviced by the lamp. Attach an adjustable chain or cord and pulley between the ceiling hook and the lamp fixture. The adjustable cord makes it easy to keep the lamp at the proper distance from the growing plants and up out of the way when maintaining them.

CAUTION! A hot HID may break if touched by a few drops of cold water. Be very careful and make sure to move the HID out of the way when servicing the garden.

Step Eight: There are some tools an indoor gardener must have and a few extra tools that make indoor horticulture much more precise and cost-effective. The extra tools help the horticulturist play Mother Nature and make the garden so efficient that they pay for themselves quickly. Purchase all the tools or hunt them up around the house before the plants are moved into the room. If the tools are available when needed, chances are they will be used. A good example is a hygrometer. If plants show signs of slow, sickly growth due to high humidity, most gardeners will not notice the exact cause right away. They will wait and guess, wait and guess and maybe figure it out before a fungus attacks and the plant dies. When a hygrometer is installed before the plants are in the garden room, the horticulturist will know from the start when the humidity is too high and causing sickly growth. The majority of long-day plants bloom according to chronological age. That is, when they are two or three months old they start to bloom. Flowers such as marigolds, petunias, pansies, cosmos, California poppies, zinnias etc. will continue to bloom once flowering starts. Long-day vegetables will set blossoms that soon drop when fruit forms in the wake of the lower. Many common vegetables such as tomatoes, peppers, egg plants, squash etc. fall into this category. Vegetables grown for their roots (carrots, potatoes, onions) generally bloom before the final underground produce is ripe. Leaf crops such as lettuce, spinach, parsley etc. are very productive indoors. The bulk of these crops are consumed and little concern about maturity is needed.

Step Nine: Read and complete: "Setting Up the HID Lamp" at the end of Chapter Two.

Step Ten: Move in the seedlings or rooted clones into the room. Huddle them closely together under the lamp. Make sure the HID is not so close to the small plants that it burns their leaves. Usually seedlings require the lamp to be at least 24 inches away.

PLASTIC DROP CLOTH

Necessary Tools	**Extra Tools**
Thermometer	pH & soil test kit
Spray bottle	Hygrometer
Pruner or scissors	Wire (bread sack) ties
Notebook	Merasuring cup & spoons
Yardstick (to measure growth)	Moisture meter

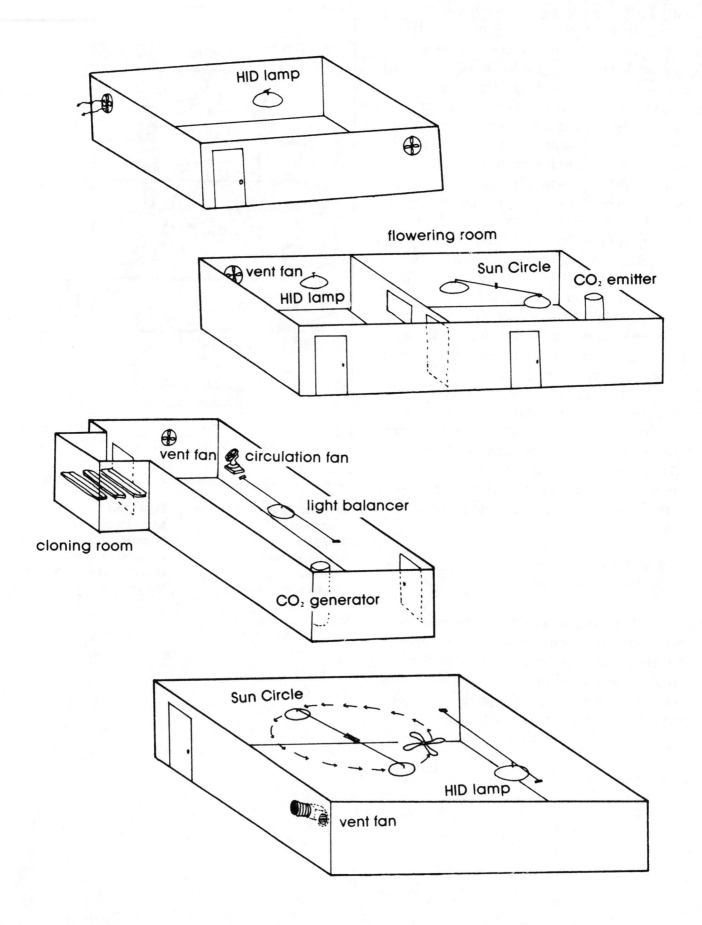

HID lamp

flowering room

vent fan

HID lamp

Sun Circle

CO₂ emitter

vent fan

circulation fan

light balancer

cloning room

CO₂ generator

Sun Circle

HID lamp

vent fan

Chapter Two
Light, Lamps and Electricity

Light is one of the major factors that contribute to plant growth. Indoors, light has been, until recent years, the main limiting factor to growing more than a small indoor garden of limited plant varieties. By understanding how a plant uses light, the indoor horticulturist can use the technology provided by the High Intensity Discharge (HID) lamps to fulfill light requirements and grow spectacular gardens. The subject of light as used by plants can become very complex. This book will look at the basic ways light affects plant growth.

A plant combines light energy with carbon dioxide (CO_2), water and nutrients to form green chlorophyll and carbohydrates, releasing oxygen as a by-product. Without light, a plant will not be able to produce green chlorophyll leaves soon turn yellow and eventually death results. With the proper spectrum and intensity of light, chlorophyll is rapidly produced and growth is rapid.

Outdoors, the sun usually supplies enough light for rapid growth. The sun also supplies much light that plants do not use. Scientists have found that plants need and use only certain portions of the light spectrum. The most important colors in the spectrum for maximum chlorophyll production and photosynthetic response are in the blue (445 nm) and red (650 nm) range. ("nm" = nanometers. One nm = 000001. meter.) Light is measured in wavelengths, the wavelengths are divided into nm.

Phototropism is the movement of a plant part (foliage) toward illumination. Positive tropism means the foliage moves toward the light.

Negative tropism means the plant part moves away from the light. Positive tropism is greatest in the blue end of the spectrum at about 450 nm. At this optimum level, plants lean toward the light, spreading their leaves out horizontally to absorb the most light possible.

The photoperiod is the relationship between the length of the light period and dark period. The photoperiod affects the life cycle of all plants. Short-day plants will stay in the vegetative growth stage as long as a photoperiod of 18 to 24 hours light is maintained. Sixteen to 24 hours of light per day will give short day plants all the light they need to sustain optimum seedling and vegetative growth. The plants will think it is the longest and sunniest day (June 22) every day of the year. Many plants can use 16 to 18 hours of light in a 24-hour period before a point of diminishing returns is reached. The light has a minimal effect on growth after 16 to 18 hours.

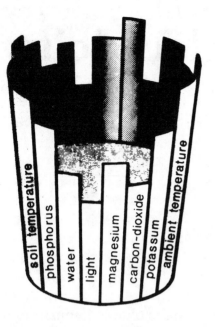

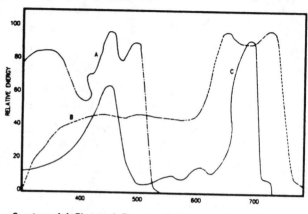

Spectrum of A. Phototropic Response, B. Photosynthetic Response, C. Chlorophyll Synthsis

A plant will only grow as fast as the least available factor will allow.

Greatest efficiency is obtained by adding supplemental light to a greenhouse crop after the sun goes down. The HID lights are not as bright as the sun and should not compete with the sun. Plants can also reach a maximum saturation point. The extra light they receive does not increase growth in relation to the amount of light shed. After this point of diminishing returns is reached, additional light has only a minimal effect. If this supplemental light is added during dark periods or on very cloudy days, plants get the entire benefit of the supplemental lighting. Many experiments have proven that adding supplemental light during the dark hours is 50 to 100 percent more productive than adding more light during sunlight hours.

Flowering is induced most efficiently in short-day plants with 12 to 14 hours of uninterrupted darkness in a 24-hour photoperiod. It is possible to gradually decrease the daylight hours while increasing dark hours to simulate the natural photoperiod. This practice follows the natural photoperiod but flowering is delayed for several weeks.

Light spectrum - photosynthetic response chart

Optimum flowering potential is reached when the 12-hour photoperiod is coupled with high levels of intense light from the red end of the spectrum. After short-day plants are two to 12 months old, altering the photoperiod to an even 12 hours, day and night, will induce flowering in two to four weeks. The 12-hour photoperiod represents the classic equinox and is the optimum daylight-to-dark relationship for flowering. For most of the plants that fall in this category, less than 12 hours of light will not induce flowering any faster and can substantially reduce flower formation and yield.

More than 12 hours of light will prolong flowering; visible signs of flower formation take much longer.

The photoperiod can also be the signal to stay in (or revert to) vegetative growth. Short-day plants must have 12 hours of uninterrupted, total darkness to flower properly. Tests have shown that even dim light during the dark period in the pre-flowering and flowering stages will prevent short-day plants from blooming. Chrysanthemums, for example, are forced to bloom at various times of the year by interrupting their nighttime with a few 10-to-30 minute bursts of bright light.

When the 12-hour dark period is interrupted by light, the plant gets confused by the light's signal saying, "It's daytime, start vegetative growth." The plant will try to revert to vegetative growth and flowering seems to take forever. Make sure to keep flowering short-day plants in total darkness no midnight visits or lit-up open doorways! Too many hours of light per day is the main reason gardeners can not get their Christmas cactus or poinsettias to bloom every year.

Gardeners growing tropical plants (orchids or bromeliads) from equatorial regions give their gardens 12 hours of light throughout the life cycle. They want to replicate the less dynamic photoperiod of the tropics. On the equator, days and nights are almost exactly the same length the year round. When this method is used, plants tend to bloom when they are chronologically ready, after thoroughly completing the vegetative growth stage.

The average house plant is "night neutral" since it will grow and bloom well with six to eight hours of darkness. These plants require 14 to 16 hours of daylight. Examples of these "night neutral" plants include most gesneraids, oxalis, Exacum affine, many begonias and most house plants.

Chrysanthemums, poinsettias, species columnea orchids and some begonias, Christmas cactus and related plants will bloom only if given a long night of 14 to 16 hours and less than eight to 10 hours of light per day.

Summer-blooming plants and vegetables need 18 hours of light per day and a short night of six hours. Geraniums, annuals, tuberous begonias and seedlings of almost all plants are in this category. In fact, African violets will double their blossom production if they are given 18 hours of light rather than 12 hours.

Foliage plants are raised for green foliage flowers are not important. These plants can have varying amounts of light and dark and growth is not affected. Examples are rex begonias, aroids, palms, marantas and ferns.

Intensity

HID's are incredibly bright! It is this brightness that makes them so useful. However, this intense light must be properly managed. Intensity is the magnitude of light energy per unit of area. It is greatest near the source of the light and diminishes with distance from the source. The drawing below demonstrates how rapidly light intensity diminishes. Plants that are 4 feet away from the lamp, get a fourth as much light as plants one foot away! The closer plants are to the light source, the better they grow. Six inches to 12 inches is a safe distance for plants to be from the lamp (tender seedlings require 24 inches to 36 inches). Any closer and plants run the risk of growing so fast that they run into the hot bulb, burning tender growing tips.

A 1000-watt standard metal halide emits 100,000 initial lumens and 88,000 mean (average) lumens - super halides emit 125,000 initial lumens and 100,000 mean lumens. The HP sodium emits a whopping 140,000 initial lumens! The indoor horticulturist is interested in how much light is *emitted* by the HID, as well as how much light is *received* by the plants. Light that is received is measured by the "Light and Distance Chart" or in watts-per-square-foot or in foot-candles (f.c.). One foot-candle equals the amount of light that falls on one square foot of surface located one foot away from one candle. One lumen is equal to the amount of light emitted by one candle that falls on one square foot of surface one foot away.

Watts-per-square feet is easy to calculate, but not very accurate. It measures how many watts are available from a light source in a given area. For example, a 1000-watt HID will emit an average of 10 watts-per-square foot in a 10-by-10-foot room. The mounting height of the

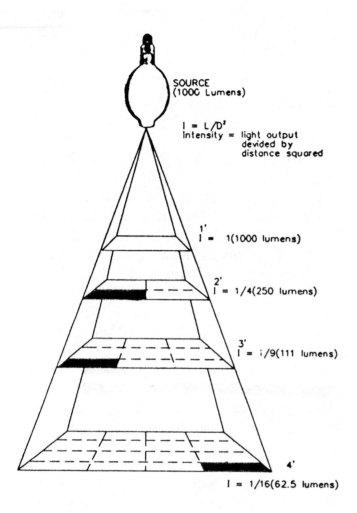

SOURCE
(1000 Lumens)

$I = L/D^2$
Intensity = light output
devided by
distance squared

1'
$I = 1$(1000 lumens)

2'
$I = 1/4$(250 lumens)

3'
$I = 1/9$(111 lumens)

4'
$I = 1/16$(62.5 lumens)

lamp is not considered in watts-per-square foot the lamp could be mounted at any height, from 4 to 8 feet.

Calculating foot-candles is the most accurate way to estimate the amount of light plants receive. Foot-candles can be measured with a light meter. The meter can measure in foot-candles, miliwatts-per-square-meter or lumens. A photographic light meter, either hand-held or built into a camera can also be used. The foot-candle meter is simply pointed at the light source or reflective surface at any location and a read-out in foot-candles is given.

When using a photographic light meter, set the ASA (film speed) at 200 and the shutter speed at 1/125 second. Focus the camera on a rigid white sheet of paper in the proposed plant location. Hold the paper so it gets maximum

illumination. Get close enough so all the camera or light meter sees is the white paper. Adjust the camera lens aperture (f stop) until a correct exposure registers on the light meter. Use the following chart to calculate foot-candles (f.c.).

f4	64 f.c.
f5.6	125 f.c.
f8	250 f.c.
f11	500 f.c.
f16	1000 f.c.
f22	2000 f.c.

Almost all the resent light research in relation to plants that is available was done by European scientists or scientists and expressed in watts-per-square-meter or miliwatts-per-square-meter. You will need to convert foot-candles to watts-per-square-meter to get the most out of this chapter. Please notice that each lamp and natural sunlight have different conversion factors. The conversion factors are found in the chart below.

Conversion Chart

Formula:
One: Multiply the foot-candle reading by the conversion factor for the light source. Look at the "Conversion Factors Chart" below to obtain the number of watts-per-square-meter.
Two: For mixed lighting (using multiple sources) determine the watts per square meter level for each light source and add the readings for the total.

Examples:
One: A site has 100 foot-candles of daylight and 100 foot-candles of HP sodium light.
Daylight: 100 X 0.055 = 5.5 watts-per-square-meter
HP sodium light: 100 X 0.034 = 3.4 watts-per-square-meter

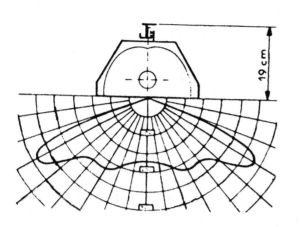

This drawing shows the light distribution curve for the PL-780, a Dutch 400 watt horizontal HP sodium lamp.

Total: 5.5 = 3.4 = 8.9 watts-per-square-meter
Two: A garden room has 100 foot-candles of HP sodium light and 100 foot-candles of metal halide light.
HP sodium light: 100 X 0.034 = 3.4 watts per square meter
Metal halide light: 100 X 0.34 = 3.4 watts per square meter
Total: 3.4 = 3.4 = 6.8 watts per square meter

Plants are too close to the lights when they are (sun) bleached or have curled or stunted leaves. Move plants demonstrating these symptoms farther away from the lamp. Plants that require more light should be set up closer to the lamp. Use a stand or overturned container to set them on.

Try this simple test with a light meter. You will see how rapidly light intensity diminishes.

One of the best ways to demonstrate how light intensity can retard a harvest is found in an outdoor vegetable garden. Have you ever planted 65-day broccoli that took 100 days to mature? Think about it. Did the plants get full sun all day long? It is assumed that the seeds

An inexpensive light meter will help you get the most out of your lamp.

were planted at the peak of the season and perfect temperatures prevailed. Plants that got less light matured slowly and produced less than ones getting full sun all day long.

 Rule of Thumb: Plants with high light requirements but receive less intense or filtered light will yield less and mature later.

Conversion Factors Chart

Light Source	Conversion factor
Daylight	0.055
HP sodium lamp	0.034
LP sodium lamp	0.022
Metal halide lamp	0.034
Cool white fluorescent	0.030
Warm white fluorescent	0.30
Fluorescent grow lamps	0.044
Incandescent lamps	0.090

Determines watts-per-square-meter for various light sources

Light Requirement Categories for All Plants

Milliwatts per square meter (mWm^2) is the irradiance produced by one-thousandth of a watt of light energy beamed into a surface of one square meter.

3,000 mWm^2: Lighting after flower induction (forcing) during the latter part of cultivation growing long-day plants, giving a little growth stimulation as well.

4,500 mWm^2: Cultivation of vegetables, flowers (for produce and flowers) through harvest young spaced vegetative plants.

6,000 mWm^2: For rooting and young plants while still packed under the HID high light vegetables, flowers (for produce and flowers) plants.

7,500 mWm^2: Rooting some nursery stock and some high-light plants.

9,000 mWm^2: Expensive plants fast and programmed crops special cases. Producing this much supplemental light in a room is very expensive.

The U.S. Department of Agriculture will provide data to help determine the amount of light (radiant energy or flux) various plants need to fulfill their light requirements in different stages of their life.

When combined with natural sunlight, artificial light is optimally used during non-daylight hours. Greenhouse growers turn the HID lights on when the point of diminishing returns is reached. The time to turn on or off the HID is when daylight reaches twice the intensity of the HID.

For Example: Turn the HID on when the daylight intensity is less than twice the intensity of the HID. Measure this point with a light meter. A photo cell can also be used to turn one or several HID's on and off when this point is reached.

Turn the HID off when the daylight intensity is greater than twice the intensity of the HID.

 Rule of Thumb: Turn HID's in a greenhouse "on" at sunset and "off" at sunrise.

Supplementary lighting has the most dynamic effect when applied to the youngest plants. It is least expensive to light plants when they are small, a very important consideration when budgets are concerned.

Spacing

Ideally plants should be spaced under lamps so that they do not touch one another. This provides for more air movement and allow enough growing space for each plant. Proper spacing also allows more even light saturation.

Bedding plants are given a level of 6,000 mWm^2 for 16 to 18 hours a day. This extra light gives the little plants a big jump on the season outdoors. The intense light also keeps many plants blooming all year long indoors.

When light intensity is too low, plants s-t-r-e-t-c-h for it. Low light intensity is often caused by the lamp being too far away. When the plant is too far away, branches usually form farther apart on the stem than if the lamp were close to plants. By keeping the lamp as close as possible, leggyness is kept to a minimum.

When light shines on a garden, the leaves near the top of plants get more intense light than the leaves at the bottom. The top leaves shade the bottom leaves, absorbing light energy, making less light energy available to lower leaves. If the lower leaves do not receive enough light, they yellow and die. But, do not pick off perfectly good leaves so lower foliage gets more light! Tall 6-to-8 foot plants take longer to grow and yield more overall than shorter 4-foot plants, but the yield of flowers and foliage is about the same. The taller plants have large flowers on the top 3 to 4 feet and spindly buds near the bottom, due to lack of light. Tall plants tend to develop flower tops so heavy that the stem cannot support the weight and they need to be tied up. Short plants support the weight of the tops better and flowers weigh more overall than leaves.

Annual flowers and vegetables should not be over waist-high before fruit and flowers set. Due to their high light requirements, these plants do not respond very well to weak light.

Several hundred two-week-old seedlings or clones may be huddled directly under a single HID. The young plants will need more space as they grow. Plants that are packed too close together sense the shortage of space and do not grow to their maximum potential. Leaves from one plant that shade another plant's leaves slow its development. It is very important to space young plants just far enough apart that their leaves do not touch. This will keep shading to a minimum and growth to a maximum. Check and alter the spacing every few days. Eight to 16 mature tomato plants will completely fill the space under one 1000-watt HID.

The stadium method is a very good way to get the most from an uneven garden profile. Tall plants go on the perimeter, while shorter plants crowd toward the center of the garden. The intensity of light all the plants receive is about the same and tall plants do not shade shorter plants. See drawing below.

 Rule of Thumb: Keep the HID 6 to 12 inches above garden. Tender clones, seedlings and transplants require 24 to 36 inches. For other than fast-growing annuals, consult the "Plant Selection Guide" in Chapter Eleven.

The HID Lamp Family

Incandescent lamps create light by passing electricity through a very fine wire or filament. HID lamps make light by passing electricity through vaporized gas under high pressure. Fluorescent and low-pressure (LP) sodium lamps create light by passing electricity through gaseous vapor under low pressure.

The stadium method places the tallest plants on the perimeter of the garden.

The chart on page 26 shows various lamps with their lumen-per-watt conversion. This formula is used to measure the lamp's efficiency: the amount of lumens (light) produced in relation to the amount of watts (electricity) consumed. Note the high lumen-per-watt conversion of the halides and sodiums.

All the HID lamps work on the same principle, passing or do arcing electricity through gas or vapor, rather than using a tungsten filament, as household incandescent bulbs. The gas is inside a heat-resistant glass or ceramic arc tube, sealed under high pressure. The materials contained in the arc tube dictate the colors or spectrum the lamp will produce, except for the effect of the phosphor coating. Passing electricity through vaporized elements is a simple principle, but putting it into action requires a little technology.

HID lamps all work on the same principles however, their starting requirements, line voltage, operating characteristics and physical shape are unique to each lamp.

CAUTION! Do not try to mix and match ballasts with lamps!

Lumens-per-watt = Lumens/Watts

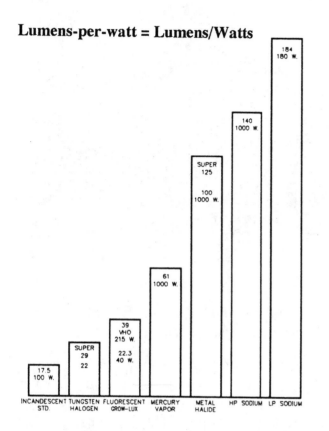

The efficiency of the LP sodium lamp is mislead-ing, because the largest wattage available is 180. One thousand watt HP sodium lamps are avail-able and with a -lumen-per-watt conversion of 140, the HP sodium is clearly the most efficient.

Just because a lamp fits a socket attached to a ballast does not mean that it will work properly in it. The wrong lamp plugged into the wrong ballast adds up to a burned out lamp!

Rule of Thumb: Buy the entire HID sys-tem - ballast, lamp, socket, bulb and timer - all at the same time from a rep-utable supplier to ensure that the ballast and lamp belong together. Make sure to get a written guarantee from the dealer. The system should carry a complete guarantee for at least one year.

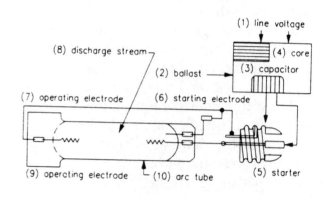

The electricity or line voltage (1) flows through the ballast (2). The ballast is the box that contains a capacitor (3) that provides a high, fast charge of electricity to start the lamps. Getting the electricity to flow between the electrodes (7) and (9) in the arc tube (10) requires a high-voltage charge or current. This current is sent through the starting mechanism of the lamp (5). In HP sodium lamps, the starting electrode and the operating electrode are one and the same.

The electricity is then arced or shot across the arc tube (10) from the starting electrode (6) to the operating electrode (9) at the other end of the arc tube. As soon as the arc is estab-lished and the gases vaporize, the arc jumps from the starting electrode to the operating electrodes (7) and (9). Once the electricity is flowing across the tube, the elements slowly vaporize into the discharge stream (8).

When the discharge stream (8) is working and the lamp warms up, the line voltage could run out of control, since there is an unrestrict-ed flow of electricity between the two elec-trodes. The ballast (2) regulates this line volt-age with a transformer, a wire coil wrapped around an iron core (4). By employing this core (4) the lamp is assured of having a con-stant and even supply of electricity

About Ballasts

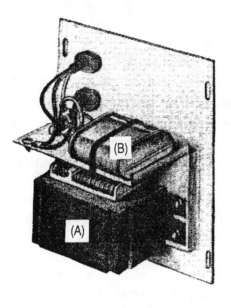

The metal ballast consists of (A) the transformer and (B) the capacitor

120 volt - 208 volt
240 volt - 277 volt

A multi-tap ballast can be used as 110 or 220 volts. Single-tap ballasts must be either 110 volts or 220 volts.

All HID's require a ballast. It is very important to buy the proper ballast for your HID. If possible, buy the assembled unit from a specialized retailer that advertises in *Growing Edge Magazine* and in this book. Electrical supply and greenhouse supply stores also carry HID's. Buy component parts if you are low on capital and want to assemble the system yourself. However, you are not assured of saving any money.

Ballast components are manufactured by Advance, Jefferson, Sola and General Electric. Assembly instructions are in the form of a wiring diagram glued to the side of the transformer. The components consist of a transformer core, cooling capacitor, containing box and wire. Capacitor manufacturers are Cornell, General Electric, Duviler and Dayton. If you are not familiar with electrical component assembly and reading wiring diagrams, purchase the assembled ballast in a package containing the lamp and hood from one of the many HID distributors or retailers.

Do not buy used parts from a junk yard or try to use a ballast if unsure of its capacity. The fact that a bulb fits a socket attached to a bal-

last does not mean all of the components are compatible. The best way to grow a miserable garden is to try to save money on the ballast.

Even though HID's have specific ballasting requirements, the ballasts have a good deal in common. The transformer consists of thin metal plates that are laminated together with a sticky, tar-like resin. This transformer core is then wrapped with wire. When operated at excessive temperatures or with poor ventilation, the resin becomes thin and the metal plates will begin to vibrate or hum super loud. This steady hum can be unnerving.

Ballasts are manufactured with a protective metal box. This outer shell safely contains the core, capacitor and wiring. Always use ballasts with all the wiring and necessary parts enclosed. Never use a ballast with exposed electrical connectors. Never build another box around a ballast. It will cause excessive heat and may even start a fire!

Ballasts operate at 90 to 150⁰ F (65⁰ C). Touch a "strike-anywhere" kitchen match to the side of the outer box to check if it is too hot. If the match lights, the ballast is too hot. It should be taken into the shop for repair before

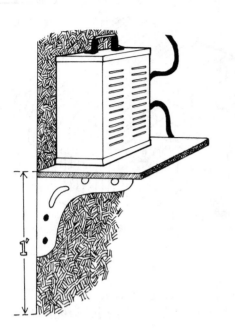

This ballast is set up off the floor on a shelf to prevent excess water from leaking in the bottom.

it creates an accident or burns out. Heat is the number one ballast destroyer!

Make sure the ballast has a handle on it. A small 400-watt halide ballast weighs about 30 pounds and a large 1000-watt HP sodium ballast tips the scales at about 55 pounds. This small, heavy box is very awkward to move with no handle.

Most ballasts at retail stores are set up for the 110-volt current found in all homes. Some may be ready for 220-volt service. It is usually easiest to use the regular 110-volt system because the outlets are more common. The 220-volt systems are normally used when several lamps are already taking up space on other 110-volt circuits. Changing all ballasts (except for Jefferson, which are manufactured either 110 or 220 volts and are not able to change) from 110 to 220 is a simple matter of moving one internal wire from the 110-volt brad to the 220 (208)-volt brad and changing the plug to a 220 type. Consult the wiring diagram in each ballast for specific instructions.

There is no difference in the electricity consumed by using either 110- or 220-volt systems. The 110-volt system draws about 9.5 amperes and an HID on a 220-volt current draws about 4.3 amperes. Both use the same amount of electricity! "Ohm's Power Law: Volts X Amperes = Watts.

A cooling fan is not necessary unless there are many ballasts in a small room and ventilation is inadequate. Air vents allow a ballast to run cooler. The vents should protect the internal parts and not be prone to letting water splash in.

Some industrial ballasts are sealed in fiberglass or a similar material to make them weatherproof. These ballasts are not recommended. They were designed for use outdoors where heat buildup is not a problem. Indoors, protecting the sealed unit from weather is not necessary and could create excessive heat.

Ballasts that are 220-volts can be looped together. Up to four ballasts may be wired in a series circuit on a 220 volt, 30 ampere circuit. This is the most efficient way to use HID ballasts. There is less resistance for electricity when ballasts are wired in series. Less electricity is lost in transmission. I advise that only electricians try this relatively simple procedure. There is a lot more current flowing with more ballasts and grounding requirements increase. Any competent electrician should be able to loop ballasts together.

The ballast has a lot of electricity flowing through it. Do not place the ballast directly on a damp floor or any floor that could get wet. Always place it up off the floor and protect it from possible moisture. The ballast should be suspended in the air or set on a shelf attached to the wall. It does not have to be very high, just far enough to keep it off a wet floor.

Ballast can be either remote or attached to the lamp. The remote ballast is the best for most indoor gardens. It can be moved easily. Placed near the floor, it can be used to radiate heat in a cool portion of the garden room. Place it outside if the room is too hot. Attached ballasts are fixed to the hood, require more overhead space, are very heavy and create more heat around the lamp.

A good ballast manufacturer will place a 10-ampere fuse inside the ballast. This is a double safeguard against electrical mishaps that destroy the lamp or cause a fire.

CAUTION! Do not touch the ballast when it is operating.

High Intensity Discharge Lamps

Artificial light from the High Intensity Discharge (HID) lamp family can be used to stimulate growth responses induced in plants by natural sunlight. This may be seen by comparing charts on HID spectral emission (pages 32 and 36) with the "Light Spectrum Chart" (page 20).

Popular HID wattages include 150, 175, 250, 400 and 1000. The 1000-watt system costs about 30 percent more than the 400-watt system, but is more efficient in its -lumen-per-watt conversion and produces more than twice as much light. By employing a light mover, uniform light distribution is no longer a problem. The smaller 400-watt systems are great for a space that is 2- to 6-feet square or a small greenhouse. The smaller 400-watt HID's are similar to the larger 1000-watt systems, only smaller. They produce less light and heat. Their color spectrum is almost identical to those of their big, 1000-watt brothers.

Mercury Vapor Lamps

The mercury vapor lamp is the oldest and best-known member of the HID family. The HID principle was first used with the mercury vapor lamp around the turn of the century. But it was not until the mid-1930's that the mercury vapor lamp was really employed commer-

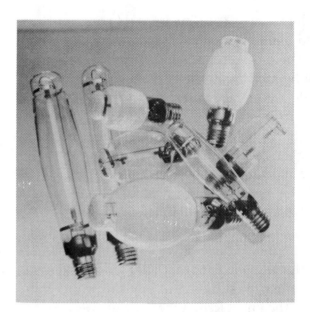

Metal halide lamps have shapely bulbous curves, while HP sodium lamps are more tubular in shape.

The lettering on the dome of the Sylvania 400 watt metal halide bulb lists a "C" for phosphor coated and "BU" for base up. The Westinghouse MS 1000/C/BU lamp is a super 1000-watt metal

cially on a large scale.

As the "Lumen-per-watt Chart" shows (page 26), the mercury vapor lamps produce only 60 lumens-per-watt. The spectral energy distribution of the mercury vapor does not fulfill the light requirements outlined by the "Photosynthetic Response Chart" (page 20). The mercury vapor is a poor lamp for horticulture. Not only is it expensive to operate, but it produces most color in areas that are not helpful to plant growth.

The old mercury vapor lamps produce light by arcing electricity through mercury and a little argon gas is used for starting. They come in sizes from 40 to 1000-watts. They have fairly good lumen maintenance and a relatively long life. Most wattages last up to three years at 18-hour daily operation.

The mercury vapor usually requires a separate ballast however, there are a few low wattage bulbs that have self-contained ballast.

People who use or try to modify these ballasts for use with another HID have all kinds of problems and still have to buy the proper ballast in the end. Remember, trying to save money on a ballast usually costs more in produce that was not realized.

In summary, the mercury vapor lamp produces a color spectrum that is not as efficient as the halide or HP sodium for indoor cultivation. It is not the lamp to use if you want any kind of garden at all! Gardeners who have used them paid more for electricity and their gardens yielded much less.

Metal Halide Lamps

The metal halide HID lamp is the most efficient source of artificial white light available to the horticulturist today. It comes in 175, 250, 400, 1000 and 1500-watt sizes. They may be either clear or phosphor-coated and all require a special ballast. The 1500-watt halide is avoided due to its relatively short (2000 to 3000 hours) life and incredible heat output. Most gardeners prefer the 1000-watt halide and those with small growing areas or low-light greenhouses the 400-watt.

Three major metal halide manufacturers are General Electric (Multivapor), Sylvania (Metalarc) and Phillips/Westinghouse (Metal Halide). Each manufacturer has a super version of the halide. The Super Metalarc, the High-Output Multivapor and The Super Metal

Metal halides are either clear or phosphor coated.

Halide fit the standard halide ballast and fixture. They produce about 25 percent more lumens than the standard halides. These super halides cost about $10 more than the standard, but are well worth the extra money.

The clear halides are the most commonly used by gardeners. The clear bulb offers the brightest white light available. It supplies the most lumens of the best possible spectrum for plant growth. The clear halide works well for seedling, vegetative and flower growth.

Phosphor-coated 1000-watt halides emit more diffused light. They are easy on the eyes, emitting less ultraviolet light than clear halides. They produce the same initial lumens and about 4,000 fewer lumens than the standard halide and have a slightly different color spectrum. Phosphor-coated halides emit more yellows, less blue and less ultraviolet light. Some gardeners prefer the diffused light of the phosphor-coated halide to the HP sodium saying it is the best all-round bulb.

The 1000-watt super clear and super phosphor-coated halides are the most common halides used indoors. Compare energy distrib-

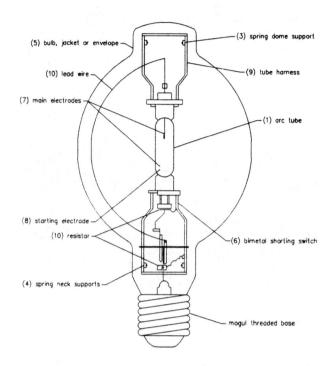

Diagram of a metal halide lamp.

ution charts and the lumen output of all three lamps to decide which lamp offers the most desirable characteristics for your garden. Typically, the home gardener starts with the 1000-watt Super Metalarc (Sylvania), High-Output Multivapor (G.E.) or Super Metal Halide (Westinghouse).

Construction and Operation

Metal halide lamps produce light by passing or arcing electricity through vaporized argon gas, mercury, thorium iodide, sodium iodide and scandium iodide within the quartz arc tube(1).

At the end of the arc tube is a heat reflecting coating (2) to control temperature during operation. Spring supports in the neck (4) and dome (3) of the outer bulb or envelope (5) mount the arc tube frame (9) in place. The bimetal shorting switch (6) closes during lamp

Burning positions of BU metal halide lamps. Metal halide "HOR" lamps can be burned in a horizontal position.

operation, preventing voltage drop between the main electrode (7) and the starting electrode (8). Most bulbs are equipped with a resistor (10) that keeps the bulb from shattering under temperature stress. The outer bulb functions as a protective jacket. It contains the arc tubing starting mechanism, keeping them in a constant environment as well as absorbing ultraviolet radiation. Protective goggles that filter out ultraviolet rays are a good idea if you spend much time in the garden room.

The five halogens include the elements fluorine, chlorine, bromine, iodine and astatine.

Initial vaporization takes place in the gap between the main electrode (7) and the starting

CAUTION! If outer bulb shatters, turn off (unplug) the lamp immediately. Do not look at or get near the lamp until it cools down. When the outer bulb breaks, it is no longer able to absorb ultraviolet radiation. This radiation is very harmful and will burn skin and eyes if exposed. Be careful!

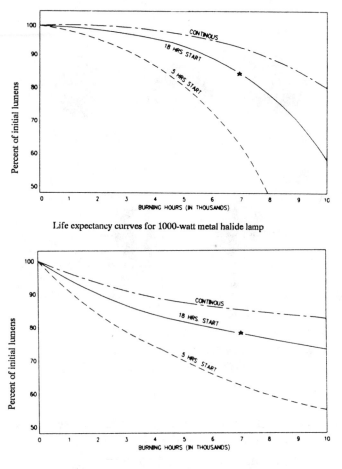

Life expectancy curves for 1000-watt metal halide lamp

Appropiate Lumen Maintenance of 1000-watt HP sodium lamp.

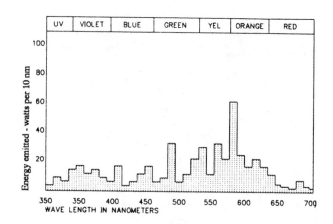

Energy distribution of 1000-watt phosphor coated metal halide

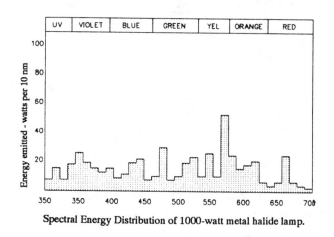

Spectral Energy Distribution of 1000-watt metal halide lamp.

Successful gardeners change the bulb before it burns out. This is about every 12 to 18 months or 6,500 hours. This ensures maximum light intensity.

electrode (8) when a high starting voltage is applied. When there is enough ionization, electricity will arc between the main electrodes (7). As the lamp warms up, the metal iodide additives begin to enter the arc stream. After they are in their proper concentrations in the arc tube, the characteristic bright white light is emitted. This process takes about 3 to 5 minutes.

Note: The metal halide arc system is very complex and requires a seasoning period of 100 hours operation for all of its components to stabilize. At first the colors produced by the bulb may vary, but once, the system is seasoned, clear white light appears.

If a power surge occurs and the lamp goes out or if the lamp is turned off, it will take 5 to 15 minutes for the lamp to restart. The gases inside the arc tube must cool before restarting. If the lamp is on a timer, it will restart automatically. There is no need to turn the timer on or off manually.

When the lamp is started, incredible voltage is necessary for the initial ionization process to take place. Turning the lamp on and off more than once a day causes unnecessary stress on the HID system and will shorten its life.

Metal halides have very good lumen maintenance and a long life. The decline in lumen output over the lamp's life is very gradual. The average life of a halide is about 12,000 hours - almost two years of daily operation at 18 hours.

Many will last even longer. The lamp has reached the end of its life when it fails to start or come up to full brilliance. This is usually caused by deterioration of lamp electrodes over time, loss of transmission of the arc tube from blackening or shifts in the chemical balance of the metals in the arc tube. I do not advise waiting until the bulb is burned out before changing it. An old bulb is inefficient and costly. Replace bulbs about every 12 to 18 months or 6,500 hours. Electrode deterioration is greatest during starting and is usually the reason for the end of lamp life. Do not start the halide more than once a day and use a timer!

The halide may produce a stroboscopic (flashing) effect. The light will appear bright, then dim, bright, dim, etc. This flashing is the result of the arc being extinguished 120 times every second. Illumination usually remains constant, but it may pulsate a little. This is normal and nothing to worry about.

Metal halides operate most efficiently in a vertical +/- 15^0 position (see Diagram A). When operated in positions other than +/- 15^0 of vertical, lamp wattage, lumen output and life will decrease the arc bends, creating non-uniform heating of the arc tube wall. The result is less efficient operation and shorter life.

Metal Halide Ballasts

Read "About Ballasts" pages 27-29. The ballast for a 1000-watt halide will operate standard, clear or phosphor-coated or super, clear and phosphor-coated halides on a 110- or 220-volt current. The bulbs can be either "BU" or "HOR". A different ballast is required for 400-watt halides it will operate all 400-watt halides: super or standard, "BU" or "HOR", clear or phosphor-coated.

The ballasts must be specifically designed for the 400- or 1000-watt halides, since their starting and operating requirements are unique.

HP sodium bulbs are the brightest available and operate in any position, 360^0.

High Pressure Sodium Lamps

The most impressive fact about the 1000-watt high pressure sodium vapor lamp is that it produces 140,000 initial lumens. That's one brilliant light! The HP sodium is also the most efficient HID lamp available.

It is available in 35, 50, 70, 100, 150, 200, 250, 310, 400 and 1000 wattages. All, may be either clear or phosphor-coated, except the 200- and 1000-watt bulbs (which are available only clear). All HP sodium vapor lamps have their own unique ballast. HP sodium lamps are manufactured by G.E. (Lucalox), Sylvania (Lumalux) and Westinghouse (Ceramalux). The Ceramalux has a color-corrected spectrum. It produces a little more blue than other HP sodiums. Iwasaki produces a very high quality HP sodium bulb. In fact, the Iwasaki bulbs are known by most gardeners as the top of the line. They produce more blue light than most other HP sodium lamps. The SON AGRO lamp manufactured by Phillips produces 30 percent more blue light than their Sun-T-Agro lamp. This HP

SON AGRO Lamp from Phillips

The newest innovation in HID lighting for horticulture is the SON AGRO lamp from Phillips. The SON AGRO improves improves production and quality of plant material. This new innovative HP sodium lamp is the only one that radiates light that resembles natural sunlight.

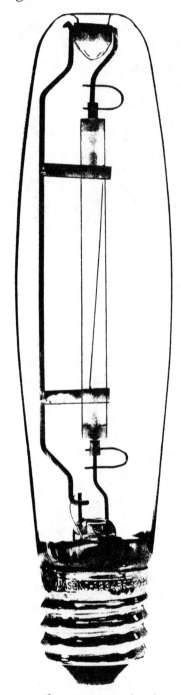

Many gardeners use only the 430-watt SON AGRO lamp.

The metal halide has been until now the only lamp that was able to supply the blue and red light that completes the spectrum which is necessary for plant growth. If you grow indoors exclusively with HID light, a combination of metal halide and HP sodium light was necessary. This is no longer the case with the introduction of the SON AGRO.

At the beginning of this chapter we learned that the majority of light used by plants is from the red end of the spectrum; but blue light is also necessary for plant growth. Along with other factors such as temperature, humidity, and nutrition, the blue light prevents unnatural stem elongation.

The 430-watt SON AGRO fits into the standard 400-watt HP sodium socket and runs with the same ballast, capacitor and ignitor. No new ballast is necessary! Simply unscrew your current HP sodium lamp and screw in the SON AGRO lamp into the same socket. That is all there is to installing the SON AGRO lamp!

Since the SON AGRO has 30 more watts than the standard HP sodium lamp, it generates 6 percent more light for the same amount of electricity used!

The SON AGRO produces 30 percent more blue light than the standard 400 watt HP sodium. The prodiction of blue light is what makes the SON AGRO so effective. This extra 30 percent blue light is just enough more to make a huge difference in plant growth.

Much research has been done on the SON AGRO lamp at the Agricultural University of Wageninegen in the Netherlands. Tests at the university compared the SON AGRO with the standard HP sodium lamp.

The tests showed that the SON AGRO consistently produced stronger flower stems. Roses produced more flowers and chrysanthemums grew more flowers and were consistently heavier.

sodium lamp was developed specifically for Dutch greenhouse growers that use lights.

Most gardeners find the best value is with the 1000-watt HP sodium rather than the 400-watt.

The HP sodium lamp emits an orange-like glow that is sometimes compared to that of the harvest sun. The color spectrum is highest in the yellow orange and red end. These colors promote flower production and stem elongation.

Light from the red end of the spectrum stimulates floral hormones within the plant, promoting more flower production. When using an HP sodium lamp, flower volume and weight may increase by 20 percent or more, depending on variety of seed and growing conditions. Many gardeners, using a 10-by-10-foot room, will retain the 1000-watt halide and add a 1000-watt sodium during flowering. This not only more than doubles available light, but increases the red end of the spectrum, causing flowers to form and grow like crazy. This 1:1 ratio (one halide and one HP sodium) is a popular combination for flowering. But many growers report the same or better results using only HP sodium lamps.

The HP sodium is the only practical lamp to use in a greenhouse. Since the sun provides all the blue light necessary, the HP sodium is used during low-light hours and during total darkness.

Construction and Operation

The HP sodium lamp produces light by passing electricity through vaporized sodium and mercury within an arc tube (1). A small quantity of xenon gas, used for starting, is also included in the arc tube.

The HP sodium lamp is totally different from the metal halide in its physical, electrical and color spectrum characteristics. An electronic starter works with the magnetic component of the ballast to supply a short, high-volt-

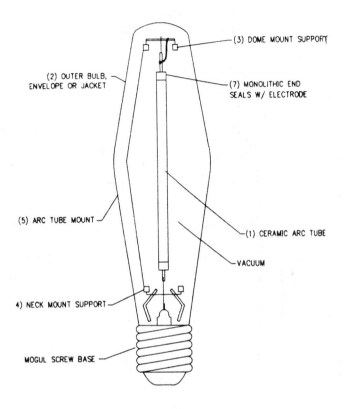

Diagram of a high pressure (HP) sodium lamp.

age pulse. This electrical pulse vaporizes the xenon gas and initiates the starting process, which takes 3 to 4 minutes. Electricity passes or arcs between the two main (electrodes 6) and (7). If the lamp is turned off or power surge occurs and the lamp goes out, the gases in the tube will usually need to cool 3 to 15 minutes before restarting is possible. As with the metal halides, if the HP sodium is on a timer, it will restart automatically.

Like the metal halide, the HP sodium has a two bulb construction, with an outer protective bulb (2) and inner arc tube(1). The 'arc tubes frame (5) is mounted by spring supports in the dome (3) and neck (4). The outer bulb or jacket protects the arc tube from damage and con-

LIFE AND LUMEN MAINTENANCE

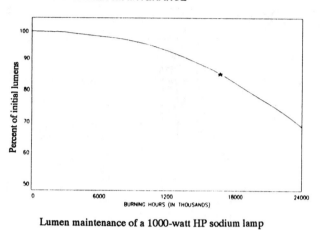

Lumen maintenance of a 1000-watt HP sodium lamp

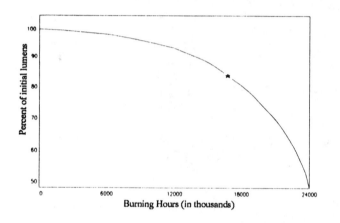

Mortality curves of a 1000-watt HP sodium lamp show a long lamp life. For best results, change the HP Sodium bulb after 15,000 hours of operation.

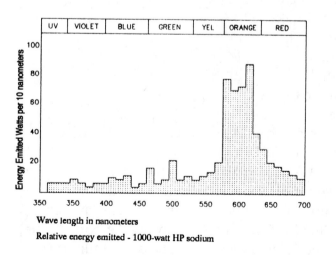

Wave length in nanometers

Relative energy emitted - 1000-watt HP sodium

tains a vacuum, reducing heat loss from the arc tube. The sodium, mercury and xenon gas are contained within the arc tube and have a constant operating temperature and the lamp may be operated in any position (360°). However, most growers prefer to hang the lamp overhead in a vertical operating position.

Life and lumen maintenance

HP sodium lamps have the longest life and best lumen maintenance of all HID lamps. Eventually the sodium bleeds out through the arc tube over a long period of daily use, the ratio of sodium to mercury changes, causing the voltage in the arc to rise. Finally the 'arc tubes operating voltage will rise higher than the ballast is able to sustain. At this point, the lamp will start, warm up to full intensity, then go out. This sequence is then repeated over and over, signaling the end of the lamp's life. The life of a 1000-watt HP sodium lamp will be about 24,000 hours or five years operating at 12 hours a day. As with other HID's, HP sodiums should be replaced before the end of their rated life.

HP Sodium Ballasts

Read "About Ballasts," pages 27-29. A special ballast is required specifically for the 400- or 1000-watt HP sodium lamp. The lamp has unique operating voltages and currents during start up and operation. These voltages and currents do not correspond to similar wattages of other HID lamps. As with the halide ballast, to save money and time I recommend purchasing it from an HID lamp store rather than in a component kit.

Never remove a warm lamp. The heat makes them expand in the socket. A hot bulb is more difficult to remove and must be forced. Vaseline or a special electrical lubricant may be smeared lightly (it takes only a dash) around the mogul socket base to facilitate screwing it in and out.

Always keep the bulb clean. Wait for it to cool and wipe it off every 2-4 weeks with a clean cloth. Dirt will lower lumen output.

Store HID's that are not being used in the same box they came in.

HID bulbs are tough and durable. They survive being shipped many miles by uncaring carriers. Once the bulb has been used a few hours, the arc tube blackens and the internal parts become somewhat brittle. After a bulb has been used several hundred hours, a good bump will substantially shorten its life and lessen its luminescence.

Conversion Bulbs

Conversion bulbs are available for metal halide ballasts. The conversion bulb operates on a metal halide system, but produces a light spectrum very similar to the HP sodium bulb. The outer bulb looks like a metal halide. The internal arc tube is very similar to that of a HP sodium. A small starter (ignighter) is located at the base of the arc tube.

The bulbs are available in either 360-watt or 940-watt sizes. The 360-watt conversion bulb operates on a 400-watt metal halide system. The 940-watt conversion bulb runs on a 1000-watt metal halide system. Since the bulb operates at a lower wattage, it is not quite as bright as a HP sodium bulb. runs at The price of the conversion bulbs is slowly becoming affordable. The price of a conversion bulb is more economical than buying a complete HP sodium system. The conversion bulb offers an excellent value to gardeners that only have one metal halide system.

Fluorescent Lamps

Until HID's were developed, fluorescent light was the most efficient and widely used

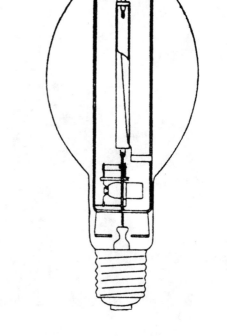

Conversion bulbs convert a metal halide system into a HP sodium system.

Disposing of an HID Lamp.
Please read the following rules of disposal before laying a faithful HID to rest:

One: Break the lamp outdoors in a container. Hit it a couple of inches from the base with a hard object. Take care to avoid shattering glass, as the bulbs are under vacuum.

Two: The lamps contain materials that are harmful to the skin, so contact should be avoided and protective clothing should be used.

Three: Once the lamp is broken, place it in a plastic bag, then throw it away.

Four: Under no conditions place the bulb in a fire.

This orchid grower uses fluorescent lamps to help illuminate her greenhouse.

form of artificial light available to the indoor gardener. Some fluorescent lamps boast a spectrum almost identical to that of the sun, but they are not bright enough to grow high-light plants efficiently.

Today, these lamps are most efficiently used as a light source to root cuttings and grow low-light plants. Fluorescent lamps are manufactured in long glass tubes or circle-line tubes and illuminate in many commercial and residential buildings. They are available in a wide variety of sizes: lengths of 18 inches, 24, 36, 48, 72 and 96 inches and standard circline-tube diameters of 8, 14, 12 and 16 inches. Longer tubes are better to use than short ones since there is a light loss at the ends of tubes. The 4-foot and 8-foot tubes and the easiest to handle and most readily available. However, 8-foot tubes are easily damaged in shipping. Buy 8-foot tubes at a retail store rather than via mail order.

Fluorescent tubes are available in several wattages or outputs. Ballasts also operate at different wattages. Both tubes and ballasts are made by several companies. The standard or regular tubes use about 10 watts per linear foot. A 4-foot tube uses about 40 watts, 8-foot, 80 watts, etc. High-Output (HO) tubes use about 50 percent more watts-per-linear-foot and emit about 40 percent more light than the standard. These fluorescents require a special ballast and end caps. Very High Output (VHO) use almost three times as much electricity and produce more than twice as much light as the standard fluorescent. VHO fluorescents are more expensive and more difficult to find. VHO tubes also require a special ballast. They can be ordered from the manufacturer or purchased from the wholesaler.

Fluorescent lamps are an excellent light source to root cuttings. They supply cool, diffused light in the proper color spectrum to promote root growth. The VHO tubes are more expensive, but are preferred for their high lumen output. None-the-less, if low on capital, a gardener may use any fluorescent lamp to root cuttings. The only drawback to using the less luminous standard or HO fluorescents is that cuttings may take a few days longer to root. Fluorescents, like HID's, diminish in intensity with distance from the light source. Since fluorescents produce much less light than HID's, they must be very close 2 to 4 inches to the plants for best results.

In many cases, as when there are many plant varieties and ages of plants under a fluorescent, it is easier to retain the lamp at one overhead level. Move the plants closer to the lamp by placing them on a block to elevate then.

A few gardeners hang extra fluorescent lamps with HID's to increase light intensity. I have found fluorescent lamps to be most efficient to grow seedlings, root cuttings and growing low-light plants. Fluorescent tubes are most effective when mounted above plants if they are the only source of light. When tubes are placed vertically around plants, they do not promote straight, even growth. If used with bright halides, fluorescents can be used as side lighting for lower leaves, but it is a difficult job to mount the fluorescent fixtures close enough to the plants to do any good. Fluorescent fixtures can also shade plants from HID light and generally get in the way.

Fluorescent lamps have a wide variety of spectrums. Sylvania makes the Gro-Lux and the Wide Spectrum Gro-Lux. The Standard Gro-Lux is the lamp to use for starting clones or seedlings. It is designed to be used as the only source of light, having the full spectrum necessary for photosynthesis and chlorophyll production. The Wide Spectrum Gro-Lux is designed to supplement natural light and covers the blue to far red regions. Westinghouse makes the Agro-Light, which produces a very similar spectrum to the sun. Warm White and Cool White bulbs used together, make excellent lamps to root clones.

Power Twist or Power Groove lamps offer additional lumens in the same amount of linear space. The deep, wide grooves in the tube give more glass surface area and more light output.

Fluorescent bulbs and fixtures are relatively inexpensive. Two, 4-foot bulbs and a fixture will usually cost from $20 to $30. Clones root best with 18 hours of fluorescent light.

Side mount reflectors have a partition between the light tubes. This partition eliminates light loss that occurs when the tubes are side by side. The side mount fixtures offer the best value. If you unable to buy fixtures with this partition, you can easily construct one from stiff white paper and tape it to the fixture.

Construction and Operation

Like the HID family, fluorescent lamps require an appropriate fixture, containing a ballast (much smaller than the HID ballast) and the ordinary 110-or 120-volt house current. The fixture is usually integrated into the reflective hood. There are several types of fixtures.

Light spectrum charts of various fluorescent lamps.

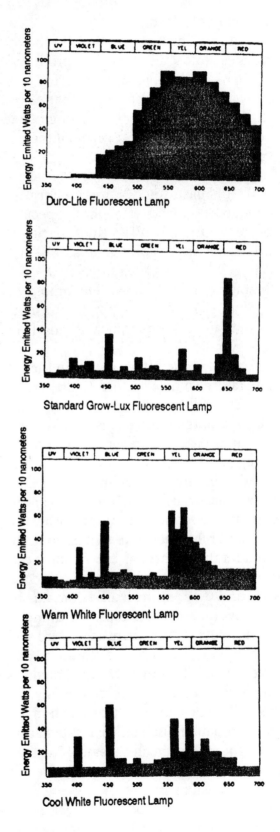

Duro-Lite Fluorescent Lamp

Standard Grow-Lux Fluorescent Lamp

Warm White Fluorescent Lamp

Cool White Fluorescent Lamp

Some have one pin on each end others are two pin types. If purchasing new tubes, make sure the bulb fits the fixture. The fixture may contain one, two or four tubes.

The ballast, which is contained in the fixture, radiates almost all of the heat produced by the system. The ballast is located far enough away from standard tubes that plants can actually touch them without being burned. VHO tubes may burn tender plants if they get too close.

The ballast or transformer regulates electricity. Most ballasts and fixtures are for use with standard 40- or 80-watt tubes. Special ballasts are required for VHO fluorescent tubes. The operating requirements of VHO lamps are greater, due to the increase in current, than for standard fluorescent lamps. I advise ordering the VHO ballast, fixture and tubes at the same time as a package and from a reputable supplier.

The ballast reduces the current in the tube to the operating voltage required by a particular lamp. The ballast will normally last 10 to 12 years. Used fluorescent fixtures (unlike used mercury vapor ballasts) are generally acceptable. The end of life is usually accompanied by smoke and a disagreeable chemical odor. When the ballast burns out, remove it (or take the entire fixture to the nearest electrical supply store) and buy a new one to replace it. Be very careful if the ballast has brown slime or sludge on or around it. This sludge could possibly contain PCB's. If the ballast contains the sludge, throw it away at an approved dump site. Most modern fluorescent lamps are self-starting, but older fluorescents require a special starter. This starter may be integrated into the body of the fixture and hidden from view or be a small metal tube (about an inch in diameter and half an inch long), located at the end of the fixture on the underside. The latter starters are replaceable the former require a trip to the electrical store.

If the ballast creates too much heat, remove it from the fixture and place it in a remote loca-

tion. Just splice the wires. Secure the remote ballast away from water and excessive heat to prevent damage. Most electrical supply stores are able to test starters. If your fluorescent fixture does not work and you are not well versed in fluorescent troubleshooting, take it to the nearest electric store to ask for advice. Make sure they test each component and tell you why it should be replaced.

The tubular fluorescent glass bulb is coated on the inside with phosphor. The mix of phosphorescent chemicals in the coating and the gases contained within determine the spectrum of colors emitted by the lamp. The bulb contains a blend of inert gases: argon, neon or krypton and mercury vapor, sealed under low pressure.

Electricity arcs between the two electrodes, located at each end of the tube, stimulating the phosphor to emit light. The light emission is strongest near the center of the tube and somewhat less at the ends. If rooting just a few cuttings, place them under the center of the fixture for best results.

Once the fluorescent is turned on, it will take a few seconds for the bulb to warm up before an arc can be struck through the tube. Fluorescent lamps blacken with age, losing intensity. I recommend replacing bulbs when they reach 70 percent of their stated service life listed on the package or label. A flickering light is about to burn out and should be replaced.

Life expectancy ranges from 9,000 hours (a little more than a year at 18 hours daily operation) with VHO tubes to 18,000 hours (2 1/2 years at 18 hours daily operation) with the standard tubes.

Change fluorescent lamps every 9 to 12 months. Use a grease pencil to mark the date that you install any light. Mark the bulb or fixture near the end or base.

Other Lamps

Incandescent Lamps

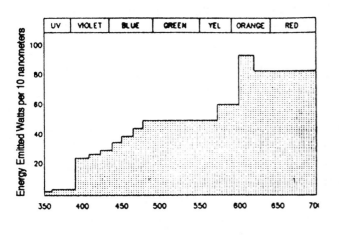

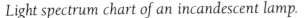

Light spectrum chart of an incandescent lamp.

The incandescent lamp is the electric lamp invented by Thomas Edison. Light is produced by sending electricity through the filament, a very fine wire inside the bulb. The filament resists the flow of electricity, heating it to incandescence (causing it to glow). Incandescent bulbs work on ordinary household current and require no ballast. Filaments may be of many shapes and sizes, but are nearly always made of tough, heat-resistant tungsten. They come in a wide range of wattages and constructions for special applications. Most lamps used in homes for Christmas trees, interior lighting and refrigerators are incandescent lamps.

There are many types of incandescent lamps. They usually use a tungsten filament with a glass bulb construction and threaded base that fits household sockets. The bulb is usually under a vacuum or contains some type of gas to minimize wear on the filament.

Most incandescents have a spectrum in the far red end, but there are some incandescent grow lamps that have a more balanced spectrum. Incandescent lamps are expensive to operate and produce so few lumens-per-watt

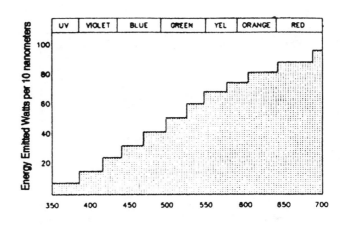

Light spectrum chart of a tungsten halogen lamp.

that they are not worth using. They are most efficiently used as a source of bottom or soil heat for clones rooting under cool fluorescent. A few gardeners use incandescents during flowering to help promote more and heavier flowers.

Tungsten Halogen Lamps

The tungsten halogen lamp was originally called the iodine quartz lamp. The outer tube is made of heat-resistant quartz and the main gas inside the quartz tube was iodine, one of the five halogens

There are several variations of the quartz halogen or quartz tungsten lamp. Today bromine, also one of the halogens, is used most often in the lamps, so the name halogen covers all of the gases in the arc tube. Tungsten lamps are very similar to incandescents. They electricity flows through a tungsten wire filament sealed in bulb. They are very expensive to operate. Their lumen-per-watt output is very low. Tungsten halogens, like incandescents, run on 110-volt current and require no ballast. They are as inefficient to operate as incandescents (See "Lumen-per-watt Chart", page 26). Their color spectrum is in the far red end. Only 10 to 15 percent is in the visible spectrum.

LP Sodium Lamps

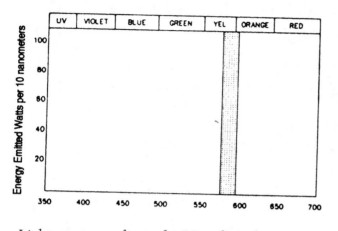

Light spectrum chart of a LP sodium lamp.

Low-Pressure (LP) sodium lamps are available in 55, 90, 135 and 180 wattages. Their - lumen-per-watt conversion is the highest of all lamps on the market today. More careful inspection of the color spectrum chart above shows that it is monochromatic or produces light only in one very narrow portion of the spectrum, at 589 nanometers (nm). The LP sodium lamp emits a yellow glow. Colors are not distinguished and appear as tones.

LP sodium lamps are supplied by Phillips/Westinghouse. Their main use has been for security, street and warehouse lighting.

Each wattage requires its own unique ballast and fixture. The ballast or transformer regulates electric current and is located inside the fixture. The fixture for a 180 watt lamp is just a little larger than a fixture for two 40 watt 4-foot fluorescent tubes.

Phillips/Westinghouse is the only supplier of LP sodium lamps. The ballast and fixture for a LP sodium system costs about $200. As with other lamps, I advise purchasing the lamp, ballast and fixture from a reputable supplier together in the same package.

The LP sodium must be used with a metal halide lamp to stimulate photosynthesis and chlorophyll synthesis. LP sodium lamps work well for side lighting or in areas with high electrical rates.

This lamp has the unique quality of maintaining 100 percent of its lumen output throughout its life. There is no gradual decrease in the lumen output over time as with other discharge lamps. The LP sodium lamp will burn out all at once, at about 18,000 hours.

The basic design of the LP sodium lamp is essentially the same as it was when first introduced to the market in 1932. Like HID lamps, the LP sodium has a two-bulb construction. The arc tube is made of lime borate glass and contains a mixture of neon, argon and pure sodium metal. The neon and argon begin to glow after electricity enters the arc tube.

As the gas mixture gives off increasing amounts of heat, the sodium metal, which is still in the solid form, begins to vaporize. A yellowish glow is soon emitted from the vaporized sodium.

Fixtures can be lightweight plastic due to low outside bulb temperatures. The LP sodium lamp conserves energy by keeping heat inside the lamp. A special reflective coating on the outer tube allows light to pass outward while heat remains inside. A vacuum is formed between the outer and inner tubes, retaining even more heat.

To ensure long life of the lamp, it should be operated horizontally. Do not let it operate at more than 20 percent +/- off horizontal.

Pure sodium metal will react with air or water and explode. There is about one gram of sodium in a 180 watt LP sodium lamp - not enough to cause a big explosion, but enough to warrant careful handling. When disposing of an LP sodium bulb, place it in a dry, plastic garbage can and break it.

Reflective Light

Reflective light also increases light intensity by as much as 30 percent. A large white 4-foot reflective hood over the lamp and flat white walls will triple the growing area.

EXAMPLE: Using a 1000-watt super metal halide with a small, 2-foot hood and no reflective walls and ceiling, the effective growing area is only 36 square feet. When a large 4-foot white reflective hood and flat white walls and ceiling are added, effective growing area is increased to 100 square feet.

Reflective hoods come in all shapes and sizes. The main features to look for in a hood are the size, the reflective ability and the specific application. Parabolic dome reflectors work very well. The light has a good chance to spread out and not be reflected around within the walls of the hood. These hoods are very popular because they are inexpensive and provide the maximum amount of reflection for the least amount of money.

Artificial light fades fast. The farther away from the light source (bulb), the less light available. This is the most critical factor when using artificial light.

The farther the light travels from the source, the less intense it is. If this light must be reflected, the closer the reflector is to the bulb, the more intense the light will be when it is reflected. For example, If the reflector is one foot from the bulb, the light that is reflected will be four times more intense than if the reflector were two feet away. Look at the "Light and Distance Chart" on page 22.

To prove all these simple premises, we constructed a black room to measure light. The room is of simple design. It is 10' X 10' square and the walls are painted flat black. The floor is covered with black tar paper. On the floor, on 12-inch centers, dots are marked to form a matrix. Each of the four walls has one foot increments marked. The flat black paint and black tar paper floor reflect a maximum of 3 percent light. This small percentage of reflection will facilitate consistent light measurements.

There were two lamps used in this test, a 1000-watt clear super metal halide and a 1000-watt HP sodium. The bottom of each bulb was hung at a distance of 3 feet from the floor. The lamps were warmed up for an hour before any measurements were taken.

A light reading was taken at each square foot of the matrix on the floor. The foot-candle reading was recorded next to a corresponding point on a chart. To complete the charts, a line was drawn connecting all of the dots on the matrix that have a value of 500, 1,000, 1,500 and 2,000 foot-candles. The charts are very interesting and demonstrate where the high-light and low-light plants should be placed.

Horizontal reflectors are much more efficient than reflectors requiring the lamp to burn vertically. Turning a lamp horizontally increases light output substantially. By turning the lamp on it's side, the arc tube is parallel with the ground. All of the light comes out of the arc tube. When the arc tube is already horizontal, half of the light it produces shines directly on plants. Only half of the light needs to be reflected. When the arc tube is in a vertical position, light is emitted out the sides of the arc tube. This light must be reflected downward before it is of any value to plants.

The hoods can be covered with white paint or constructed from a reflective. First and foremost, they should be made of a material that is lightweight, since they will be hanging from the ceiling. The hood should have a heat vent outlet around the bulb so that it will not collect heat. Excessive heat around the bulb could cause premature burn-out.

The hoods can be made of galvanized steel, polished or painted aluminum. The color is usually flat white, but some companies paint them glossy white (see discussion below on flat white paint). Sheet metal hoods tend to be much less expensive than aluminum or stainless steel But, sheet metal is heavy. The other differences in reflective quality are similar to the differences between flat white paint and reflective mylar, discussed later. Polished aluminum hoods scratch easily and are expensive.

For maximum reflection, paint the inside of the reflector with titanium white paint. Tests we completed showed titanium white reflectors

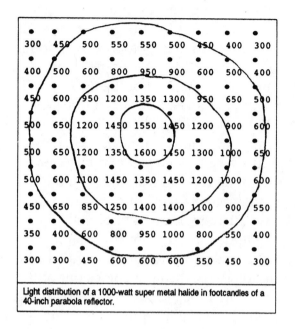

The charts show that a compact horizontal reflector delivers 40 percent more light than a 45-inch cone-shaped reflector. The 40-inch parabolic reflector delivers 19 percent more light than a 45-inch cone-shaped reflector.

Light distribution of a 1000-watt super metal halide in footcandles of a 40-inch parabola reflector.

The charts show that a 40-inch parabolic reflector delivers 24 percent more light than a 45-inch cone-shaped reflector.

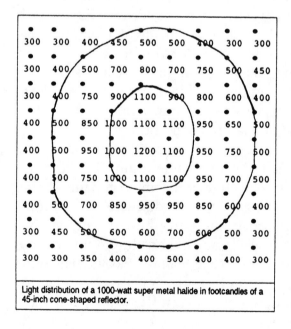

Light distribution of a 1000-watt super metal halide in footcandles of a 45-inch cone-shaped reflector.

The tests above compare a 45-inch cone-shaped reflector and a 40-inch parabolic dome reflector.

produce 5-10 percent more light.

The 4-foot parabolic hoods are usually manufactured in 9 parts. The smaller size facilitates shipping and handling. The customer assembles the hood with small screws and nuts.

HP sodium lamps mounted horizontally use a small, very effective hood for greenhouse culture. The hood is mounted just a few inches over the long horizontal HP sodium so that all the light is reflected down toward the plant beds but the small hood creates a minimum shadow. One manufacturer's hood for its HP sodium has a protective glass covering to protect the lamp from water spray when irrigating.

One option is to remove the reflective hood if the garden is too tall. With no hood, the lamp burns cooler and the white ceiling provides some reflection. If the lamp is too close to the ceiling (less than 24 inches) install a non-flammable heat shield to protect the ceiling. See instruction Number Two in "Setting Up the Lamp," pages 56-58.

White, reflective walls should be 12 inches or less from the plants for optimum reflection. Ideally, the walls should be moved around the plants. This way, the walls always provide the optimum amount of reflection. The easiest way to install mobile walls is to hang the lamp near the corner of a room. Use the two walls in the corner as reflective walls. Fabricate two outside walls that are mobile. They will need to be fabricated out of light plywood, sheet rock or white visqueen plastic.

Hanging white visqueen plastic is a great way to white out a room. People use it for several reasons. White visqueen is inexpensive,

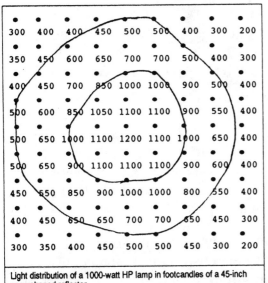

300	400	400	450	500	500	400	300	200
350	450	600	650	700	700	500	400	300
400	450	700	850	1000	1000	900	500	400
500	600	850	1050	1100	1100	900	550	400
500	650	1000	1100	1200	1100	1000	650	400
500	650	900	1100	1100	1100	900	600	400
450	650	850	900	1000	1000	800	550	400
400	450	650	650	700	700	650	450	300
300	350	400	450	500	500	450	300	200

Light distribution of a 1000-watt HP lamp in footcandles of a 45-inch cone-shaped reflector.

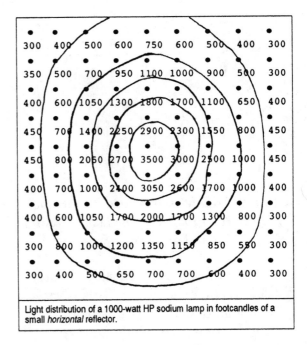

300	400	500	600	750	600	500	400	300
350	500	700	950	1100	1000	900	500	300
400	600	1050	1300	1800	1700	1100	650	400
450	700	1400	2250	2900	2300	1550	800	450
450	800	2050	2700	3500	3000	2500	1000	450
400	700	1000	2400	3050	2600	1700	1000	400
400	600	1050	1700	2000	1700	1300	800	300
300	800	1000	1200	1350	1150	850	550	300
300	400	500	650	700	700	600	400	300

Light distribution of a 1000-watt HP sodium lamp in footcandles of a small *horizontal* reflector.

Light distribution of a 1000 watt HP sodium lamp.

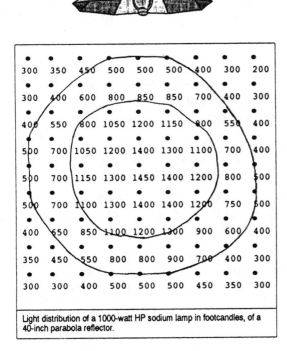

300	350	450	500	500	500	400	300	200
300	400	600	800	850	850	700	400	300
400	550	800	1050	1200	1150	900	550	400
500	700	1050	1200	1400	1300	1100	700	400
500	700	1150	1300	1450	1400	1200	800	500
500	700	1100	1300	1400	1400	1200	750	500
400	650	850	1100	1200	1300	900	600	400
350	450	550	800	800	900	700	400	300
300	300	400	500	500	500	450	350	300

Light distribution of a 1000-watt HP sodium lamp in footcandles, of a 40-inch parabola reflector.

The tests above compare a 45-inch cone-shaped reflector, a 40-inch parabolic dome reflector and a compact horizontal reflector.

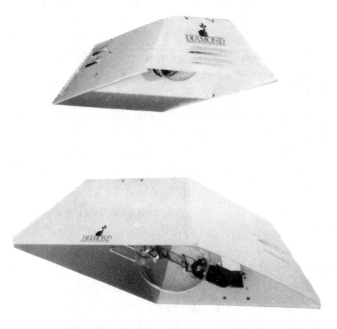

This hood from Diamond Lights is typical of the efficient horizontal reflectors.

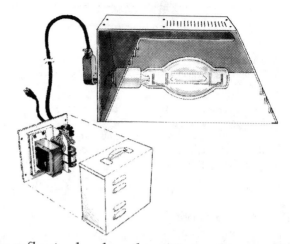

This innovative HID reflective hood is manufactured by Green Air Products. The hood stays less than 1000 F., even on hot summer days.

The reflective hood on this 400-watt horizontal reflector by Hydrofarm spreads the light out into a broad beam.

expandable, removable and reusable. It may also be used to construct walls. This is very handy when a gardener wants to partition off one or several rooms. The walls can expand as the garden grows. The plastic is waterproof, so it may be used on the walls as well as the floor. White visqueen is easy to work with. It may be cut with scissors or a knife, stapled, nailed or taped. Generally, people hang the plastic sheets wrapped around a 1-by-2's nailed to the ceiling. The white visqueen actually forms a mobile wall around the garden. It is easy to keep the walls close to the plants for optimum reflection. To make the white walls opaque, hang black visqueen on the outside. The dead air space between the two types of visqueen increases insulation.

The only disadvantages of white visqueen plastic are that it is not as reflective as flat white paint, it may get brittle after a couple of years of use under an HID lamp and it is difficult to find at retail outlets.

Whitewash is an inexpensive alternative to white paint. It is a little messy to apply and it is thin, so several coats will have to be applied. If fungus or moisture is a problem, like the kind found on wet concrete basement walls, the mess is worth the trouble. For mixing directions, see pages 66-67.

Using flat white paint is one of the simplest, least expensive, most efficient ways to create optimum reflection. Artist's white or titanium white paint is more expensive, but very reflective. It is recommended for reflective hoods. Semi-gloss white is not quite as reflective as flat white, but it is much easier to wash and keep clean. A gallon of good flat white paint costs $15 to $20. One gallon should be enough to "white out" the average garden room. Use a primer to prevent bleed through of stains or if walls are rough and unpainted. The vent fan should be installed before painting. Fumes can cause headaches and nausea.

Why is flat white so reflective? When light shines on a green object, green pigment in the object absorbs all colors but green from the spectrum and the green light is reflected. This is why we see the color green. Flat white contains little or no light-absorbing pigment. Flat white essentially absorbs no light it is almost all reflected, except for a small amount that somehow gets lost. Flat white is whiter and reflects better than glossy white. Glossy white is manufactured with more light-absorbing varnish. The glossy surface lends itself to bright spots and glare. Flat white contains less varnish and inhibits the path of reflective light much less. It also has a mat texture, actually providing more reflective surface.

REFLECTIVE CHART

MATERIAL	Percentage of Light Reflected
Reflective Mylar	90 - 95
Flat white paint	85 - 93
Semi-gloss white	75 - 80
Flat yellow	70 - 80
Aluminum foil	70 - 75
Black	less than 10

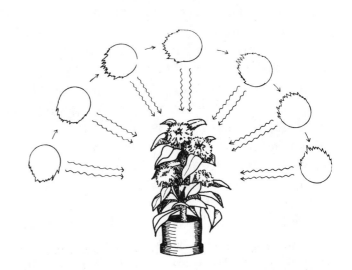

This drawing simulates the path of the sun over a single plant.

Reflective mylar provides one of the most reflective surfaces possible. It looks like a very thin mirror. Unlike light absorbing paint, reflective mylar reflects almost all light. It is simply taped or tacked to the wall. The trick to setting it up is to make it lay down flat against the wall. When it is loose or wavy, light is reflected poorly.

Aluminum foil is one of the worst reflective surfaces possible. The foil always crinkles up, reflecting light in the wrong directions, actually wasting light. It also reflects more ultraviolet rays than other surfaces. Take a look at the reflective chart. Aluminum foil is not very reflective!

More Growing Light for Less Money

There are several ways of getting a more even distribution of light in the garden. Use several 400-watt HID's, installing side lighting or rotate the plants. The most efficient way is to replicate the movement of the sun through the sky. This is done two basic ways. Both methods move the lamp back and forth overhead so it covers more area.

One: The plants get more even distribution of light. Even growth is promoted. When the HID is stationary, plants tend to grow toward the lamp. When the lamp is always in the same place, the plants grow up around it, severely shading the rest of the garden. Rotating the plants every few days so they receive more even

light distribution solves this problem. It is much easier to move the lamp rather than the plants.

Two: A lamp moving overhead increases the intense light that the majority of plants receive. This is not a substitute for more lumens from an additional lamp. It is a more efficient way to use an HID. Since the lamp will be directly above more plants, they all will receive more direct, intense light. Young clones and seedlings may s-t-r-e-t-c-h, becoming leggy, to get more light if the lamp travels too far away. Start using the light movers after the plants are 12 inches tall and have several sets of leaves.

Three: Light is received by the plants from more directions. Total light energy is optimum for all plants, as long as one plant is not shading another. This promotes even growth.

Light Movers

A light mover is a device to move a lamp back and forth across the ceiling of a garden room to provide a more even distribution of light. The methods employed to move the lamp across the ceiling may be motorized or manual, fast moving or moving only once or twice a day. The speed at which the lamp moves is of minimal importance. But the more often it traverses the garden, the more even the profile of the garden will be and the closer plants can be to the lamp. The unit should not move so fast that the lamp wobbles, making it unstable. It is not necessary for the lamp to move exactly like the sun whether the lamp moves from east to west is of no consequence. The path it takes should be a consistent, one that distributes light evenly. If the lamp is allowed to stay in the same position for two or three days before it is moved, plants will get uneven light distribution. Motorized units have an advantage in this respect, since they are moving at a constant rate all the time.

These light movers may be purchased from an ever-increasing number of suppliers or constructed by the gardener. There are only two things to be on the lookout for when constructing your own: (1) strength and (2) ease of movement. First and foremost, the rigging overhead must be able to support the weight of the lamp and hood. If the system were to come crashing down on the garden it could cause a real problem. Besides wrecking your precious garden, it very well could start a fire. Make sure it is secured to the ceiling! The electric cord should not slow down or affect the movement of the light mover in any way. Second, the system should be easy to move. If it is easy to move, chances are that you will move it. Homemade made light movers work best for gardeners who are able to look after their garden two or three times a day, moving the lamp every time.

There are two basic kinds of light movers. The first is a linear system. These systems move in a straight line simulating the sun's path through the heavens. This system increases the intense light to plants in a linear oval. The square footage covered by the system depends on the length of the track and the number of lamps employed. The system uses a track affixed to the ceiling. The lamp moves back and forth across the ceiling, guided by the track. The lamp is hooked to the light mover with an extendible chain or cord so it can be as close as possible to the plants. These units vary as to the length and speed the lamp travels. Some are designed for one lamp, while others are able to move up to six lamps efficiently. A 6-foot linear light mover increases optimum coverage of light from 36 to 72 square feet.

A homemade alternative to the commercial linear light track is the clothesline unit. It is simple to construct. Eyebolts are attached at opposite ends of the ceiling or ceiling corners. Pulleys are attached to the eyebolts. Between the pulleys, a small diameter, heavy-duty nylon cord is strung in a loop. The HID is attached to the bottom of the loop. This is just like

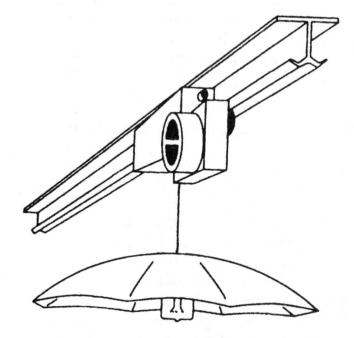

Light Rail 3 by Gualala Robotics

Various commercial light movers.

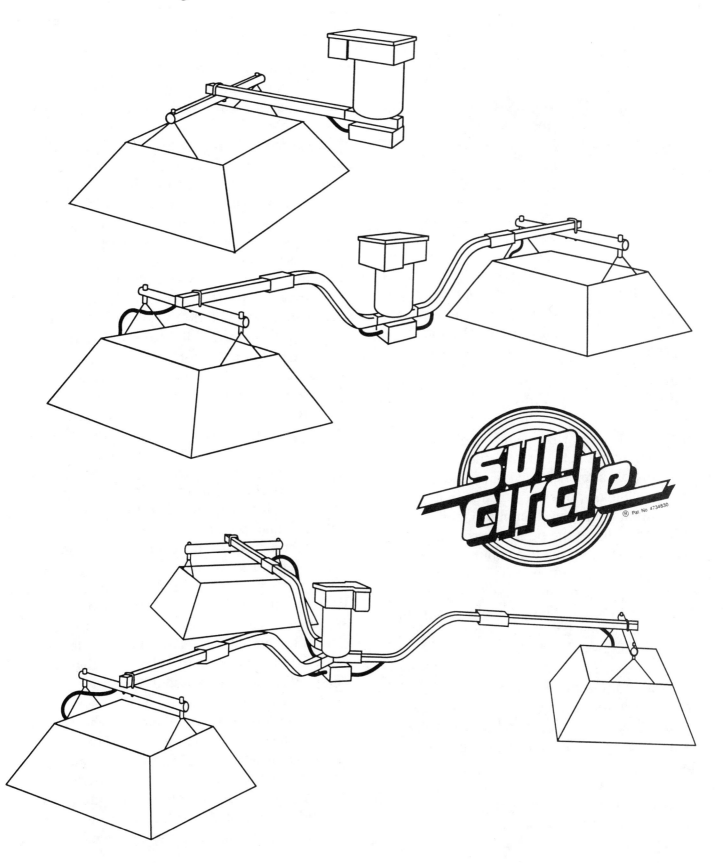

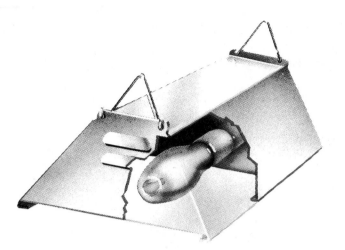

This small 175-watt metal halide lamp from Hydrofarm will provide enough light for a small garden. It can also be used for side lighting in larger gardens.

many clotheslines used in tall city buildings that have access from only one end. After the lamp is mounted on the looped cord, it may be moved back and forth as often as desirable - the more often the better. Another variation of the principle stretches a nylon cord across the ceiling. A single pulley is attached to it. Attach the lamp to the pulley, then move the lamp back and forth on the pulley overhead. One industrious person made a light mover out of an old garage door opener. The possibilities are endless. When using these types of units, make sure to watch the profile of the garden. Try to give the garden the most even distribution of light possible.

The second type of light mover is the arc method. It rotates in a pivoting motion. The unit swivels from a boom on a wall or the ceiling overhead. The lamp(s) take an arc-shaped path, covering a little more area than the linear method.

There are two basic types of arc method: (1) wall mount units that swing back and forth in a partial arc on a motorized hinge. (2) ceil-ing mount units that rotate 360⁰ in a circle. The lamp(s) in both types are suspended by an adjustable chain attached to a telescoping boom(s).

Another type of arc method is a homemade model employing 1-inch plumbing pipes. It bolts to the ceiling or is mounted on a wooden frame that is in turn affixed to the ceiling. This unit, like the clothesline unit, is non-motorized. The gardener simply moves the lamp to a different location daily or as often as necessary to maintain an even garden profile.

Commercial light movers give more intense light to more plants for less money. Light movers make it possible to use fewer lamps and get the same yield. An increase of 25 to 35 percent in intense light coverage is afforded by light movers. Two lamps mounted on a motorized light mover will do the job of three stationary lamps. Motorized light are preferred because they help maintain an even garden profile. Since the HID is already drawing about 9.2 amperes and it is hooked up to a 15- or 20-ampere circuit, it would take a new circuit to hang up another HID. The commercial movers is easily plugged into the same timer and socket as the lamp. Since the motor for the light mover uses about one ampere (75 to 100 watts) of current, it may be attached to the same circuit as the lamp with little risk of overload.

Light movers are normally used for only part of a plant's life. When there are just a few plants, they are huddled directly under the lamp. Using a light mover on too many seedlings or clones causes them to s-t-r-e-t-c-h. One of the good things about homemade units is they do not have a particular cycle they must complete. They are operated by hand and can be placed in any location for as long as desired.

Planter boxes or containers on wheels offer a good alternative to light movers. The containers are rotated daily. The wheels make this job easy. The light reaches every corner of the garden without having to move the lamp. This method has essentially the same effect as moving the lamp overhead, but is more work because all the plants have to be moved, rather than only one or two lamps.

The 400-watt bulbs offer more even light distribution and the lamp can be closer to the plants since they have less heat buildup than 1000-watt HID's. The 400-watt bulbs offer certain advantages, especially if space is a problem. One gardener uses two of them in a narrow 4-by-8-foot room with amazing success. Another apartment dweller has the brightest closet in town! The 400-watt halides do have a longer life than the 1000-watt lamps, but share the same lumen maintenance curve. For the amount of lumens produced, their initial cost is much higher. However, their life is twice as long - about 20,000 hours. If the 400-watt HID's give you the best value for an even distribution of light, several ballasts may be looped together on the same 220 volt circuit. Ask an electrician for help. Do not use a 400-watt lamp in a 1000-watt system! It will work for the first 24 to 48 hours, then BOOM! The lamp and maybe the ballast will stop working and who-knows-what else!

Side lighting is another way to provide nearly the same amount of light to the entire garden. Of course this uses more electricity, but it increases the amount of light available to the plants. Probably the most efficient lamp to use in this case is the low-pressure (LP) sodium, since its -lumen-per-watt conversion is the highest available. The lamps are mounted where light intensity is marginal, along the walls, to provide side light.

Fluorescent lamps could also be used, but the -lumen-per-watt conversion is much lower. Remember the LP sodiums must be used with a halide, which supplies all the blue light the plants need. If you really want to get the most intense light possible in the garden, you may want to employ both side lighting and a light mover.

Cuttings and young seedlings are huddled below the HID when small and moved into larger containers when they are crowding one another. When they are far enough apart that

the light does not afford complete coverage, it is time to use a light mover. Before this time, a light mover might not give them enough intense light and growth might be leggy. However, use a light meter to check to make sure each plant variety gets adequate light.

About Electricity

The basics of electricity really do not need to be understood to grow indoors. Understanding the basics may save you money, time and the shock of your life. First, simple electrical concepts and terms are defined and briefly discussed. Once these terms are understood, you will be able to see the purpose of fuses, wire thickness (gauge), amperes on a circuit, the importance of ground and the necessity to develop safe habits.

Before anything electrical is touched, please remember the rule below.

 Rule of Thumb: Work backward when installing electrical components or doing wiring. Start at the bulb and work toward the outlet. Always plug in the cord last!

Alternating-Current - an electric current that reverses its direction at regularly occurring intervals.

Ampere (amp) - the measure of electricity in motion. Electricity can be looked at in absolute terms of measurement just as water can. A gallon is an absolute measure of a portion of water a coulomb is an absolute measure of a portion of electricity. Water in motion is measured in gallons per second and electricity in motion is measured in coulombs per second. When an electrical current flows at one coulomb per second, we say it has one ampere.

Breaker box - an electrical circuit box containing breaker circuit switches.

Breaker switch - an ON/OFF safety switch that

CAUTION! Do not handle electricity when you are standing in a puddle of water.

will turn the electricity OFF when the circuit is OVERLOADED.

Circuit - the closed path that electricity travels. If this path is interrupted, the power will go off. If this circuit is given a chance, it will travel a circular route through your body! Never give it a chance!

Conductor - something that is able to carry electricity easily. Copper, steel, water and the human body are good electrical conductors.

Direct Current - an electrical current that flows only in one direction.

CAUTION! The HID lamp operated on an overloaded circuit will blow fuses, switch off breakers and burn wiring. It could wreck the HID system, even start a fire. Pay attention!

Fuse- an electrical safety device consisting of a fusible metal that MELTS and interrupts the circuit when overloaded. Never replace fuses with pennies or aluminum foil They will not melt, which interrupts the circuit when overloaded. This is an easy way to start a fire!

Fuse box - an electrical circuit box containing fuses.

Rule of Thumb: Use only one 1000-watt HID for each 15 to 20 ampere circuit.

Ground - a means to connect electricity to the ground or earth. Safety is the reason for ground. If a circuit is properly grounded and the electricity travels somewhere it is not supposed to, it will go via the ground wire into the earth and be rendered harmless. Electricity will travel the path of least resistance. This path must be along the ground wire. It is all right to have several ground wires for extra security.

The ground is formed by a wire (usually green or bare)copper that runs parallel to the circuit and is attached to a metal ground stake. All the circuits in the home are then attached to the ground stake. Metal cold-water pipes serve as excellent conductors for the ground. They are all attached to one another. Water pipes conduct electricity well and are all in good contact with the ground.

The entire system - pipes, copper wire and metal ground stake - conduct any misplaced electricity safely into the ground.

The ground wire is the third wire with the big round prong on a male plug. The ground runs through the ballast all the way to the hood.

HID systems must have a ground that runs a continual path from the socket through the ballast to the main fuse box then to the house ground. See drawing above.

Hertz - fluctuations or cycles in electricity within a conductor (wire). In the United States,

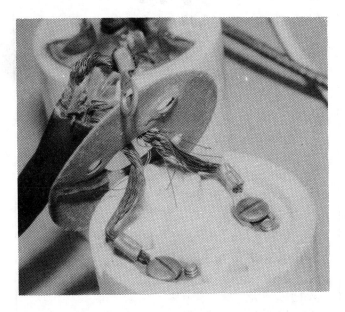

Inadequate wire and poor connections almost caused a fire.

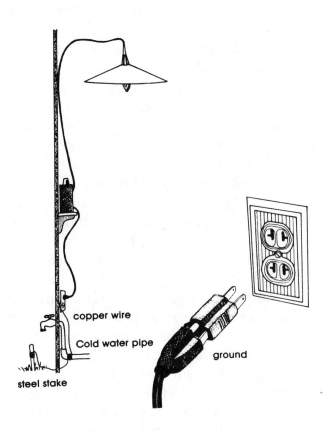

copper wire

Cold water pipe

ground

steel stake

A complete grounded circuit is essential for safety. If you use a ground adapter, make sure the socket is grounded separately.

alternating-current electricity runs at 60 HERTZ or cycles per second.

Ohm's Power Law - law that expresses the strength of an electric current: volts x amperes = watts.

Short circuit - side or unintentional circuit formed when conductors (wires) cross. A short circuit will normally blow fuses!

Volts - air, water, gas - virtually anything can be put under pressure. Pressure is measured in pounds per square inch (PSI). Electricity is also under pressure or electrical potential this pressure is measured in volts. Most home wiring is under the pressure of approximately 110 or 220 volts.

Watt - a measure of work. Watts measure the amount of electricity flowing in a wire. When amperes (units of electrons per second) are multiplied by volts (pressure) we get watts. 1000-watts = 1 kilowatt.

A halide lamp that draws about 9.2 amperes X 120 volts = 1104 watts. Remember Ohm's Power Law: amps X watts = volts. This is strange the answer was sup-

posed to be 1000-watts. What is wrong? The electricity flows through the ballast, which requires energy to run. The energy drawn by the ballast must then amount to 104 watts.

Watt-hours - the amount of watts used in an hour. One watt-hour is equal to one watt used for one hour. A kilowatt-hour is 1000 watt-hours. A 1000-watt HID will use one kilowatt per hour and the ballast will use about one watt. Electrical bills are charged out in kilowatt hours (KWH) (See "Chart on Cost of Electricity", page 55).

Wire and Wiring

Electrical wire comes in all sizes (gauges) and they are indicated by number. The higher the number the smaller the wire the lower the number the larger the wire (See drawing below). The standard wire in most homes is 14-gauge. Wire size is important for two reasons (1) ampacity (2) voltage drop. Ampacity is the amount of amperes a wire is able to carry safely. Electricity flowing through wire creates heat. The more amps flowing, the more heat created. This heat is wasted power! To avoid this wasted power, the proper thickness of wire must be used: at least 14 gauge. It must be well insulated and must have a ground wire.

In addition, forcing too much power (amperes) through a wire also creates voltage drop. Voltage (pressure) is lost in the wire. For example: if you force an 18-gauge wire to carry 9.2 amperes at 120 volts not only would the wire heat up, maybe enough to blow fuses, but the voltage at the outlet would be 120 volts, while the voltage 10 feet away could be as low as 108. Would you like to pay for this unused 12 volts? The farther electricity travels, the more heat is generated and the more voltage drops.

Note: Voltage drop is wasteful and causes lamps to function very inefficiently. A lamp designed to work at 120 volts that receives only 108 volts (90 percent of the power it was intended to operate at) would produce only 70 percent of the normal light. Use at least 14-gauge wire for any extension cords and if the cord has to carry power over 60 feet, use 12-gauge wire.

A simple electrical circuit requires two wires. One wire runs from the source of power to the load (from the electrical outlet to a ballast for example) and the other wire completes the circuit back to the source of power. There always should be a third or ground wire along with the circuit wires.

Voltage in homes ranges from 110 to 125. Most calculations use 125 volts. The only way

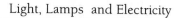

8 10 12 14 16 18

Wire is rated by number; the smaller the number, the larger the wire.

Wires are usually
Black = hot
White or red = common
Bare, blue or green = ground

When wiring a plug-in or socket:

The hot wire attaches to the brass or gold screw.

The common wire attaches to the aluminum or silver screw.

The ground wire always attaches to the ground prong.

Take special care to keep the wires from crossing and forming a short circuit.

to tell the exact voltage available at the outlet is to measure the electricity with a voltmeter.

Outlets and sockets must have a solid connection. If they are jolted around, allowing the electricity to jump, the prongs will burn a fire could result. Check plug periodically to ensure that they have a solid connection.

If a new circuit or breaker box is necessary, hire an electrician or purchase *Wiring Simplified*, by H.P. Richter and W.C. Schwan. It costs less than $5. and is available at most hardware stores. Installing a new circuit in a breaker box is very easy, but installing another fuse is more complex. Before trying anything of this scope, read up on it and discuss it with several professionals. You could be in for the shock of your life!

About Electricity Consumption

There are many ways to save energy to compensate for the increase in consumption of electricity. One friend moved into a home that had all electric heat and a fireplace. He installed three HID lamps in the basement that generated quite a bit of heat. The excess Supplemental heat was supplied by wood burned in a fireplace insert. Even running three lamps, the electric bill was less than it had been with electric heat!

A one-to-three-bedroom home can run two or three 1000-watt lamps and a four-or-five-bedroom home can operate three to five lamps with little or no problem. Any more lamps usually require new incoming circuits or the use of present circuits is severely limited. Some friends bought a new, efficient water heater and saved $17 a month! Another indoor gardener set her water heater for 130⁰ (55⁰ C) instead of 170⁰ (76⁰ C). This simple procedure saved about 25 kilowatt-hours per month!

Note: Do not turn the water heater any lower than 130⁰ F (55⁰ C). Harmful bacteria can grow below this safe point!

HID lights are most likely to be used economically where hydroelectric power is plentiful such as the West Coast and the Tennessee-Kentucky area. Some power companies are not able to sell all the power they generate during certain hours of the day. These power companies use coal or nuclear energy to generate electricity. Many of these companies generate electricity during the daylight hours for factories and office buildings, but after 4 or 5 p.m., the power plant will not need to generate electricity however, it is impractical and uneconomical to shut the plant down. Electrical rates after 4 p.m. are generally greatly discounted. It will probably take quite a bit of power usage to get a good discount, but the rates of some companies are as low as one-third of the cost of prime-time day usage.

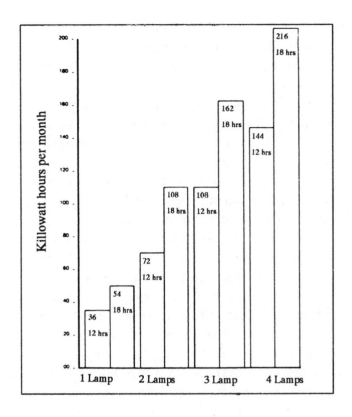

This bar graph compares electric consumption of lamps at 12 and 18 hours of daily use.

Cost of Electricity Chart

Price per killowatt hour	12 hour days		18 hour days	
	day	month	day	month
$.02	.24	7.20	.36	10.80
$.03	.36	10.80	.54	16.20
$.04	.48	14.40	.72	21.60
$.05	.60	18.00	.90	27.00
$.06	.72	21.60	1.08	32.40
$.07	.84	25.20	1.26	37.80
$.08	.96	28.80	1.44	43.20
$.09	1.08	32.40	1.62	48.60
$.10	1.20	36.00	1.80	54.00

Setting Up the HID Lamp

Step One: Before setting up the HID system, read "Setting Up the Garden Room" in Chapter One, pages 15-18 and complete the step-by-step instructions.

Step Two: Both the lamp and ballast radiate quite a bit of heat. Care must be taken when positioning them so they are not so close (6 to 12 inches) to plants or flammable walls and ceiling that they become hazardous. If the room is limited in space, with a low ceiling, placing a protective, non-flammable material, such as metal or asbestos, between the lamp and ceiling provides much more space. If the room is 6-by-6-feet or smaller, an exhaust fan will be necessary to keep things cool. It is most effective to place the remote ballast near the floor. It can also be placed outside the garden room if the temperature is too high, which is unlikely when a good vent fan is used. When hanging the lamp on the overhead chain or pulley system, make sure electrical cords are unencumbered and not too close to any heat source.

Step Three: Buy a timer! A timer will be necessary for you to play Mother Nature successfully. The reasons for having a timer are obvious. If the HID system is not equipped with a timer, the only way to turn it on and off is to plug and unplug it, a shocking and colorful experience. Mother Nature provides a rigid schedule for plants to count on and live by. When the horticulturist assumes her role, will he or she remember to turn the lamp on and off at exactly the same time each and every day for several months? Or will he or she even be there each and every day, at the same time, twice a day, all year round? (see: photos of various timers.)

Step Four: To start the HID lamp, it will be necessary to find the proper outlet. A 1000-watt

This sophisticated timer by Green Air Products offers exacting control.

HID lamp uses about 9.5 amperes(amps) of electricity on a regular 110 to 120 volt house current.

A typical home has a fuse box or a breaker box. Each fuse or breaker switch controls an electrical circuit in the home. The fuse or breaker switch will be rated for 15, 20, 25, 30 or 40 amps of service. These circuits are considered overloaded when more than 80 percent of the amps are being used. The fuse will have its amp rating printed on its face and the breaker switch will have its amp rating printed on the switch. To find out which outlets are controlled by a fuse or breaker, switch remove the fuse or turn the breaker switch off.

Test every 110-volt outlet in the home to see which ones do not work. All the outlets that do not work are on the same circuit. All outlets that work are on another circuit. When you have found a circuit that has few or no lights, radios, TV's, stereos etc. plugged into it, look at the circuit's amp rating. If it is rated for 15 amps, just plug one 1000-watt HID into it. A leeway of 5.5 amps is there to cover any power surges or incongruities in electricity supply. If the circuit is rated for 20 or more amps, it may be used for the HID lamp as well as a

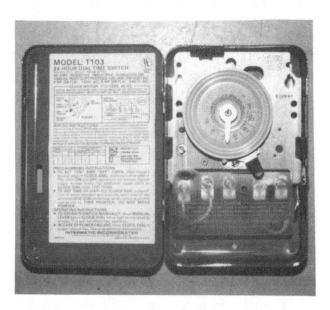

This grounded timer is rated at 40 amps and is designed for up to three lamps and a light mover.

few other low-amp appliances and lights. To find out how many amps are drawn by each appliance, add up the number of watts drawn by each appliance, then divide by 120.

Example:
A circuit with a 20-amp fuse containing the following items
1400-watt toaster oven
100-watt incandescent light bulb
20-watt radio
1520 total watts divided by 120 = 12.6 amps in use

The above example shows 12.6 amps are being drawn when everything is on. By adding 9.2 amps, drawn by the HID to the circuit, we get 21.8 amps drawn - AN OVERLOADED CIRCUIT. There are three solutions to this problem: (1) Remove one or all of the high amp consuming appliances and plug them into another circuit. (2) Find another circuit that has few or no amps drawn by other appliances. (3) Install a new circuit. A 220-volt circuit will make more amps available per circuit if using several lamps.

Never replace a smaller fuse with a fuse that has a higher amperage rating. The fuse is the weakest link in the circuit. If a 20-amp fuse is placed into a 15-amp circuit, the fuse is able to conduct more electricity than the wiring. When this happens, the wires burn, rather than the fuse. An overloaded circuit can easily result in a house fire. Please be careful.

CAUTION! An HID lamp operated on and overloaded circuit will blow fuses, switch off breakers or burn wiring. It could wreck the HID system, even start a fire. Pay attention!

Rule of Thumb: Use only one 1000-watt HID per 15 to 20 amp (110-volt) circuit. Do not break this rule!

Use an extension cord that is at least 14-gauge wire or heavier if the plug will not reach the outlet desired. The thicker 14-gauge extension cord is more difficult to find and may have to be constructed. A smaller 16- or 18-gauge cord will not conduct adequate electricity and will heat up, straining the entire system. Cut the 14 gauge extension cord the exact length the farther electricity travels, the weaker it gets and the more heat it produces, which also strains the system.

Step Five: Always use a 3-prong grounded plug. If your home is not equipped with working 3-prong grounded outlets, buy a 3-prong grounded plug and outlet adapter. Attach the ground wire to a grounded ferrous metal object, such as a grounded cold-water pipe or a heavy copper wire driven into the earth to a form a ground. Screw the ground into the outlet face. You will be working with water under and around the HID system. Water conducts electricity about as well as the human body . . . guaranteed to give you a charge!

Step Six: Once the proper circuit is selected, the socket and hood mounted overhead and the ballast in place on the floor (but not

When installing the bulb, make sure that it is screwed securely into the socket.

plugged in), screw the HID bulb finger-tight into the socket. Make sure the bulb is secured in the socket firmly. The threaded metal base of the bulb should not be seen from under the socket, to make certain there is a good connection. When secure, wipe off all smudges on the bulb to increase brightness.

Step Seven: Plug the three-prong plug into the timer that is in the "off" position. Plug the timer into the grounded outlet, set the timer at the desired photoperiod and turn the timer on. The ballast will hum, the lamp will flicker and slowly warm up, reaching full brilliance in about five minutes.

Step Eight: When using more than one HID, it is easiest to plug in each lamp individually. This way, flexibility is maintained. If another lamp needs to be hung up or removed, it is easy and does not require more wiring into a central system.

Troubleshooting the HID Lamp

When your light does not shine, your garden does not grow. Finding the reason a HID system does not work is simple and easy when the steps below are followed.

Step One: First, the problem must be isolated. Is the ballast receiving electricity? Plug in the ballast. If it hums, it is receiving electricity. If there is no hum, check the plug and outlet for a firm connection. Check the timer using another light to ensure it functions properly. If there is still no hum, remove the covering over the ballast check for solid wire connections.

The transformer is the big steel or aluminum box check it for burns. If you see any burns, take the transformer to a halide dealer for replacement. The starter (HP sodium only) and capacitor look like an oblong tin can. They are burned out if the sealed lip around each end is pinched out or the bottom is bulging (convex). The lip should be completely smooth and unwrinkled. If you can shake the capacitor and hear liquid inside, it is also burned out. When a starter or capacitor is burned out, it must be replaced.

Step Two: If the ballast works, the problem must be in the bulb or the wiring between the ballast and the bulb. First check to make sure the bulb is screwed firmly into the socket. A loose bulb is the most common reason the bulb will not work. Once the bulb is securely screwed into the socket, check all the connections for heat and firm contact. Always unplug the ballast before touching bare wire or connections. Check the arc tube in bulb for darkness. If the bulb is two to five years old, it could be burned out.

CAUTION! Be extremely careful when handling the capacitor. It can hold an extremely powerful electrical charge for months.

Step Three: If a fuse burns out or a breaker switch turns off, there is an overloaded circuit. See information about "Setting Up the HID Lamp" on pages 56-58.

Step Four: If the lamp flickers or pulsates, do not worry. After about 100 hours of operation, the lamp halogens in the arc tube will stabilize and appear to pulsate less. Color changes may also occur. Color changes are normal and will not effect the life or the brilliance of the bulb.

Step Five: HID bulbs become brittle after several hours of use. Handle used bulbs as little as possible to avoid breakage. Wipe finger prints from the bulb after handling to retain full brilliance. When restarting lamp, wait about 15 minutes for the bulb to cool before it will restart.

Back Issue and Subscription Order Form

____ **Vol. 1 #1** — Out of Print

____ **Vol. 1 #2** Basil Production for the Small Grower / Propagation in Rockwool / Biological Pest Control / The Fine Art of Micropropagation / Hydroponic Nutrient Solutions / Phytofarms of America / Toxins in the Garden / Environmental Dynamics: Part II / Wine-Red Strophana

____ **Vol. 1 #3** Bananas: Grown in Oregon / In-Store Hydroponics in Houston / Pest Management for Hydroponics / Bioponics: Part I / Hydroponics for the Home Hobbyist / Quebec's Hydroponic Tomatoes / Shiitake Mushrooms

____ **Vol. 1 #4** Build Your Own Hydroponic System! / Plant Selection for Hydroponics / Water Should Taste Good to Plants! / Basil Production: An Update / Mid-South Greenhouse / Look Out Holland, Here Comes B.C.! / Grow Your Own Mushrooms Indoors / Softwood Cloning for Beginners

____ **Vol. 2 #1** Aero-Hydroponics / A Computer in Your Garden / Hydroponic or Organic? / Deep Water NFT / The Earth as Greenhouse / The Sip of Life: Cutting Survival / Optimizing High Pressure Sodiums / Growing Oyster Mushrooms Indoors

____ **Vol. 2 #2** Low-Tech, High-Performance Hydro / Allelopathy: Bio-Weapon of the Future / Bioponics: Part II / Recycling Nature's Gifts / Brooklyn Botanic Garden / NASA's Ames Research Center / SLUG: Garden for the Environment / (Very) Basic Hydroponics

____ **Vol. 2 #3** Rockwool: Cube and Slab Gardens / Foliar Feeding: Fast Food for Plants / Hydroponic Herbs at Home / Artificial Lighting in Horticulture / Bioponics: Part III / Desert Botanical Gardens / Assault on Eden! / Shiitake Growing Indoors / Computer Control Systems

____ **Vol. 2 #4** Thigmomorphogenesis / Hydroponic/Aquaculture Food Systems / Bioponics - Part IV / Drip Irrigation: The Basics / A 'Sound' Diet for Plants / New Efficiency for Home Lighting

____ **Vol. 3 #1** The Origin of Botanical Species / New World Fruits / Hardy Kiwi for Every Climate / The Garden Hacker / Plant Plane Hydroponics / The Struggle for Sunlight / Sununu Effect vs the Greenhouse Effect

____ **Vol. 3 #2** Carbon Dioxide Enrichment / White Owl Waterfarm / Subirrigation Systems Indoors / Subirrigation on the Cheap / Nitrogen Fixing Plants / The Domesticated Citrus

____ **Vol. 3 #3** Growing Bananas Indoors / Hydroponics for the Rest of Us / The Garden Hacker: Part III / Planetary Healing with Biology / Nature's Pharmacy: Medicinal Plants / Clean Air Update / Water Wise Garden

____ **Vol. 3 #4** Bedroom Garden / Goldfish Production / Designing With Nature / Gardening at the South Pole / Small Scale Solutions / Cloning / The Garden Hacker: Part IV / The $50 Greenhouse

____ **Vol. 4 #1** Hydroponics — A Global Perspective / Iceland — Land of Fire, Ice and Flowers / Paradise Found — Indoor Palms / Pest Control for Greenhouse Growers / Seeding Diversity, Reaping a Future / Sokol's Gourmet Sprouting Co. / Understanding Plant Names

____ **Vol. 4 #2** Hydroponics—Dynamic Sustainable Agriculture / Coffee, Tea or Hot Chocolate - Hot Drinks You Can Grow / Biological Alchemy and the Living Machine / A Moment of Hope by John Todd / Bioponics: Part V - Enzymes for Hereditary Potential / Mutation Breeding: Part I - Bypassing the Birds and the Bees / High-Tech Nursery / The Role of Gases in Nutrient Solutions / An Orchard of Lettuce Trees / Demystifying Plant Propagation / Hydroponic Solutions for Beginners

____ **Vol. 4 #3** The Lives of a Plant: Part 1/ Seeds - Embryonic Plants / The Orchid Environment - An Artificial Alternative / A Down-to-Earth Space Garden / Mutation Breeding: Part II / Healing a Wounded Planet / The Fruit/Herb Dryer / More Oxygen for your NFT

____ **Vol. 4 #4** Hydro-Organics—Organic Hydroponic Solutions / Bioponic Greenhouse / A Microbial Culture Chemostat / Organic Nutrient Extractor / System Earth—Urban Hot Spots / Rain Gutter Hydroponic System / The Lives of a Plant: Part 2 / Site Selection for Beginners / The Search for the Perfect Seedless Grape / The Fabric of Plant Diversity

____ **Vol. 5 #1** Hydroponics in Schools / Leaf Analysis / Mist Propagation and Fog Systems / Oxygen Intensive Water Culture / Basic Backyard Breeding / Pesticides in Our Communities / Winterize Indoor Plants / Systems for Beginners

____ **Vol. 5 #2** Building a Better Tomato / Computerize Your Garden / Gardening on Ice / Agriculture for the Millennium-Part I / Wheelchair Garden / More Green from Your Garden / Genius of Simplicity

____ **Vol. 5 #3** Soliviva Greenhouse / Lemon Substitutes / Computer Control Systems / Non-circulating Hydroponic System / Check Your Nutrient IQ / Best Compost Pile Ever / Treating Horticultural Soils With Microwaves / Biological Controls for Specialty Collections / Agriculture for the Millennium

____ **Vol. 5 #4** Under the Dome: Biodome de Montreal / An Introduction to Herb Mint / Frankenfood / Biological Systems for Glasshouse Horticulture / Lighting for Beginners Part I-The Meaning of Light / Biological Controls for Specialty Collections Part II

____ **Vol. 6 #1** Cultivating Passiflora / Commercial Hydroponics / Mushrooms / Water Gardening / Visit to an Experimental Beijing Market / Lighting for Beginners - Part II

____ **Vol. 6 #2** Windowsill Herb Garden / Fatal Attraction: the Fascinating World of Carnivorous Plants / A Taste of Things to Come / Tissue Culture / Hydroponics: Beyond the Basics / Greenhouse Growing Southern Style / Fruit Cocktail Planting / The Methane Greenhouse

____ **Vol. 6 #3** E=MC²: A Lesson in Plant Growth / Port-O-Plot: Growing Edibles in Containers / Zero Gravity Gardening / Garden of the Future / Sweet or Fiery...Peppers are Hot! / What's in Your Soil? / Biological Revival / Greenhouse Covering...Uncovered

____ **Vol. 6 #4** Hydroponics: Making Waves in the Classroom/ The Rice Paddy Kid / In Praise of Prairie Plants / A World Ahead...The Leaders in Hydroponic Technology / Wildlife Habitat Gardens / Cherry Cheaters / Biological Revival Part II / Gardening in Cyberspace

---

The Growing Edge — please send me:

☐ Back issues (checked above) .... $ _____
☐ 1 year subscription (4 issues, U.S. only) $17.95
 ☐ check here if renewal
☐ 2 year subscription (8 issues, U.S. only) $34.00
☐ First Class 1 year subscription (U.S. & Canada) $24.95
 (Sent First Class in a protective envelope)
 ☐ check here if renewal
☐ Overseas subscription (1 year, 4 issues) $45.00
 (Sent Air mail in a protective envelope)
 ☐ check here if renewal

Total Cost (U.S. funds only) .... $ _____

Please send order to:

Name _____

Address _____

City _____

State/Province _____

County _____ Zip or Postal Code _____

I have enclosed payment: Personal check, money order (U.S. funds. Personal checks will delay delivery), or bill my charge card: VISA, MASTERCARD, DISCOVER OR AMERICAN EXPRESS.

No. _____ _____ _____ _____ Exp. Date: _____ /_____

Telephone number (charge card orders): _____

Cardholder Name _____

Signature _____

NEW MOON Charge card orders 1-800-888-6785 (U.S. only)
Please send form and payment to:
NEW MOON PUBLISHING
P.O. Box 1027 • Corvallis, OR 97339
PUBLISHING ☎ (503) 757-8477 / ✉ (503) 757-0028

GVP-GI

Chapter Three
Soil and Containers

Flowers and vegetables flourish in rich organic soil or soilless mixes. Outdoors, when planted in the earth, roots will branch out and penetrate deep into the soil in search of water and nutrients. Outdoors, plants tend to grow above ground at the same rate as they grow below the surface. The roots spread out beyond the drip line. If the root system is inhibited from growing, the entire plant's growth is inhibited. It is important to remember how much root space plants need and provide adequate soil or growing medium to meet those needs. In the indoor environment, roots must be contained in a pot or planter box. It is virtually impossible to provide an indoor soil environment exactly like that found outdoors. This is why much care must be taken when selecting soil and containers.

About Soil

Air, water, minerals and organic matter are important non-living elements of soil. Spaces between soil particles are conduits for air and water. Plenty of space must be available in soil for air and water to move freely. Minerals, minute particles of fragmented rock, must be in a soluble form to be used by plants. Slightly acidic water solution, bacteria and other soil life change minerals into this soluble form.

Humus, decomposed organic matter, is the binding fiber. Organic matter fuels the soil's bacteria. Heat, air and water are also needed for these bacteria to act and all are promoted by good soil structure and texture. When the soil warms, the bacteria activity increases. It is through bacterial activity that nutrients are changed into compounds that can be absorbed by plants.

Soil is made up of many mineral particles mixed together with living and dead organic matter that incorporates air and water. Three factors contribute to the root's ability to grow in soil: (1) texture (2) pH and (3) nutrient content.

Soil Texture

Texture is governed by the size and physical make up of the mineral particles. The proper soil texture is required for sufficient root penetration, water and oxygen retention and drainage, plus many other complex chemical processes.

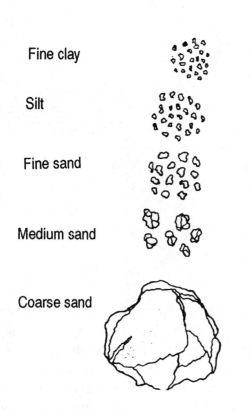

Fine clay

Silt

Fine sand

Medium sand

Coarse sand

The soil's water- and air-holding ability, as well as root penetration are a function of texture.

To get the feel of your soil's texture, pick up a handful of moist (not soggy) soil and rub it through your fingers. Clay soil feels and looks slippery. Sandy soil feels and looks gritty. Silty soil, in-between clay and sand almost feels greasy but less slippery than clay. When gently squeezed, the ideal soil for most indoor gardens should barely stay together and have sponge-like effect when the hand slowly opens up to release pressure. Most outdoor garden soils must be amended to perform best indoors.

About Soil Amendments

Soil amendments increase the soil's air- and water-retaining ability. Soil amendments are either mineral or organic.

Mineral soil amendments are all near neutral on the pH scale and contain few if any nutrients of their own. Mineral amendments decompose through weathering and erosion, which does not effect soil pH. The amendments are also very lightweight, an important point to consider when containers have to be moved often.

Perlite (sand or volcanic glass expanded by heat like popcorn) holds water and nutrients on its many irregular surfaces and works especially well for aerating the soil. This is a good medium for people planning to "push" plants with heavy fertilization. It drains fast and does not promote salt buildup. Perlite is available in three grades: fine, medium and coarse. Medium and coarse are the choice of most gardeners for a soil amendment.

Pumice (volcanic rock) is very light and holds water, nutrients and air in its many catacomb-like holes. It is a good amendment for aerating the soil and retaining moisture evenly. Pumice is a popular hydroponic growing medium.

Vermiculite (mica processed and expanded by heat) holds water, nutrients and air within its fiber and gives body to fast draining-soils. Fine vermiculite also works very well as a medium in which to root cuttings. This amendment holds more water than perlite or pumice. It works best for water retention in small pots or for people who do not like to water. Vermiculite is used for hydroponic wick systems because it holds so much moisture. Vermiculite is available in three grades: fine, medium and coarse. Always use the fine grade to root cuttings or start seeds. If fine is not available, crush the coarse or medium grades between your hands, rubbing the palms back and forth. As a soil amendment for potted plants, coarse vermiculite is the best choice.

Organic soil amendments break down through bacterial activity, slowly yielding humus. Humus is a soft, spongy material that binds minute soil particles together improving the soil texture. Composting organic soil amendments require nitrogen to carry on their bacterial decomposition. If they do not contain at least 1.5 percent nitrogen, the organic amendments will extract it from the soil, robbing roots of nitrogen. When using organic amendments, make sure they are thoroughly composted (at least one year) and releasing nitrogen rather than using it from the soil. A good sign of soil fertility is a dark, rich color and sweet smell.

Some gardeners prefer to use mineral amendments because there is no bacterial activity that alters nutrient content and pH. Others prefer rich, thoroughly composted organic matter that not only amends texture, but supplies available nutrients. Leaf mold, well-rotted garden compost and many types of thoroughly composted manure usually contain enough nitrogen for their decomposition needs. Purchasing organic soil amendments at a garden center or nursery will help control quality. Carefully look over the bag to see if it guarantees that it contains no harmful insects, larva eggs, fungus or harmful micro-organisms.

Garden compost and leaf mold may be rich and organic, but can also harbor harmful insects and diseases. For example, the compost pile is a favorite breeding ground for cutworms. Just one cutworm in a 5-gallon pot means certain death for the defenseless flowers.

Barnyard manure may contain toxic levels of salt and copious quantities of weed seeds and fungus spores. If using manure, purchase it in bags that guarantee its contents or make sure it is well-rotted. There are many kinds of manure cow manure, horse manure, rabbit manure, chicken manure and the less common pig and duck manure. Manures can also be used as soil amendments. Their nutrient content varies, depending on the diet of the animal and the decomposition factors.

Peat is partially decomposed vegetation (sedge grasses and mosses). The decay has been slowed by the wet and cold conditions of

Vermiculite, sand and manure make a popular and inexpensive mix.

the Northern U.S. Canada and other northern latitudes where it is found. The most common types of peat are formed from sphagnum and hypnum mosses.

Sphagnum peat moss is light brown and the most common peat found at commercial nurseries. It retains water well, absorbing 15 to 30 times its own weight. This gives the soil body. It contains essentially no nutrients of its own and the pH ranges from 3 to 5. After decomposing several months, the pH can get very acidic if, fine dolomite lime is not added to compensate and stabilize the pH.

Hypnum peat moss is more decomposed, darker in color with a higher pH (5 to 7). This peat moss is less common and contains more nutrients than sphagnum peat moss. This peat is a good soil amendment but it cannot hold as much water as sphagnum moss.

Peat moss is very dry and difficult to wet the first time. When using peat moss as a soil amendment, it is easiest to dry-mix all of the components, then wet the mix using a wetting agent such as liquid concentrate soap (2 or 3

Orchids thrive in mineral amendments like pumice and vermiculite.

Mushroom compost is an excellent organic soil amendment. Most growers use about one third mushroom compost with two thirds soil.

drops per gallon). Another trick to mixing peat moss is to kick the sack a few times before opening. A few kicks help break up the bail much faster and with less mess.

pH and Lime

pH is a scale from 1 to 14 that measures acid-to-alkaline balance. 1 is the most acidic, 7 is neutral and 14 is most alkaline. The pH of a soil is one of many conditions that affect plant growth. Clay soils are usually acid and many sandy soils are alkaline. Most plants grow best in a slightly acidic soil with a pH between 6.0 and 6.8. Within this range, roots can absorb and process available nutrients. If the pH is too low (acid) manganese can concentrate to toxic levels and calcium. phosphorus and magnesium availability is limited. In an alkaline soil, with a pH above 7.0, phosphorus, iron, copper, zinc, boron and manganese availability is limited. Hydroponic solutions perform best in a pH range a little lower than for soil. The pH range for hydroponics is from 5.5 to 6.8, 6.0 being ideal for most plants.

There are several ways to measure pH. A pH soil test kit, litmus paper or an electronic pH tester may be found at most nurseries and garden centers. When testing pH, take two or three samples and follow the directions for the soil test kit, litmus paper or electronic pH tester to the letter. There are several inexpensive soil test kits ($10-50) on the market. Make sure you buy a kit with a set of directions that you understand. I prefer the inexpensive electronic meters to measure soil pH and a $50-70 model to measure hydroponic pH.

If using litmus paper, collect soil samples that demonstrate an average of the soil. Place the samples in a clean jar and moisten with distilled water. Place two pieces of the litmus paper in the muddy water. After 10 seconds, remove one of the pieces. Wait a minute and remove the other one. Both pieces of litmus paper should be the same color. The litmus paper container should have a pH color chart on the side. Match the color of the litmus paper with the colors on the chart to get a pH reading. The only way litmus paper could give a false reading is if the fertilizer contains a color tracing agent or the pH of the distilled water used for the test was not a neutral 7.

There are many brands of electronic soil pH testers. They are inexpensive ($15 to $70), very convenient and fairly accurate. Pay special attention to the soil moisture when using the meter. Most electronic testers are designed to work in soil that is very moist. When checking pH regularly, the electronic tester is much more economical than test kits and more convenient than litmus paper. The electronic unit will test pH an infinite number of times, while the small chemical test kits are good for only about a dozen tests. For an accurate test, clean the probes of the pH meter after each test with an abrasive agent to wipes clean any corrosion; pack the soil tightly around the probes and water soil with distilled or neutral pH water before testing.

Check the pH of the water being used. Sometimes the pH of the water is too low or too high. After repeated watering, an unacceptable pH can substantially alter the pH of the soil, especially soils high in organic amendments. Coastal, rainy climates generally have acidic water, while desert regions are prone to alkaline water. A pH problem may surface in the late autumn when all the leaves fall and vegetation is decomposing. This biodegradation process is acidic by nature and may create an artificially low pH. The acidic leaves lower the pH of the outside soil and in turn lower the pH of the ground water. This problem is most common among smaller municipal and well-water systems. Larger water facilities generally monitor and correct pH so there are fewer problems for the gardener. Be on the lookout for any major environmental changes that could affect the water pH. It is very important to keep an eye on the pH at all times.

This digital pH meter helps keep the pH in the "safe" range.

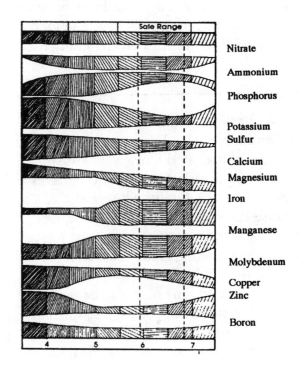

The nutrients listed in this chart are most readily available in the safe pH of 5.9 to 6.8.

Small tomato seedlings are emerging from Jiffy-7 pellets.

 Rule of Thumb: Check pH at least once every two weeks.

Soil pH should be between 6 and 7 for maximum growth and nutrient uptake in most plants.

Commercial potting soil seldom has a pH above 7.5. A lower pH is more usual - even as low as 5.5. The ideal range would be between 6 and 6.5. Most potting soils have a tendency to be a bit acidic since they are generally used

Whitewash is made from hydrated lime and table salt. The recipe is printed on sacks of hydrated lime. Whitewash is not as viscous as latex paint and requires a few coats. I really like whitewash because it sticks to damp concrete basement walls and is antiseptic against fungus. Whitewashing is the most effective way to safely "white out" damp, sweaty walls. Hydrated lime may also be used as a garden room fungicide. Just sprinkle it on the floor and around the room. It will kill fungus on contact. Bordeaux fungicide mix uses hydrated lime and copper sulfate.

for indoor, perennial, acid-loving plants. The easiest way to maintain and raise the pH is to mix in one cup of fine dolomite lime per cubic foot of potting soil. Mix dolomite lime thoroughly into dry soil. Mix the soil again in the container after it has been watered to ensure a thorough even mix.

Fine dolomite lime has been a favorite pH stabilizer of gardeners for many years. It is virtually impossible to apply too much dolomite as long as it is thoroughly mixed. It stabilizes the pH safely. That is, by adding dolomite to the soil when planting, the pH is guaranteed to remain stable, even with changes in the water supply and acidic fertilizer applications, but dolomite lime is a compound of magnesium and calcium. Both of these secondary nutrients are needed by flowers and vegetables to flower and fruit. Many fertilizers do not supply adequate amounts of calcium and magnesium. Dolomite does not save the soil from excess salt buildup only you, and regular leaching will take care of toxic salts. When purchasing dolomite, ask for the finest (dust-like) grade available. The dolomite should be as fine as possible so it is readily assimilable. Coarse dolomite could take as long as a year before it *starts* to break down enough for the plants to assimilate.

Make sure to mix fine dolomite thoroughly with the soil when planting. Improperly mixed, the dolomite will form a cake or layer that burns roots and deflects water.

 Rule of Thumb: When planting, add one cup of fine dolomite lime to each cubic foot (or one ounce per gallon) of planting medium to stabilize the pH and provide calcium and magnesium.

Hydrated lime is very similar to dolomite lime, but as the name hydrated implies, it is very soluble. Hydrated lime works acceptably to alter pH after planting. Mix it thoroughly with warm water and apply with each watering. Some horticulturists use a mix of one fourth hydrated lime and three fourths dolomite lime. This mix provides lime that is immediately available to neutralize the pH and the dolomite lime has a long-lasting effect. It is not advisable to use more than one cup of hydrated lime per cubic foot of soil. With only hydrated lime in a soil mix, it is released so fast that it can become toxic to plants. If you do add too much, heavy leaching will wash it out within a couple of weeks.

Use quicklime (calic lime) only in small doses it can be toxic to plants. Calcic lime contains only calcium and is not a good choice to induce plant growth. It does not have the buffering qualities of dolomite, nor does it contain any magnesium.

There are several ways to raise the pH. Each requires putting some form of alkali in the growing medium or water. Examples include calcium carbonate, potassium hydroxide, sodium hydroxide, lime and several other compounds. Both hydroxides are caustic and require special care when handling. They are normally used to raise the pH of hydroponic nutrient solutions. The easiest and most convenient way to raise and stabilize the pH of soil is to add fine dolomite lime and hydrated lime before planting.

 Rule of Thumb: To raise the pH one point, add three cups of fine dolomite lime to one cubic foot of soil. An alternate fast-acting mix would be 2 1/2 cups of dolomite and half cup of hydrated lime to one cubic foot of soil.

There are many ways to lower the pH. If the water has a pH that is slightly high, distilled white vinegar will solve the problem. Calcium nitrate or nitric acid, used mainly in hydroponic systems and sulfur also work very well to lower pH. If using fertilizers containing these nutrients, keep close watch on the pH they could lower it substantially.

If uncertain how much solution to apply to alter the pH, give a dosage of half as much as

Types of Lime

Agricultural or ground limestone (calcium carbonate) is one of the most common forms of lime and an excellent choice. It is slow acting and will remain in the soil for several years.

Dolomite lime (calcium magnesium carbonate) combines calcium with magnesium to formulate an excellent pH-altering substance and adds two much used nutrients as well. Always buy slow-acting dolomite in the finest form available so it becomes available sooner. Even the finest grade will remain in the soil for up to five years.

Ground oyster shells contain calcium carbonate and small amounts of phosphorus. These shells are commonly available at feed stores. They are used as chicken grit to supply calcium. Oyster shells are *very* slow acting, regulating the pH for years.

Hydrated lime (calcium hydroxide) is quick acting and caustic to plants and microorganisms. Use only in small amounts if used at all.

Quicklime (calcium oxide), manufactured by searing or burning limestone, is fast acting, but caustic and may burn or kill plant and soil microorganisms.

Wood ashes are a source of lime as well as potassium (potash) and many ashes contain magnesium. Hardwood ashes are about twice as alkaline as softwood ashes. Wood ashes are soluble and leach out of the soil rapidly.

 Rule of Thumb: To lower the pH of water one point, add one teaspoon of white distilled vinegar per gallon of water. Check pH of the solution before watering; the pH of vinegar varies according to type and manufacturer.

recommended, then check it. Wait about 15 minutes and check it again. Now add the balance of the chemical or as much as needed to achieve the desired result.

After altering the pH, check it, then check it again several days later. Continue checking the pH weekly to make sure it remains stable.

 Rule of Thumb: If soil pH is under 5 or over 8, it is easiest and less expensive in the long run, to change soil rather than experimenting with changing the pH.

Pulverized eggshells, clam or oyster shells and wood ashes have a high pH and will raise pH. It takes many, many eggshells to fill a cup and it takes a long time for the shells to break down to affect the pH. Wood ashes usually have a pH of about 11, are soluble and easy to over-apply. Many times ashes come from fireplaces or wood stoves that have been burning all kinds of trash (plastic and colored inks) and are contaminated.

Soil Temperature

Raising the soil temperature speeds chemical processes and hastens nutrient uptake. Ideally, the soil temperature should range from 65 to 75° F (18 to 24° C). The soil can be heated by means of heat cable or pad placed in or under soil. Heat cable may be purchased at most nurseries. Some gardeners use a waterbed heating pad to heat a large bed. It is an inexpensive alternative to heating the air. Soil can be heated passively by placing the container up off the floor on blocks to allow the flow of warm air underneath. Using this method, an additional heat source may not be needed. Do not heat the soil or nutrient solution over 75° F (24° C). Heating the soil will dehydrate and cook the roots!

Potting Soil

Potting soil fresh out of the bag generally supplies rapid-growing annuals with enough nutrients for the first month of growth before supplemental fertilization is necessary. Secondary and trace elements are usually found in sufficient quantities and unnecessary to add, except for fine dolomite lime. If you grow organically, supplemental fertilization can be replaced by organic soil amendments and fertilizers. See Chapter Four, "Organic Fertilizers" pages 87-89.

Potting soil from a nursery is the easiest soil to use for indoor cultivation. It is usually pH balanced, contains adequate levels of most nutrients, retains water and air evenly, drains well and allows easy root growth. Most potting soils, except those containing unusually large amounts of organic fertilizer amendments, will be depleted of nutrients within three or four weeks. After this time, supplemental fertilization will usually be necessary. Potting soils tend to be very localized, since they are so heavy and shipping costs prohibitive. There are many good brands to choose from. Ask your nurseryperson for help in selecting one. None-the-less, make a point of checking the pH yourself.

Mushroom compost is an inexpensive potting soil amendment. Frequently mushroom compost has been sterilized chemically so that only mushrooms would grow in it. The law usually requires that after mushroom gardeners discard the rich compost that it sit fallow for a year or more before it is can be used. The fallow time allows for all the harmful sterilants to leach out. The compost is normally very fertile and has a marvelous texture. Check at your local nursery or extension service for a good source of mushroom compost. Some of the most abundant vegetable harvests use mushroom compost as the main growing medium.

Potting soils containing more than 50 percent vermiculite, pumice or perlite may tend to stratify when heavily saturated with water before planting. The light mineral amendments tend to float, with the heavier organic matter settling to the bottom. If this happens, mix the water-saturated soil thoroughly with your hands until it is evenly mixed before planting or transplanting.

Potting soil can get somewhat expensive when used only once, then discarded. If it is used for more than one annual crop then reused for several years, undesirable micro-organisms and insects may have time to get started. Nutrients are depleted, water and air retention are poor and compaction leads to poor drainage. There is an inexpensive alternative to potting soil: soilless mix.

Soilless Mix

Soilless mix is a very popular, inexpensive, lightweight sterile growing medium that has been used in nurseries for many years. It is generally made from one or all of the following: pumice, vermiculite, perlite, sand and peat moss. Soilless mix allows for good, even root growth. It can be pushed to amazing lengths with total control and best of all, it is very inexpensive!

Soilless mix is preferred by commercial nurserypeople and indoor gardeners alike. It has good texture. It contains essentially no nutrients of its own, unless fortified with nutrients and is generally at or near 7 on the pH scale. Soilless mix works very well for gardeners who tend to overwater or overfertilize or like to "push" plants with heavy fertilization. It drains fairly rapidly and may be leached efficiently to stop nutrients from building up to toxic levels. Soilless mix can be purchased ready-mixed in bags of Jiffy Mix, Terra-lite, etc. Some gardeners say these mixes hold moisture too long and they add 10 to 50 percent perlite to help drainage. These commercial soilless mixes are fortified with small amounts of all necessary nutrients. The fortified nutrients generally last for about a month. None-the-

less, it is a good idea to use a fertilizer containing trace elements. After one month, supplemental fertilization is generally be necessary to sustain vigorous growth in annuals.

Soilless components can be purchased separately and mixed to the desired consistency. Mix small amounts right in the bag. Larger batches should be mixed in a wheelbarrow or on a concrete slab.

Note: Mixing soil or soilless mix is a dusty, messy, miserable job. Mix it outdoors and wear a respirator. A light misting of water will help quell dust.

 Rule of Thumb: Mix soilless amendments outdoors and when they are dry. Use a respirator to avoid dust inhalation.

Coarse sand, fine vermiculite or perlite works well for rooting cuttings. Sand and perlite are fast draining, which helps prevent damping-off. Vermiculite holds water and air longer and makes cloning easier. Soilless mix also allows for complete control of critical nutrient and root-stimulating hormones for taking cuttings.

Texture of soilless mix should be coarse, light and spongy. This allows drainage with sufficient moisture and air retention, as well as providing good root penetration qualities. Fine soilless mix holds more moisture and works well with smaller containers. Soilless mixes using more perlite and sand drain faster, making it easier to fertilizer heavily and not lead to excessive salt buildup. Vermiculite and peats hold water longer and work well for small pots, rooting cuttings or for good water retention.

pH is generally a neutral 7. If using more than 15 percent moss in your mix, add the appropriate amount of dolomite or hydrated lime to correct and stabilize pH. Check the pH every week or two; continued watering can promote a lower pH. Soilless mixes tend to maintain a neutral pH. They are mostly composed of mineral particles that are not affected by organic decomposition, which could change

Examples of the many soilless mixes:

1/3 peat moss	1/8 peat moss
1/3 perlite	1/8 coarse sand
1/3 vermiculite	1/4 perlite
	1/2 vermiculite
1/8 peat moss	
1/8 coarse sand	1/2 peat moss
1/4 vermiculite	1/2 perlite
1/2 perlite	

Add the proper amount of dolomite or hydrated lime to each mix to bring pH up to neutral. See Rule of Thumb page 66.

pH. The pH is affected very little by acidic fertilizers or by water with a high or low pH.

Nutrients are not contained in soilless mix unless they are fortified or added by the gardener. Feed frequently with a soluble complete N-P-K fertilizer containing all necessary trace and secondary elements.

Note: When using sand to root cuttings or as an additive to soil or soilless mix, make sure it is washed, coarse, sharp sand it will drain much better than fine sand. Do not use beach or ocean sand, it contains toxic levels of salt. Sand is the heaviest soil amendment; if too much is used, it will settle to the bottom, while the lighter components, perlite and vermiculite remain on top.

Rockwool root cubes or Jiffy 7 Pellets and Oasis cubes are very convenient and lend themselves to growing cuttings or seedlings with a strong root system. Peat pots are small compressed peat moss containers with an expandable outside wall. The flat pellets pop up into a seedling pot when watered. They work very well for sowing seeds or even rooting cuttings. Just place the seed or cutting in the wet peat pot or root cube and keep it evenly moist. For cuttings, make sure to crimp the top in around the stem so constant contact is made between the stem and the root cube or peat pot. When roots show through the side, set pot or cube into a larger pot. There will be virtually no transplant shock. They do tend to dry out and contract, which exposes stems. Be sure to check peat pots or root cubes daily, keeping them evenly moist but not drenched. Root cubes and peat pots do not contain any nutrients. Seedlings do not require any nutrients for the first week of growth. Feed seedlings after the first week and cuttings as soon as they are rooted. One gardener likes to feed cuttings and seedlings a weak manure tea when they are planted and with each watering for the first two weeks.

Soil Mixes

If you plan to mix your own potting soil from backyard garden soil, please read the section "About Soil" carefully. Mixing you own soil is a good way to save money especially when using large amounts of potting soil. But, mixing your own potting soil takes some experience to achieve the best results. Regardless of the components that you choose to mix in your own special compost mix, make sure to mix them thoroughly. If using garden soil, be sure to find the richest, darkest soil with a good texture. Adding 30 to 70 percent perlite, vermiculite, peat moss or compost will probably be necessary to attain the best texture. Even well-draining garden soils tend to compact and need more coarse matter to retain good drainage, water and air retention. Check the pH before digging soil to make sure it is within the acceptable 6 to 7 range. Add fine dolomite regardless of the pH.

Alternatives that require more work are to sterilize amendments by baking in the oven at 16^0 F for 30 to 45 minutes. The stench can be horrible and it is a messy project. Cooking the compost in a pile that reaches 160^0 F (71^0 C) bakes all the bad insects and diseases while retaining the beneficial organisms.

Compost

Composting is easy, rewarding and profitable. The basics are simple: collect organic matter, pile it up and let it rot. All you do is keep microorganisms and bacteria in the pile well supplied with the proper proportions of air, food and water.

The relationship between the amount of carbon and nitrogen found in all compost material is called the carbon/nitrogen (C/N) ratio. The best compost materials have a C/N ratio of 1/30, expressed simply as 30. For example, barnyard manure has a C/N ratio of 15 and sawdust about 400. Manure composts rapidly, while sawdust may take two years or more to decompose. The higher the number, the higher the carbon content. The closer to 30 the C/N ratio, the faster the compost will heat and break down. Look for green organic materials such as grass clippings or leaves to ensure the fastest composting. Do not use meat products, which will attract scavengers. With the proper materials supplying adequate organic nitrogen, a compost pile can be started any time of the year, even in the middle of winter.

Turning any compost pile will add air and accelerate decomposition. If smell is a problem, cover the pile with plastic or a thin layer of soil.

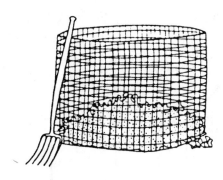

Pile framed with wire

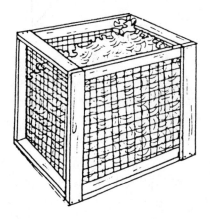

Pile framed with removable wire and wood sides

There are two basic types of compost piles - hot and cold.

Hot compost piles are fueled by adequate nitrogen-rich organic matter, air and moisture that are always available for microorganisms to change the compost into humus. A critical mass of at least 3 feet by 3 feet allows the compost pile the insulation and volume to "cook" rapidly. Decomposition is so fast that finished compost is often ready in 2-4 weeks. Hot composting is recommended when using compost to amend potting soil. The high temperatures ensure a safe mix with no harmful microorganisms, insects, etc.

Cold compost piles lack adequate amounts of air, moisture, nitrogen-rich

Free standing compost pile

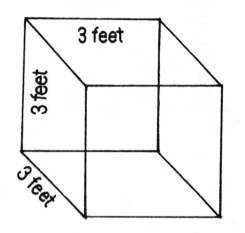

The hot compost pile must have a critical mass of at least 3 feet square.

material or the critical mass of 3 feet square. Decomposition is slow but steady, taking a year or longer. Turning the pile adds air, speeding decomposition.

Air

A layer of wood chips or dry brush below the pile helps air to circulate up under the heap, where it is most needed. A 2-4-inch layer of dry organic matter sandwiched between green matter every 12 inches supplies sufficient aeration. Very diverse sizes and textures of the organic matter also creates a perfect air environment. For the lowest work level, the pile needn't be turned. Enough air for decomposition is supplied when the organic matter is of various sizes and textures. The outer layer of debris on the pile forms a seal around the pile. Any disagreeable odors stay inside the heap.

When air is inadequate, decomposition slows and the pile starts to smell. Turning the pile is more work but aerates the heap faster, helps curtail unpleasant odors and speeds decomposition.

A length of 4-inch perforated drain pipe, a tube of wire mesh, bundled cornstalks or bamboo inserted down into the center of the compost pile forms a ventilating stack, which will help aerate the pile.

Heat

Heat speeds decomposition. The temperature in the center of the compost heap should be at least 55° F (13° C). Decomposition also takes place at lower temperatures, but is slower. Temperatures from 140 to 160° F (60-71° C) kill almost all plant diseases, harmful insects, weed seeds and roots. A "hot" compost pile will generate temperatures of up to 170° F (77° C) for up to a week or more. Check the temperature of the compost pile by inserting a thin metal into the center of the pile for a few minutes. If the rod is warm when removed, it's probably hot enough. A soil or food thermometer will give an exact reading at different locations of the pile.

Moisture

The moisture content of a compost pile should be between 40 and 60 percent. Moisture level is easy to check: the pile will have the consistency of a wrung-out sponge or "glisten" with wetness.

Steam rises from the pile as heat builds. So much water is used that the center of the pile may become dry. Insert a probe into the pile to test for heat and moisture. Ideally, the probe should come out warm, moist and with no foul odors. Add water to the pile if necessary.

Too much moisture causes poor air circulation and is signaled by a dank smell and slimy compost. Turn the pile and add dry matter to aerate. A plastic cover or layer of soil will also keep it from smelling and deflects excess rainwater.

Add water while building the heap if very dry material is used to ensure even moisture distribution throughout the pile.

Finished Compost

Finished compost, (humus) is fertile, dark and crumbly with a sweet, earthy smell. Finished compost can be applied to all crops, any time of the year, as a soil amendment/fertilizer or as a mulch/fertilizer sidedressing. Don't worry about overdoing it!

Even though finished compost is "stable" and will not break down rapidly, it keeps better when covered to prevent leaching out of nutrients. Use the finished compost within six months or many of the beneficial qualities will be lost.

Location

Build compost piles on a level ground surface with good drainage. Cultivate the soil below to break it up, so it will absorb nutrients and provide a safe haven for earthworms when the pile gets too hot. Easy vehicle access is important if you expect to have grass clippings and other chopped green matter delivered by landscapers or neighbors.

A compost pile should be convenient to access. Locate it close enough to the house so that adding kitchen scraps is easy.

Collect the kitchen scraps, excluding meat and fish products, in a gallon plastic container with a lid that seals. Throw the kitchen scraps into the center of the pile so they do not attract scavengers.

The heap can be unsightly and occasionally smell, if not properly maintained, so locate it out of view.

Do not move the compost pile from place to place. The soil below builds up a population of beneficial bacteria and microbes that will migrate into the pile. Decomposition progresses faster when these microbes and bacteria are readily available.

Good Compost Material

Note: All organic matter decomposes faster when bruised and/or chopped into small pieces.

Plant residues: Any and all trimmings and thinnings from your organic garden. The greater the variety of organic matter the better. Diverse compost materials maintain good air circulation and keep matting to a minimum.

Grass clippings are probably the best all-round compost material. They contain plenty of nitrogen and compost very quickly. Fresh composting grass clippings often reach temperatures in excess of 150^0 F (66^0 C)! Many of your neighbors will be happy to dump their chemical-free grass clippings on your compost pile.

Note: Grass clippings may develop dry or wet pockets and should be mixed with more coarse debris and turned.

Kitchen waste: Coffee grounds, egg shells, oyster and crustacean shells, vegetable scraps, sour milk, anything organic. Fish and meat scraps should be avoided because they attract scavengers and can smell.

Leaves break down faster if green and chopped, autumn leaves decompose much more slowly. City maintenance crews pick up leaves each fall. Call your local city maintenance to get the specifics on how to get a load of leaves delivered to your house.

Conifer foliage: Pine, fir and cedar needles break down fairly slowly. They make a good layer for aeration.

Weeds are okay if the pile gets hot enough in the center to cook the roots and seeds to a nonviable state. But avoid adding perennial weeds with strong, sprouting underground root systems to cold piles.

Fair Compost Materials

Ash: Wood and paper ashes add potassium (potash) but these leach out quickly and provide few long-term benefits.

Lime (dolomite): - An occasional dusting "sweetens" and stabilizes the pH. Microbes work the best in a pH that is just below the neutral 7.0.

Greensand and granite dust add potassium.

Paper: Shredded newspaper and recycled paper break down a little faster than new, unshredded paper. Do not use slick, wax or ink-colored paper; the inks may contain heavy metals.

Peat moss tends to form dry pockets.

Rock phosphate and bone meal add phosphorus.

Sawdust robs the compost pile of nitrogen, needed for decomposition. If used, add nitrogen to compensate for the nitrogen loss. Weathered sawdust, like weathered straw, decomposes faster than fresh.

Sod and soil add weight.

Wood chips, hedge clippings and small branches should be cut into small pieces or run through a chipper if possible. Add in small amounts for aeration. Wood chips break down slower and take longer than other, faster decomposing ingredients and such are best added directly to surface as mulch.

Charcoal briquettes do not break down. Furnace coal contains excessive amounts of sulfur and iron.

Chemical fertilizers are not all good compost activators.

Insecticides, herbicides, rodenticides, if concentrated, may kill any life in the heap. But grass clippings treated with herbicides, such as Weed 'n Feed, create no problems in hot, active piles.

Cooked kitchen scraps putrefy and attract scavengers and should be covered with soil if used.

Diseased plants with such afflictions as club root, dry rot, leaf spot or blight should be avoided. Potato stems and leaves can be carriers of blight.

Dung: Cat, dog or any meat-eating animal's feces can transmit parasites harmful to humans.

High-cholesterol greases and fats break down slowly and attract scavengers.

Metal: Aluminum, plastic, greasy, painted metals could contain toxic materials that should not be added to compost.

Mud, sand and gravel have no nutrient or bacterial value and add weight, but can aid in aeration.

Perennial weeds: crabgrass, dandelions, etc. that sprout from roots, are okay to add if the compost pile is hot enough to "cook" them to death.

Quicklime (calcium oxide) destroys humus.

Soapy dishwater could contain sulfates, but biodegradable soaps, such as Ivory, cause no harm.

Soil does not enhance compost and slows aeration, but can be effective in thin layers.

Compost Activators

Compost activators provide protein and bacteria. The right bacteria usually exists in a "cooking" compost pile and are unnecessary to add.

New compost piles: To speed decomposition in new piles, borrow a couple of handfuls of compost from the center of a neighbor's pile to spread on your pile. Several commercial compost activators are also on the market.

Natural activators include alfalfa meal, blood meal, bone meal, well rotted compost, cottonseed meal, fish meal, fish waste, seaweed, hoof meal, horn meal, manure and organic soil. Sprinkle them over the compost pile when building and cover with more layers of compost.

Many gardeners have no trouble using organic compost. Others lose their entire garden or have poor yields due to disease in the compost. Many good compost recipes are available from monthly publications such as *Sunset, Organic Gardening, National Gardening Magazines* and from the companies specializing in organic composts.

Before using compost, pour it through 14-inch-mesh hardware cloth (screen). Place a heavy duty framed screen over a large garbage can or a wheelbarrow to catch the sifted compost. This will break up the humus before it is mixed with the soil and amendments. After adding the amendments, the mix may be resifted for additional mixing. Earthworms found on the screen should be returned to the medium. Cutworms are promptly squished.

Gardeners using one-third worm castings one-third perlite and one-third organic matter have had excellent results. Many gardeners mix a third to half perlite with a bag of rich potting soil that has lots of worm castings. Worm castings are heavy, compacting the roots and leave little or no air space to the roots. Adding perlite aerates the soil.

Here are three basic examples of the many possible combinations of soil mixes.

Add fine dolomite lime to each one of these soil mixes, whether or not the pH is off. See Rule of Thumb, page 66.

1/3 worm castings   1/3 perlite
1/3 manure   1/3 worm castings
1/3 coarse sand   1/3 peat moss

1/3 worm castings
1/3 peat moss
1/3 compost

Use a wheelbarrow to collect sifted compost.

Containers

This lime tree needs to be flushed with water. Note the cut in photo on the left that shows the excess salt build-up on the side of the pot.

A bright halide and coarse, fast-draining soil help create a perfect natural environment for this crop of cacti.

Containers come in all shapes and sizes. They can be constructed of almost anything clay, metal, plastic, wood and fiber are the most common. Just about any kind of container will do, as long as it is large enough, thoroughly clean and has not been used for any petroleum or other toxic products. See the chart on "Minimum Container Size" page 77. Clay, fiber and wood containers breathe better than plastic or metal. Clay pots are heavy and notorious for absorbing moisture from soil inside, causing the soil inside to dry out quickly.

Grow bags are a good, inexpensive, long-lasting alternative to rigid containers. In fact, some people use the sack the potting soil came in as a container. Once the soil is inside and moist, the bag holds its shape. The bags tend to expand and contract with the soil, lessening the chance of burned root tips that grow down the side of pots.

Fiber or pulp pots are very popular and inexpensive, but their bottoms frequently rot out. Painting the inside of the fiber container with latex paint will extend the life.

Automatic self-watering pots are used for African violets and most other gesneraids. These kind of pots work very well for slower-growing perennials. One end of a wick made from coarse string or yarn soaks in water, the other end is packed into the soil. The porous yarn or string wicks water to the soil.

Other than making sure containers are clean, there are two important factors to consider: drainage holes and size.

Drainage holes should let the excess water drain easily, but not be so big that soil in the bottom of the container washes out onto the floor. Pots can be lined with newspaper if drainage is too rapid or soil washes out drain holes. Covering holes will slow drainage, so be wary!

The size of container is of utmost importance. Annual flowers and vegetables grow very rapidly, requiring a lot of root space for vigorous growth. If the roots are confined, growth slows to a crawl. A good example is

Rule of Thumb: Have at least two half-inch or four quarter-inch holes per square foot of container bottom. When using a tray under the pot, do not let excess water sit in the tray longer than three days. This stagnant water causes root rot and fungus.

found at most retail nurseries about midsummer. Tomato plants that are still in small 4-inch or gallon pots that will be fully mature and have a few ripe tomatoes. Notice the branches do not extend much beyond the sides of the container and dripline, the plants are tall and leggy with curled-down leaves. They have an overall stunted sickly appearance. These plants are pot- or root-bound. They could be kept alive or maybe even forced to grow a little by fertilizing with the exact balance of necessary nutrients. This is a lot of work, it is easy to overfertilize and the plant will always be a runt.

Annual plant roots develop and elongate quickly, growing down and out away from the main taproot. When roots reach the sides of the pot, they grow straight down. Soil contracts and separates from the inside of the container's wall. The root hairs along this gap are responsible for absorbing water and nutrients. They are left helpless to dry out and die. One way to help solve this contraction problem is to run your finger around the inside lip of the pot, cultivating the soil, filling the crack between the pot and soil. Check this gap every few days. Also, maintaining evenly moist soil will help keep root hairs on the soil perimeter from drying out.

It is important to transplant before the plant is pot-bound and stunted. Once a plant is stunted, it will take several weeks to grow enough new roots and root hairs to resume normal growth.

The best way to solve the pot-bound problem is to plant annual seedlings or cuttings directly into a five or six gallon pot. This method requires fewer containers and less

Large planters on casters are easy to maneuver in the garden room or patio and provide more root space for plants.

Minimum Container Size

Age/Months Container Size

0-1   4-inch
1-2   1 gallon
2-3   2 gallon
3-4   3 gallon
4-5   5 gallon
4-6   10 gallon

This chart shows the approximate size container for peppers at various ages.

Rule of Thumb: Allow one gallon of soil for every month the annual will spend in the container. A three-to-six-gallon pot will support a seedling or cutting for three to six months.

work. It is less stressful to both plants and transplanter.

Pots are the most common containers for indoor use. They are inexpensive and readily available. Complete individual water and nutrient control is possible with pots. An individual plant can be quarantined from the rest of the garden or dipped in a medicinal solution. When plants are small, they can be huddled tightly together under the HID lamp and moved farther apart as needed.

A drip watering system makes irrigation easy. These systems use low-pressure plastic pipe with friction fittings. Water flows down the pipe and out the emitters, one drop at a time. The emitters are attached to the main hose and are either spaghetti or nipple type. There are several kits on the market or you can construct your own system from component parts.

The drip system offers several advantages. Once set up, it cuts watering maintenance. Fertilizer can also be injected into the system. Fertilization is easy, but the same amount of nutrient is doled out to each plant on the water line. One gardener loves the convenience and constant feeding ability of the system. She injects a fertilizer solution into the system with each watering. She notes that plants grown using a drip system are able to survive in smaller containers. Root growth is minimal, since the nutrients and water are in constant supply. In fact, a soilless mix and a drip system is essentially a non-recovery hydroponic system.

The drip system can also be attached to a timer so that it irrigates when you are on vacation. This is very convenient, but can promote negligence. The garden needs daily care! If it is automated, it may discourage you from physically checking the moisture or looking at every plant daily. Automation is great, but is not a substitute for good gardening practices.

Large planters can be placed on the ground or set up on blocks or casters to allow air circulation underneath. Increased circulation lessens the chance of fungus growth and

keeps the soil warmer than if it were sitting on a cold floor. The planters range in size from 2 feet by 2 feet by 12 inches to 10 feet by 4 feet by 24 inches. The roots have 2 to 3 times as much soil to grow in and much less side surface for roots to run into and grow down. Roots are able to intertwine and grow to their maximum potential.

Plants or cuttings left in one-gallon pots until they are a month or two old, then transplanted to the large planter box before they are root-bound. This allows young plants to be bunched together under the lamp and receive maximum light intensity. Once plants start crowding and shading one another, they can be bent outward and tied down to a trellis that is nailed to the sides of the planter. Large planters work very well and are highly recommended because they require less maintenance. A large mass of soil retains water and nutrients much longer and more evenly.

Raised beds can be installed right on the earthen floor of a garage or basement. If drainage is poor, a layer of gravel or a dry well is laid under 12 to 24 inches of soil, with a 2-by-12-inch board border for the raised bed. If the bed is subterranean, it might be very close to the water table. When it rains, the water collects underneath and might flood the garden. The garden seldom needs watering, but plants are kept a little too wet and there might be a buildup of nutrients in the soil that cannot be leached effectively.

If drainage does not present a problem and you are able to grow in a raised bed, by all means do so. The large soil mass gives a chance to build up a good organic base after several crops. There will need to be organic activity within the soil. Your job is to make sure it is the good, not the bad, micro-organisms that live in the bed. When mixing soil or adding amendments, use the best possible organic components and follow organic principles. There should be good drainage and the soil should be as deep (12 to 24 inches) as possible. The more organic matter present, the more fertile the soil will be.

A good deal of heat can be generated by
the organic activity. This not only speeds nutrient uptake, but helps heat the room as well.
Ventilation is necessary to lower heat and
humidity. It also keeps the room free of fungus
and bad bugs. The organic garden sounds
great, but replicating the great outdoors can be
a lot of work.

Chapter Four
Water and Fertilizer

Water and fertilizer work hand in hand. The nutrients in fertilizer dissolve in water. Water carries nutrients through the plant. Water is essential to plant growth, making up more than 75 percent of a plant's weight.

The root hairs absorb water, nutrients (fertilizer) and oxygen in the soil and carry them up the stem to the leaves. This flow of water from the soil through the plant is called the transpiration stream. A fraction of the water is processed and used in photosynthesis. The water evaporates into the air, carrying waste products along with it, via the stomata in the leaves. This process is called transpiration. Some of the water also returns manufactured sugars and starches to the roots.

Unfortunately, common tap water may contain high levels of alkaline salts, sulfur or chlorine and may have a pH out of the acceptable 6 to 7 range. Water containing sulfur is easily smelled and tasted. Saline water is a little more difficult to detect. Water in coastal areas is generally full of salt because it washes inland from the ocean. This problem is worst in Southern California and other coastal areas.

Chlorine and salt are added to many household water systems. Chlorine, in small doses, does not seem to affect plant growth, but salt-softened water should be avoided. Enough salt will kill any plant! Chlorine does tend to make soil acidic after repeated use.

The best way to get chlorine out of water is to let it sit one or two days in an open container. The chlorine will evaporate as a gas when it comes in contact with the air. An aquarium heater works well to heat the water of a reservoir to maintain it at room temperature. Heating also makes the chlorine dissipate faster. If chlorine alters soil pH noticeably, it can be adjusted with hydrated lime. Salts from saline water or fertilizer residue can build up to toxic levels quickly in container gardens. Excessive salts inhibit seed germination, burn root hairs and the tips and edges of leaves. Excess salt buildup in the soil can easily be leached out by pouring two gallons of water per gallon of growing medium. Repeat leaching once or twice if burn is severe. Leaching will wash out any toxic buildup of salts. If you use soft or saline water or have any unwanted substances in the soil; leach containers every month or two. Hard or well water may be alkaline and can contain notable amounts of calcium and magnesium. Both nutrients are put to good use by flowering and fruiting plants. It is doubtful that hard water could contain enough

These geraniums use as much water under a HID as they would under natural sunlight in the middle of a hot summer day.

calcium or magnesium to toxify the soil. It is still a good idea to leach the soil at least every two months. Generally, water that is OK to drink is OK for plants.

Watering

There is no wet and dry rule about how much water to apply or when to apply it.

 Rules of Thumb: Apply tepid (70 to 80⁰ F, 22 to 27⁰ C) water. Plants process tepid water rapidly and it penetrates the soil better. Tepid water does not shock tender root hairs or leaves.

Water early in the day so excess water will evaporate from soil surface and leaves. Keeping foliage and soil wet leads to fungus attack.

Large plants use much more water than small plants, but there are many more variables than size that dictate a plant's water consumption. The age of the plant, container size, soil texture, temperature, humidity and ventilation all contribute to water needs. Change any one

of these variables and water consumption will change. Good ventilation is essential to promote transpiration, water consumption and rapid growth. The healthier a plant, the faster it grows and the more water it consumes.

Many gardeners irrigate on a wet and dry cycle. They water, then let the soil dry out to about 2 inches below the soil surface before the next watering. Other gardeners keep moisture more consistent by irrigating more often. A fertilizer solution is often added with each watering.

Annual flowers and vegetables do not like soggy soil. Soil kept too wet drowns roots, making it impossible for them to breathe. Slow growth and possible fungus attack result. Tiny root hairs dry up and die if the soil dries out, even in pockets. It seems to take forever for the roots to grow new hairs.

A moisture meter takes most of the guesswork out of watering. They can be purchased for $10 to $30 and are well worth the money. The meter can tell exactly how much water the soil contains at any level or point. Sometimes soil develops dry pockets and loses its ability to hold water evenly. Dry soil pockets are most common when soil components such as peat are not thoroughly mixed. Checking moisture with a finger is an educated guess and disturbs the root system. A moisture meter gives an exact moisture reading without bothering the roots as much.

 Rules of Thumb: Irrigate small seedlings and cuttings when the soil surface is dry. The surface is dry almost daily on cuttings rooting in sand or vermiculite with good drainage and no humidity tent,

Irrigate larger plants in the vegetative and flowering stages when soil is dry 2 inches below the surface. Flowering plants use high levels of water to carry on rapid floral formation. Letting a flowering plant wilt between watering stunts flower and fruit formation.

Line pots up so it is easy to keep track of the ones that have been watered.

The trick is to apply enough water so that all of the soil gets wet and not let too much run out the drain holes creating a mess. A leaching effect that carries away nutrients is caused by excessive watering. None-the-less, a little drip (about 10 percent) out the drain holes is beneficial.

Overwatering is a common problem, especially with small plants. Too much water drowns roots by cutting off their supply of oxygen. If you have symptoms of overwatering, buy a moisture meter! It will let both you and your garden breathe easier. Sometimes, parts of the soil are overwatered and other soil pockets remain bone-dry. Cultivating the soil surface, allowing even water penetration and using a wetting agent will overcome this problem.

One of the main causes of overwatering is poor ventilation. Plants need to transpire and water needs to evaporate into the air. If there is nowhere for this wet, humid air to go, gallons of water are locked in the garden room to literally hang in the air. Good ventilation carries the wet air away, replacing it with new dry air. If using trays to catch runoff water, use a turkey baster (large syringe) or sponge to draw the excess water from the tray.

 Rules of Thumb about watering: Large plants transpire more than small ones. Maintain good ventilation. Check the soil of each plant for moisture.

Signs of over watering include: curly, yellow leaves, constant soggy soil, fungus and slow growth. Over watering may affect a plant and the inexperienced gardener might not see any glaring symptoms for a long time.

Under-watering is less of a problem, but common in smaller pots. Small containers dry out quickly and may need daily watering. If forgotten, poor water-starved plants become stunted. Most gardeners panic when they see their beautiful garden wilted in bone-dry soil.

A water meter makes watering very exact.

If the soil is nearly or completely dry, take the following steps: Add a few drops (one drop per pint) of a biodegradable, concentrated liquid soap such as Castille or Ivory concentrate to the water. It will act as a wetting agent, helping the water penetrate soil more efficiently and guard against dry soil pockets. Most soluble fertilizers contain a wetting agent. Apply about a fourth to half as much water/fertilizer as the plant is expected to need. Wait 10 to 15 minutes for it to totally soak in, then apply more water/fertilizer until the soil is evenly moist. If trays are underneath the pots, let excess water remain in the trays a few hours or even overnight before removing it with a large turkey baster.

A readily accessible water source is very convenient; it saves time and labor. A 10-by-10-foot garden, containing 24 healthy tomato, pepper and cucumber plants in six-gallon pots could need 10 to 30 gallons of water per week. Water weighs eight pounds a gallon. Thirty gallons X eight pounds = 240 pounds! That's a lot of containers to fill, lift and spill. Carrying water in containers from the bathroom sink to

An inexpensive drip watering system makes watering a snap.

the garden is all right when plants are small, but when they get large, it is a big, sloppy, regular job. Running a hose into the garden saves much labor and mess. A lightweight, half-inch hose is easy to handle and less prone to damage plants. The water source should have hot and cold water running out the same tap and be equipped with threads. A hose may easily be attached and tepid water used to water the garden. A dishwasher coupling can be used if the faucet has no threads. The hose should have an on/off valve at the outlet, so water flow can be controlled while watering. A rigid watering wand will save many broken branches when you're leaning over to water in tight quarters. Do not leave water under pressure in the hose. Garden hose is meant to transport water, not hold it under pressure, which may cause it to rupture.

To make a siphon or gravity-fed watering system, place a barrel at least 4 feet high in the garden room. If humidity is a problem, put a lid on the barrel or move it to another room. The attic is a good place because it warms the

water and promotes good pressure. Place a siphon hose in the top of the tank or install a PVC on/off valve near the bottom of the barrel. An inexpensive device that measures the gallons of water added to the barrel can be purchased at most hardware stores. It is easy to walk off and let the barrel overflow. A shut-off float valve can also be installed in the barrel so there is a constant supply of water.

Fertilizer

Flowers and vegetables grow so fast under HID lamps that ordinary potting soil can not supply all necessary nutrients for rapid healthy growth. Fertilizing makes extra nutrients available for sustained vigorous growth.

There are more than 16 elements known to be necessary for plant life. Carbon hydrogen and oxygen are absorbed from the air and water. The rest of the elements, called nutrients, are absorbed mainly from the soil or fertilizer. The primary nutrients (nitrogen (N), phosphorus (P) and potassium (K)) are the elements a plant uses the most. Almost all fertilizers show the N-P-K percentages in big numbers on the front of the package. They are always listed in the same N-P-K order. For example, a 23-19-17 fertilizer has 23 percent nitrogen, 19 percent phosphorus and 17 percent potassium.

Calcium (Ca) and magnesium (Mg) are secondary nutrients or elements. They are sometimes classified with N-P-K as macronutrients. Iron (Fe), sulfur (S), manganese (Mn), boron(B), molybdenum (Mo), zinc (Zn) and copper (Cu) are trace elements or micronutrients. Trace elements are usually found in sufficient quantities in potting soil and in complete fertilizers for healthy plant growth and do not need to be added. Unless fortified, soilless mixes may be severely lacking in secondary and trace elements. It is still a good idea to use a fertilizer containing trace elements. Secondary and trace elements are usually not listed on fertilizer labels.

Primary Nutrients

Nitrogen (N) is the most important nutrient. It regulates the plant's ability to make proteins, essential to new protoplasm in the cells. Nitrogen is essential to the production of chlorophyll and is mainly responsible for leaf and stem growth as well as overall size and vigor. Nitrogen is most active in young buds, shoots and leaves. Annuals love nitrogen and require high levels during vegetative growth.

It is most actively used by young buds, shoots, and leaves. Most forms of nitrogen are water soluble and are quickly washed, or leached, from the soil. Consequently, nitrogen is required often. To calculate "actual" nitrogen, multiply the (N) percentage on the fertilizer label by the weight of the fertilizer. For example, blood meal is usually marked as 12-0-0 which means that it is 12 percent nitrogen by weight. Therefore, 5 pounds of blood meal times 12 percent nitrogen is 0.5 pounds, the actual weight of nitrogen in the substance.

Phosphorus (P) is necessary for photosynthesis and provides a mechanism for energy transfer within the plant. Phosphorus is associated with overall vigor and seed production. Plants use highest levels of phosphorus during the germination, seedling and flowering stages of growth.

Potassium (K) or potash (K_2O) is essential to the manufacture and movement of sugars and starches, as well as growth by cell division. Potassium increases chlorophyll in foliage and helps regulate stomata openings so plants make better use of light and air. Potash encourages strong root growth and is associated with disease resistance and water intake. Potassium is necessary during all stages of growth.

Secondary Nutrients

Magnesium (Mg) is found as a central atom in every chlorophyll molecule. It is essential to the absorption of light energy. Magnesium aids in the utilization of nutrients. It also neutralizes soil acids and toxic compounds produced by the plant. Add Epsom salts (magnesium sulfate) to your fertilizer mix at the rate of 2 teaspoons per 3 gallons of water.

Calcium (Ca) is essential to cell manufacture and growth. Plants must have calcium at the growing tip of each root. Calcium is essential to cell manufacture and growth. Plants must have some calcium at the growing tip of each root. The easiest way to supply calcium is to add steamed bone meal or colloidal phosphate to the soil.

Trace elements are essential for plant growth and must be present in minute amounts, but little is known about the exact amounts that are needed. They also function as catalysts to plant processes and nutrient utilization. Trace elements include iron, manganese, boron , molybdenum, zinc, chlorine, and copper. Trace elements are usually in most soils. However, extreme acidity or alkalinity may make them unavailable to plants. Liberal applications of compost or organic matter of all kinds will often remedy this problem.

Fertilizers

The goal of fertilizing is to supply the plant with proper amounts of nutrients for vigorous growth without toxifying the soil by over fertilizing. A five- or six-gallon container full of rich, fertile potting soil will supply all the necessary nutrients for a month or longer. After the roots have absorbed most of the available macronutrients, they must be added to the soil to sustain vigorous growth. Unless *fortified*, soilless mixes require N-P-K fertilization from the start. I like to start fertilizing fortified soilless mixes after the first week or two of growth.

Most commercial soilless mixes are fortified with secondary and trace elements. Use a complete fertilizer containing secondary and trace elements in mixes that are not fortified.

A plant has different fertilizer needs as its metabolism changes throughout life. During germination and seedling growth, intake of phosphorus is high. The vegetative growth stage requires high amounts of nitrogen for green leaf growth; phosphorus and potassium are also necessary in substantial levels a general-purpose N-P-K fertilizer is recommended. In the flowering stage, the plant is less concerned with vegetative growth. phosphorus intake is highest nitrogen and potassium are less important. Using a super bloom fertilizer, low in nitrogen and potassium and high in phosphorus will promote larger flowers. A high nitrogen content usually promotes greener, leafy growth during flowering. Plants need some nitrogen during flowering. Without nitrogen, older foliage may yellow and die prematurely.

Fertilizers are either (water) soluble or gradual release. Both soluble and gradual release fertilizers can be organic or chemical.

Soluble fertilizers lend themselves to indoor container cultivation. They are preferred by commercial nurserypeople and many indoor gardeners. Soluble fertilizers dissolve in water and can be added or washed (leached) out of the soil easily. It is easy to control the exact amount of nutrients available to plants in a soluble form. Versatile soluble fertilizer can be applied in a water solution to the soil or misted directly on the leaves. Foliar feeding supplies nutrients directly to the leaves where they are used.

Chemical Soluble Fertilizers can be granular fertilizers or liquid. The granular fertilizers can easily be over-applied, creating toxic soil. It is almost impossible to leach them out fast enough to save the plant.

Osmocote™ chemical fertilizers are time-release. They are used by many nurseries because they are easy to apply and require only one application every few months. Using this type of fertilizer may be convenient, but exacting control is lost. Osmocote is best suited for ornamental container that are on a low maintenance schedule.

Peters™ fertilizer has been the choice of professional nurserypeople for many years. Indoor gardeners love it because the salts are pure and easy to work with. It is formulated with chelating agents to prevent settling out of elements, contains necessary secondary and trace elements. Peters has no chloride carbonates or excess sulfates, preventing buildup of excess salts. It is excellent for use with both soil and soilless mixes. Peters comes in many different N-P-K formulas. Those most commonly used indoors are listed.

The following Peters formulas are mixed from a half-tablespoon to a tablespoon per gallon of water and applied with each watering.

General Purpose (20-20-20) is readily available at most nurseries and used during the seedling and vegetative stages*.

Peat-Lite Special (20-10-20) works very well during vegetative growth in both soil and soilless mixes. Less phosphorus helps contain roots. It contains high levels of secondary and trace nutrients**.

Geranium Special (15-15-15), also used during vegetative growth, works very well for low pH situations. Geranium Special has a non-acidic source of nitrogen and reduced ammonium toxicity potential**.

Blossom Booster (10-30-20) contains a high level of phosphorus, which is necessary during flowering. It increases bud set, count and size**.

Variegated Violet Special (5-50-17) offers an accepted method of holding variegation in a plant's leaves. It reduces nitrogen, greatly increases phosphorus and holds a minimum potassium level. Some gardeners use it as a "super bloom" fertilizer.

*Trace elements: magnesium 0.5%, iron .05%, manganese .0031%, boron .0068%, zinc .0025%, copper .0036%, molybdenum .0009%

**Trace element content: magnesium .15%,

Material	N	P	K	Notes
Blood (dried or meal)	12-15	1.2	1	soluble
Bone meal (unsteamed)	2-4	15	25	calcium, TE
Bone meal (steamed)	2-3	18-25	.2%	Ca, TE
Canola meal	0	1.2	1.3	iron, TE
Cottonseed meal	7	2	2	acidic
Poultry manure (dry)	3-4	2-4	1-2	soluble, TE
Compost	1-2	1	1	TE
Cow (steer) manure	.6-2	.3	.5-	1excess salts
Coffee grounds	2	.3	.7	acidic
Feathers (dry or meal)	12-15	0	0	some TE
Fish meal	8	7	2	soluble
Goat manure	.5	.4	.4	TE
Granite dust	0	0	4-5	some TE
Potash rock	0	6-8	0	some TE
Greensand (glauconite)	-	1	5-7	iron, Mg., TE
Guano (bat)	2-5	8-10	1-2	soluble, TE
Guano (seabird)	10-15	5	2	soluble, TE
Hoof & horn meal	6-15	2	0	TE
Horse manure	.6	.4	.4	TE
Paper ash	0	.1	2-3	high pH
Soft phosphate	0	18-24	0	calcium, TE
Seaweed (liquid)	.5	.5	.3	soluble, TE
Seaweed (meal)	1	1	1	soluble, TE
Sheep manure	.8	.4	.5	TE
Swine manure	.6	.4	.2	TE
Wood ash (hardwood)	0	1.5	7-10	soluble
Wood ash (softwood)	0	.8	5	soluble
Worm castings	3.5	1	1	TE

TE = Trace elements

iron .10%, manganese .056%, boron .02%, zinc .0162%, copper .01%, molybdenum .01%

Miracle-GroR is the old reliable house plant and vegetable food. It comes in several formulas and may be found at just about any store with a gardening section. Miracle-Gro lists secondary and trace elements on the guaranteed analysis panel: copper .05%, chelated iron .10%, manganese .05% and zinc .05%.

Tomato (18-18-21) formula also contains magnesium .05%. Many vegetables and flowers have very similar nutrient requirements. This formula is great for seedling and vegetative growth.

All-Purpose (15-30-15) formula is preferred by gardeners during flowering. The high concentration of phosphorus helps rapid bud formation.

I have only mentioned just two of the most common fertilizers available commercially. I suggest that you try several brands of fertilizer to find the one that is best for you and your gardening conditions. It is *very* important to experiement with fertilizer to get the best

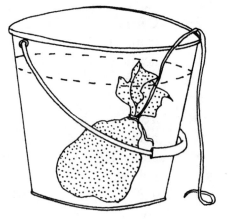

Organic fertilizer is placed inside of nylon stocking. This "tea bag" is soaked in water to brew your own organic fertilizer tea.

growth. Especially with hydroponic systems, fertilizer selection is critical for best results.

Organic Fertilizers

Organic produce boasts a sweeter taste, but implementing an organic indoor garden requires horticultural know-how. The limited soil, space and the necessity for sanitation must be considered when growing organically. Outdoors organic gardening is easy because all the forces of nature are there for you to seek out and harness. Indoors, essentially none of the natural phenomena are at play. Remember, you must create everything indoors Mother Nature creates outdoors. The nature of growing indoors does not lend itself to long-term organic gardens, but some organic techniques have been practiced successfully.

Most indoor organic gardens use potting soil, rich in worm castings, peat, sand, manure, leaf mold, compost and dolomite lime. In a container, there is little or no space to build the soil by mixing composts and organic nutrients to cook down. Even if it were possible to build soil in a container, it would take months of valuable growing time. It is easiest and safest to throw old, depleted soil outdoors and start new plants with fresh organic soil.

Organic nutrients, manure, worm, castings blood and bone meal etc. work very well to increase the soil's nutrient content, but nutrients are released and available at different rates. The nutrient availability may be difficult to calculate, but it is hard to over-apply organic fertilizers. Organic nutrients work best when used in combination with one another. This gives a more consistent availability of nutrients. A mix of 20 to 40 percent worm castings with other organic amendments yields a strong, readily available nitrogen base. A later application bat guano boosts flowering.

An indoor garden using raised beds allows true organic methods. The raised bed has enough soil to hold nutrients, promote chemical activity and ensure a constant supply of nutrients.

The nutrients in organic fertilizers may vary greatly depending upon source, age, erosion, climate, etc. The above figures are only approximate. For exact nutrient content, consult the vendor's specifications.

The Tea Bag

Five- or 10-gallon pots do not contain enough soil to hold all the organic nutrients a plant will need throughout life. This dilemma is solved by using organic tea. The tea is a bit messy, even smelly, but very effective. Tea concoctions contain just about any soluble organic nutrient diluted in water.

Worm castings and chicken manure, high in nitrogen and bat guano, high in phosphorus, are the most common ingredients in U-mix organic teas. These soluble nutrients are immediately available to plants. There are many different mixtures of organic tea. Just mix the organic nutrient(s) with water let it sit overnight. Mix it again, then strain out the heavy stuff by pouring the solution through a cheesecloth or an old nylon stocking before applying. The tea may be applied as often as each watering.

The growth or yield attained by using either chemical or organic fertilizers is about the same. The chemical fertilizers do not build soil and can build up to toxic proportions quickly. Organic fertilizers on the other hand, continually build the soil, promote better texture and structure and foster soil organism growth. The addition of organic fertilizers over a long period enhances the soil life and unlike chemicals does not contribute to its sterility.

Plants must convert organic nutrients to a chemical form before they are usable. This chemical change happens regardless of the source of the nutrients.

"Semi-organic" and "organically based" fertilizers are not actually organic fertilizers. They normally supplement these mixes with superphosphate and potassium sulfate.

Bone, kelp and seed meals in 40 to 50 pound sacks are more difficult to find at retail nurseries, but can be found at farm-supply stores.

Transplanting Seedling and Cutting Fertilizers

Vitamin B[1] is recommended for a smooth move of cuttings, transplants and seedling growth. There are many similar products that work just as well or better. Vitamin B[1] helps ease transplant wilt and shock. Using vitamin B[1] makes transplanting fast and easy.

A mild manure tea that is made from guano, manure and some form of seaweed make excellent seedling fertilizers. Remember that seedlings have few roots and are very frail. Always give them half or quarter strength fertilizer tea.

Trace Element Fertilizers

Seaweed, either liquid or powdered, is packed with trace elements that are immediately available to plants. Seaweed is the number one trace element fertilizer of environmentally conscious gardeners.

Mix FTE (Fritted trace elements) with the soil or soilless mix for a long-lasting, slow-release application of six to 12 months. The elements are encased in a pulverized glass complex that resists heavy leaching. The nutrients are available at a more constant rate throughout life. This is a form of gradual release fertilizer and is the only one that I recommend. The FTE formula is safer to use than the soluble formulas, but may be overdone also. Once overdone, FTE may not be leached out. Apply only one-third teaspoon per cubic foot of soil.

The guaranteed analysis of Peters FTE is: molybdenum 5.0%, iron 14.0%, copper 1.5%, zinc 5.0%, boron 0.8%, molybdenum 0.07%.

Mixing

To mix, dissolve powder, crystals or liquid into a little warm (90 to 100° F, 32 to 38° C) water make sure it is totally dissolved, then add the balance of the tepid water. This practice will ensure that the fertilizer and water mix evenly.

Containers have very little soil in which to hold nutrients. Toxic salt buildup may become a problem. Follow dosage instructions to the letter. Adding too much fertilizer will not make plants grow faster. It may change the chemical balance of the soil and supply too much of a nutrient or lock in other nutrients, making them unavailable to the plant.

Fertilizing

When do plants need fertilization? This may be determined by visual inspection, mak-

Dissolved salts (DS) meters, also referred to as electrical conductivity (EC) meters, are fundamental to precise control of overall nutrient content in the growing medium.

ing an N-P-K soil test or experimenting on a test plant(s). No matter which method is used, remember that plants in small containers use available nutrients quickly and need frequent fertilizing; plants in large planters with more soil have more nutrients available and require less frequent fertilizing.

Visual inspection: If plants are growing well and have deep green, healthy leaves, they are probably getting all nutrients necessary from the soil. The moment growth slows or leaves begin to turn pale green, it is time to fertilize. Do not confuse yellow leaves caused by a lack of light and yellow leaves caused by a nutrient deficiency.

Making an N-P-K soil test will reveal exactly how much of each major nutrient is available to the plant. The test kits mix a soil sample with a chemical. After the soil settles, a color reading is taken from the liquid, then matched

to a color chart. The appropriate percentage of fertilizer is then added. This method is very exact, but more trouble than it is worth for most hobby gardeners.

Many gardeners prefer to experiment on two or three test plants. This method yields experience and develops horticultural skills. Cuttings work especially well for this type of experiment. The idea is simple: give the test plants some fertilizer and see if they green up and grow faster.

How much fertilizer do plants need? The answer is simple. Just mix fertilizer as per instructions and water as normal or dilute fertilizer and apply more often. If you want to get the most out of fertilization, use a DS meter. Remember, small plants use much less fertilizer than large ones. Fertilize early in the day, so plants have all day to absorb and process the fertilizer.

It is almost impossible to explain how often to apply fertilizer. We know that large plants use more nutrients than small plants. The more often fertilizer is applied, the less concentrated it should be. Frequency of fertilization is one of the most widely disagreed upon subjects in the horticultural industry. Indoor, containerized plants may be pushed to incredible lengths. Some of them will absorb amazing amounts of fertilizer and grow well. Some gardeners fertilize vegetables and annual flowers with as much as one tablespoon per gallon (Peters 20-20-20 or 10-30-20) with each watering! Heavy fertilization works best with growing mediums that drain readily and are easy to leach, such as soilless mix. Other gardeners use only rich organic potting soil with fine dolomite lime added. No supplemental fertilizer is applied at all.

A siphon applicator found at most nurseries will mix soluble fertilizers with water. The applicator is attached to the faucet with the siphon hose submerged in the concentrated fertilizer solution. The hose is attached to the other end. Often applicators are set at a 1:15 ratio. That is, for every unit of liquid concentrate fertilizer, 15 units of water will be mixed with it. Sufficient water flow is necessary for the venturie (suction) to work properly. Misting nozzles restrict this flow. When the water is turned on, the fertilizer is siphoned into the system and flows out the hose. Fertilizer is generally applied with each watering, since a small percentage of fertilizer is metered in.

A garbage can, set 3 to 4 inches off the floor with a garden hose fitting at the bottom, will act as a gravity-flow source for fertilizer solution. The container is filled with water and fertilizer. With this system, the water temperature is easy to keep warm and fertilization is much easier.

When it comes to fertilization, experience will tell more than anything else. There are hundreds of N-P-K mixes and they all work! When choosing a fertilizer, make sure to read the entire label and know what the fertilizer claims it can do. Do not be afraid to experiment on a few test plants.

Once you have an idea of how often to fertilize, put the garden on a regular biweekly, weekly, bimonthly, every watering, every other watering or every third watering feeding schedule for consistent results. A schedule usually works very well, but it must be combined with a vigilant, caring eye that looks for overfertilization and signs of nutrient deficiency.

 Rule of Thumb: Leach soil with one to two gallons of fresh water per gallon of soil every month or two. This is the best form of preventive maintenance against toxic salt buildup in the soil. Leaching too often (weekly) washes all the nutrients out of the soil.

Foliar Feeding

Foliar feeding (misting the leaves with fertilizer solution) makes some nutrients available and usable immediately. Food is absorbed

Foliar feeding is the quickest way to deliver nutrients to a plant.

directly into the leaves. Foliar feeding is a good way to keep toxic nutrient levels from building up in the soil, but, like soil fertilization, may be overdone. Apply all foliar fertilizers 1/8 to 1/4 strength. Do not over foliar feed! Daily foliar feeding with a weak solution, for example, leaches the nutrients from the leaves, just as excessive watering leaches nutrients from the soil. A good foliar feeding program would start after the plant's first month of growth. Apply fertilizer solution with a fine spray. See "About Spraying," pages 154-157.

Foliar feeding is more work, but creates almost instantaneous results. Nitrogen-deficient plants have turned from a pale yellow to a lime green in 12 short hours! In the case of nutrient-deficient soil, foliar feeding offers a simple quick cure. The nutrients are supplied directly and used immediately. Soil condition and pH are not affected, but root absorption may improve. A combination of soil and foliar feeding is common. Good organic foliar fertilizers are fish emulsion and bat guano. Of course, it must be strained through a tea bag and the sprayer should not be prone to clogging. Dilute them the same as for regular fertilization for foliar feeding.

Nutrient Disorders

There are many things which can go wrong with indoor plants that are confused with a lack of fertilizer. The pH of both the growing medium and water is of prime importance. If the pH is not between 6 and 7 (5.4 to 6.8 for hydroponic units) some nutrients will be locked in the soil, even if the nutrient is present. The plant is not able to absorb it chemically because the pH will not let it. For example, a full point movement in pH represents a tenfold increase in either alkalinity or acidity. This means that a pH of 5.5 would be 10 times more acidic than a pH of 6.5. A pH below 6.5 may cause a deficiency in calcium. If this happens, root tips could burn and leaves could get leaf spot fungus. A pH over 7 could slow down the plant's iron intake and chlorotic leaves with yellowing veins could result.

Incorrect pH contributes to most serious nutrient disorders. Too many people worry about fertilizer application and do not pay attention to the pH! See "pH Chart," page 65. Check each of the vital signs and fine tune the environment, especially the soluble salts and ventilation, before deciding that plants are nutrient-deficient.

Nutrient deficiencies do not normally occur in fresh potting soil containing dolomite lime or in a fortified soilless mix that contains all necessary trace elements. This fresh planting mix is coupled with a regular fertilization schedule.

Two basic problems occur with nutrients deficiencies and excesses.

Deficiency, indicated by lime-green leaves is treated by applying a general-purpose fertilizer. The macro-nutrients are all used at similar rates and a single nutrient seldom builds to toxic levels. If a deficiency is suspected, leach the soil heavily. Start a new fertilization program. Adjust the pH to 6.0-7.0 and use a complete fertilizer containing all the trace elements.

Excess or overfertilization is indicated by very-dark green leaves and burnt tips. Treat by

This lime tree is being leached (flushed) with about five gallons of water to wash all the toxic salt from the soil.

leaching the soil of excess nutrients.

Over fertilizing can become one of the biggest problems for indoor gardeners. Too much fertilizer causes a buildup of nutrients (salts) to toxic levels and changes soil chemistry. When overfertilized, growth is rapid and super-lush green until toxic levels are reached. When the toxic salt (fertilizer) level is reached, leaf tips burn (turn yellow, then black). If the problem is severe, the leaves will curl under like a bighorn sheep's horns. Over fertilization is easy to diagnose in the early stages (two or three weeks before symptoms appear) when using a soluble salts (DS) meter. For more information on the DS meter, see *Gardening: The Rockwool Book*, by George F. Van Patten.

The chance of overfertilization is greater in a small amount of soil. It can hold only a small amount of nutrients. While a large pot or planter can hold much more soil and nutrients safely, it will take longer to flush if overdone.

To treat severely overfertilized plants, leach soil with two gallons of water per gallon of soil, so as to wash all the excess nutrients out. The plant should start new growth and be looking better in one or two weeks. If the problem is severe and leaves are curled, the soil may need to be leached several times. After normal growth resumes, start foliar feeding or apply diluted fertilizer solution.

Primary Nutrient Disorders

Nitrogen deficiency: Nitrogen is the most common nutrient found deficient. Growth slows; lower leaves turn yellow and eventually die. Remedy by fertilizing with nitrogen or N-P-K fertilizer. For fast results, foliar feed.

Excess nitrogen causes plants to grow too fast. Stems become spindly and the leaves, lush green. But the plant tissue is soft, weak, and more susceptible to damage from insects, disease, drought, heat and cold. Flowering and fruit set is delayed.

A lack of phosphorus is often confused with a nitrogen deficiency because both have many of the same symptoms. One way you can distinguish between them is that phosphorus-deficient plants will have dull green leaves and often the stems will turn shades of purple. Overall growth is slow, maturity is delayed, and flower and fruit development are retarded. Phosphorus-deficient citrus fruits are stunted and have puffy skins. Phosphorus in soils and in fertilizers or other soil amendments is generally found in forms that have low solubility. Therefore, these materials, such as rock phosphate, should be thoroughly blended with the soil before planting. Because bacterial activity is reduced in acid soils, it may need more phosphorus because less is able to be "fixed." It is uncommon for phosphorus to leach out of the soil.

Excess phosphorus: Toxic signs of phosphorus will take a long time to surface. It causes older leaves to turn yellow, growth to be stunted, and new leaves to be smaller. Older leaves at the bottom of nitrogen-deficient plants start turning yellow and may drop. Treat toxicity by leaching the soil with fresh water.

Discolored leaf tips on this false aralea plant tell the experienced gardener that toxic salt buildup is occurring in the soil.

A lack of potassium: Potassium deficiency occurs occasionally. Many times potassium deficient plants are the tallest and appear healthy. But the lower leaf tips turn yellow, followed by whole leaves that turn dark yellow and die. The potassium is usually present in the soil, but locked in by high salinity. First, leach the toxic salt out of the soil, then apply foliar N-P-K fertilizer.

Excess potassium is very unlikely. About one percent of the potassium in the soil is available to plants. Insoluble potassium is found in organic matter and minerals. It moves within the soil slowly. Weathering, the wearing away of soil, releases potassium into solution. Potassium and other plant nutrients must be in soluble form to be available to roots.

Secondary Nutrient Disorders

Secondary nutrient deficiencies are easily avoided by mixing one cup of fine dolomite lime per cubic foot of soil before planting. Dolomite supplies soil with magnesium and calcium.

Magnesium (Mg) is the most common secondary nutrient to be found deficient. It is naturally deficient in soilless mixes, but is also found deficient in soil. Lower leaves yellow, veins remain green, the tips and then the entire leaf turns brown. The leaf tips usually turn upward, then die. The entire plant could discolor and die within a few weeks. Cure by watering as usual, adding one teaspoon Epsom salts to every two quarts of water. If the deficiency progresses to the top of the plant, turning the growing shoots lime-colored, you will notice the greening-up effect there first. In a few days, it will move down the plant, turning lower leaves progressively greener. Continue a regular watering schedule with Epsom salts added until symptoms totally disappear. In a soilless mix, you may want to use Epsom salts regularly, but it will not be necessary if the fertilizer contains magnesium.

Calcium (Ca) deficiency is uncommon, but when noticed, it may be too late to remedy. Signs of deficiency are a yellowing and dying back of leaf edges. Mixing fine dolomite lime with the soil before planting is the best way to prevent this ailment. If you must, use a trace element formula containing calcium to treat the deficiency.

Micronutrient Disorders

Sulfur (S) is almost never a problem. Many fertilizers contain some form of sulfur. Deficiency shows when leaves turn pale green and general-purpose N-P-K fertilizer fails to cure the problem. Very seldom is it a problem, but if it is, remedy with trace element fertilizer.

Iron (Fe) deficiency is somewhat common indoors. An iron-deficient (chlorotic) plant is yellowing between the veins, with the veins of the leaves remaining green. Leaves may start to drop if it is severe. Chlorosis (yellowing) is generally caused by a high pH rather than a lack of iron. To remedy, correct pH. If necessary, foliar feed with fertilizer containing soluble chelated iron.

Other micronutrients - manganese, boron, molybdenum, zinc and copper- are rarely deficient in any soil. By using commercial potting soil, fortified soilless mix or N-P-K fertilizer with trace elements, you are guaranteed that all necessary trace elements are available. Fertilizers that contain only trace elements are available, but may be very tricky to use. Trace elements are necessary in minute amounts and reach toxic levels easily. Do not use a chemical trace element fertilizer more than once every two months or unless it is absolutely necessary. Liquid seaweed is the safest trace element formula to apply. Seaweed is natural, soluble and difficult to over apply.

In Conclusion

Nutrient uptake can be immediate, providing the plants are fertilized with a soluble food that is absorbed through the leaves. Foliar feeding can be a "quick fix" for acute nutrient deficiencies. The easy and inexpensive organic way to provide nutrients to plants is to feed the soil with a complete organic fertilizer, add compost and let the soil "process" its nutrients for the plants. This slow-release method promotes good overall plant vitality.

Chapter Five
Hydroponic Gardening

The roots of hydroponics come from two Greek words that were put together: *hydro* meaning "water" and *ponos* meaning "labor". Today hydroponics is the science of growing plants without soil, most often in a soilless mix. With hydroponics, two very important factors may be totally controlled: nutrient and oxygen intake via roots.

Hydroponic gardening, like HID gardening, is easy and fun once the concept and principles are understood. There are a few basic rules that must be followed to make a good system productive. First, let's look at how and why hydroponics works.

In the basic hydroponic system, the inert soilless medium contains essentially no nutrients of its own. All the nutrients are supplied by the nutrient (fertilizer) solution. This solution passes over the roots or floods around them at regular intervals, later draining off. The extra oxygen around the roots is able to speed the plants' uptake of nutrients. Plants grow faster hydroponically because they are able to assimilate nutrients faster. They are able to take in food as fast as they are able to utilize it. In soil, as in hydroponics, the roots absorb nutrients and water; even the best soil rarely contains as much oxygen as a soilless hydroponic medium.

Hydroponics works well for horticulturists who are willing to spend a few extra minutes a day in their garden.

The garden requires extra maintenance. Plants grow faster and there are more things to check. In fact, some people do not like hydroponic gardening because plants grow too fast and require additional care.

Hydroponic gardening can become overwhelming for the novice gardener if too complex of a system is implemented at first. If you are a novice gardener and want to garden hydroponically, try setting up a basic system. Once you have gained experience and feel comfortable with hydroponics, move to a more elaborate system. Remember, if you buy all the new little hydroponic garden gadgets available, you may start more projects than you can manage effectively. If you are contemplating constructing and inventing your own unit, get your hands wet with a tried and true system first. It will take a month or two to work out most of the bugs in a homemade unit.

Hydroponic gardening is exacting and not as forgiving as soil gardening. The soil works as a buffer for nutrients and holds them longer than the inert medium of hydroponics. Some very advanced hydroponic systems do not even use a soilless mix. The roots are suspended in the air and misted with nutrient solution. The misting chamber is kept dark so algae does not compete with roots. This form of hydroponics is called aeroponics.

Plants properly maintained, grown hydroponically under HID lamps tend to grow more lush foliage and at a faster rate than plants grown in soil. The real benefit with hydroponics is realized later in the plant's life. When roots are restricted and growth slows in containerized plants, hydroponically grown plants are still getting the maximum amount of nutrients.

The principles involved in hydroponics are simple and direct, but the application of these principles can become very complex. Gravel is the inert medium most commonly used to hold the roots and stabilize the plant while the nutrient solution passes over the roots in one of many ways. The nutrient solution drains away from the roots, so the oxygen will have a chance to work with the roots to draw in the nutrients. These are the basic principles of hydroponics. The nutrient solution, its application and the growing medium are the main variables.

Different Systems

The way the nutrient solution is applied distinguishes the various systems. Hydroponic systems may be classified as *active* or *passive*. An active system actively moves the nutrient solution. Examples of active systems include: flood and drain and top feed.

Passive systems rely on the capillary action of the wick and the growing medium. The nutrient solution is passively absorbed by the wick, medium and roots. The mediums that are commonly used in a wick system are vermiculite, sawdust, peat moss etc. For rapid growth, the average wick system keeps the medium too wet consequently, not enough air

This easy to operate hydroponic garden simplifies growing.

The wick system of hydroponic gardening cuts watering frequency. Simply fill the lower reservoir with a mild fertilizer solution.

is available to the roots. However, the wick system works very well if engineered properly. The soilless medium, the number of wicks, their gauge and texture are the main variables involved in a wick system.

The wick system has no moving parts. There is nothing mechanical to break, replace or malfunction. Wick systems also boast a low initial cost. Once set up and functioning properly, they require little work to maintain. Wick systems are perfect for slow-growing perennials such as African violets and rex begonias.

Hydroponic systems are further classified as recovery and non-recovery. Non-recovery means just what it says. Once the nutrient solution is applied to the inert growing medium, it is not recovered. These systems use sand, gravel, sawdust, expanded clay or rockwool as the medium. No nutrient solution is recovered less is applied, promoting less waste, complication and labor. Non-recovery systems were common for commercial applications where the soilless medium is plentiful and the soil is not arable. Today, environmental concerns and regulations have curtailed most dumping of nutrient solutions. And for good reason! Nutrient solutions are packed with nitrates and phosphates, not to mention concentrations of other chemicals. These chemicals, if dumped without regard on the ground concentrate in ground water creating a toxic environment. Recirculating systems are much more environmentally friendly. It is acceptable to use the used nutrient solution to fertilize your outdoor garden. Remember to spread it around and do not dump it on one spot where it can buildup to create a toxic waste dump!

The flood and drain and top feed methods are *active* recovery systems. They actively work by moving a volume of nutrient solution into contact with the roots. Recovery, because the nutrient solution is recovered after it has drained off and will be used again. These systems tend to use mediums such as pea gravel, light pumice rock or crushed brick that will

Aeroponics

In an aeroponic system plants' root zone is suspended in a dark space. No growing medium is used. The roots are misted in this dark chamber at regular intervals. The humidity in the chamber remains at or near 100 percent. The roots have the maximum potential to absorb nutrients in the presence of air. There is only air and nutrient solution in the chamber; no soil or soilless medium is there to impair absorption.

The growth achieved with this system can be phenomenal, but control must be very exact. The system may take some time to fine tune so that the air and nutrients act symbiotically to affect uptake.

On the negative side, there is no medium to act as a water/nutrient bank. If the pump fails, the roots soon dry out and plants die. If the pH or the nutrient solution becomes imbalanced, there is nothing to help stabilize them.

Aeroponics is very productive to root cuttings. A system similar to the one below has 40 to 50 holes in the top of the chamber. The cuttings are simply stuck in the holes and suspended in the misting chamber. They are misted with nutrient solution/rooting hormone up to 10 times per hour 24 hours per day.

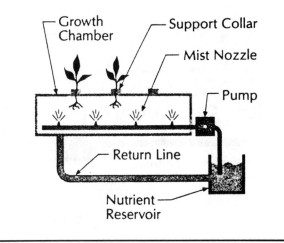

NFT Systems

NFT (Nutrient Flow/Film Technique) hydroponic systems are one of the most productive available. They operate on a very simple principle. The roots grow into a shallow capillary mat located in a light-tight grow bed. Nutrient solution flows over the roots up to 24 hours per day. The majority of the roots actually grow on top of the thin matting. The nutrient solution flows over the roots. This system allows the maximum amount of air and nutrients to be absorbed by the roots. Growth is unbelievable in a fine tuned NFT hydroponic system.

The system is very easy to maintain and clean up. The capillary matting along with the root mass is removed from the system and discarded. The growing beds and reservoir are cleaned before new capillary matting and cuttings/seedlings are reintroduced.

With no medium to hold water and nutrients, remember that this system is not very forgiving. The system depends on the flow of nutrient solution. When this flow is interrupted long enough for the roots to dry, plants suffer severely.

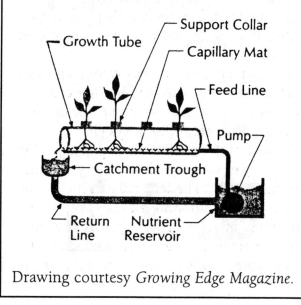

Drawing courtesy *Growing Edge Magazine*.

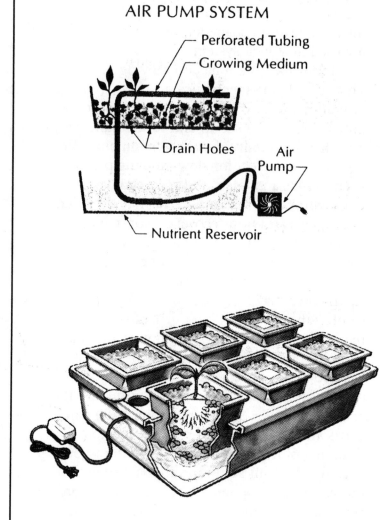

AIR PUMP SYSTEM

drain fairly rapidly and hold lots of air, . The flood method is a very productive and simple system used in many commercial hydroponic operations and home systems. This system has proved to be low-maintenance and easy to use.

The top feed method is a little more intricate, but used in hydroponic units with excellent results. There are many very efficient top feed systems. The nutrient solution is delivered by a hose overhead. (See drawing, page 84).

In a flood system, the water floods into the bed, pushing the carbon dioxide-rich, oxygen-poor air out of the root zone. When the nutri

FLOOD AND DRAIN SYSTEM

TOP FEED SYSTEM

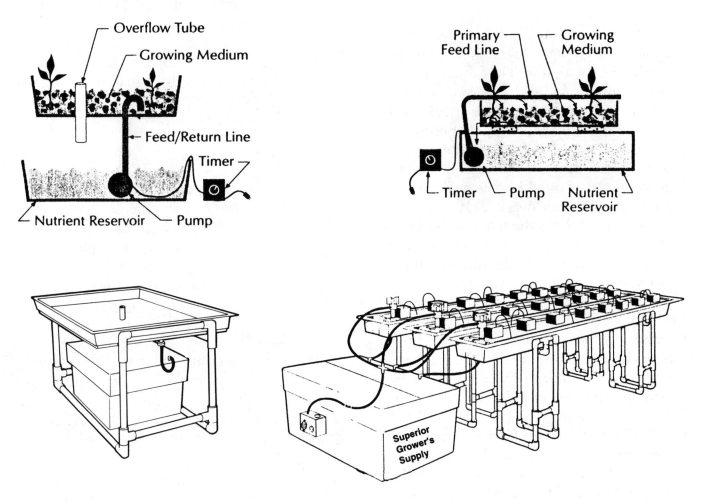

ent solution drains, it draws the new oxygen-rich air into the growing medium. Top feed systems apply the nutrient solution to the base of each plant with a small hose aerating the solution as it flows through the air.

The Growing Medium

The purpose of the growing medium is to harbor oxygen, water and nutrients plus support the root system of a plant. As with soil, the texture of the soilless medium is of utmost importance. The texture should be one that lets the solution drain rapidly enough for the

roots to get a good supply of oxygen. A fast-draining medium that holds little water for a long time is ideal for active recovery hydroponic systems.

Fibrous materials, such as vermiculite and peat hold much moisture within their cells. These types of mediums are most effective in passive, capillary action wick systems.

The size of the medium is important. The smaller the particles, the closer they pack and slower they drain. The larger the particles, the faster they drain and more air they hold.

Irregular materials have more surface area and hold more water than round ones, which hold less water. Avoid gravel with sharp edges

This wick system garden is nearly maintenance free. The containers can be removed in this simple wick system garden.

that could cut a plant's roots if it fell or was jostled around. Round pea gravel, smooth, washed gravel, crushed brick or some form of lava are some of the best mediums for growing flowers and vegetables in an active recovery system. Rock should be of igneous (volcanic) origin. This type of rock tends to have a neutral pH and will not break down under hydroponic growing conditions. Gravel is the most widely used hydroponic growing medium for flowers and vegetables. It holds moisture and nutrients without staying too wet. The best gravel to use for growing indoors is a pea gravel that is one-eighth- to three-eighths-inch in diameter. Ideally, over half of the medium should be about a quarter-inch in diameter.

Hydrofarm supplies a ceramic hydroponic medium called Geolite that could be better than gravel. In any case, wash gravel and ceramic rock thoroughly to get out all the dust, which turns to sediment.

The medium should be clean so as not to react to nutrients. For example, gravel from a limestone quarry is packed with calcium car-

bonate and old concrete is full of lime. When mixed with water, calcium carbonate will raise the pH. The concrete is toxic to plants. Other mixtures made from pebbles or anything near the ocean could be full of ocean salt. If you suspect the medium is toxic, it may be easier to get another load of medium than to try to flush away the salts.

Rockwool

Rockwool is the neatest invention since halide lamps! It is an inert, sterile, porous, non-degradable growing medium that provides firm root support. Like all soilless mediums, rockwool acts as a temporary reservoir for nutrients. This affords the grower a tremendous amount of control over plant growth through nutrient uptake.

This relatively new growing medium consists of thin strand-like fibers made primarily from limestone or granite but can be made from almost any kind of rock. There are two basic types of rockwool, horticultural grade and insulation grade. The horticultural grade has the appearance of strand-like fibers similar to pressed cotton candy. The insulation grade has the appearance of lent collected by a cloths dryer. Insulation grade is just what the name implies. It is insulation that is used in residential and commercial construction. Rockwool has been used for many years as home and industrial insulation. In fact, the walls in your home may be packed full of rockwool. The insulation grade lacks many of the qualities of the horticultural grade. I do not recommend using the insulation grade as a growing medium. Regardless of the type of rockwool, insulation or horticultural grade does not resemble any other growing media.

Definite advantages are reaped when growing in this soilless substrate. It is economical, consistent and easy to control. Best of all, rockwool's fibrous structure will hold up to 20 percent air even when it is completely saturated.

Rockwool was introduced into the U.S. in 1985. The American horticultural community has been slow to accept rockwool as a growing medium. Some commercial greenhouse growers have switched to rockwool, but many home gardeners have not even heard of rockwool.

Rockwool has been used in European greenhouses for more than 20 years. It was first discovered in Denmark in 1969. Growers began using rockwool to overcome the ban on soil-grown nursery stock imposed by some of the European communities. Today, an estimated 50 percent of all Western European greenhouse vegetables are grown exclusively in rockwool.

Other mediums like peat and soils are becoming more expensive to produce and can easily vary in quality. This fact, coupled with the high cost of sterilization, prompted European growers to explore new alternatives.

Rockwool can be used in both recovery and non-recovery hydroponic systems. As explained earlier, the nutrient solution in a recovery system is constantly changing. Fertilizer salts soon build up to toxic levels as plants use selected nutrients in the solution. The nutrient solution must be monitored constantly and adjusted to provide the exact concentration of nutrients for optimum growth. However, with a non-recovery system, the excess nutrient solution drains off and is not recovered. The plants get all the nutrients they need and any nutrients that are not used will simply drain off. A fresh nutrient-rich solution is used for the next watering. As explained earlier, this process is much less common than a few years ago. The excessive runoff creates environmental problems.

Enough nutrient solution is applied to get a 10 to 20 percent drain or leaching effect. Leaching flushes out excess salts from the medium and applies adequate nutrient solution to the medium.

European growers switched to rockwool because it is inexpensive and easy to control.

Rockwool is the growing medium of choice in Holland. This entire greenhouse is watered automatically.

Rockwool slabs contain pepper plants in neat rows.

Rockwool is produced from volcanic rock alone or a combination of volcanic rock, limestone and coke. The rigid components are melted at temperatures exceeding 2,500 F. This molten solution is poured over a spinning cylinder, very similar to the way cotton candy is made using liquefied sugar. As the molten solution flies off the cylinder under centrifugal force, it elongates and cools to form fibers. These fibers could be likened to cotton candy

To transplant seedlings grown in rockwool cubes, simply set the one-inch cube in a pre-drilled hole in the larger cube. The roots branch out into the slab quickly.

fibers. The product of these fibers, rockwool, is then pressed into uniform blocks, sheets, cubes or granules. The blocks are rigid and easy to handle. They can be cut into just about any size desirable. Granulated rockwool is easily placed into growing containers or used like vermiculite and perlite as a soil amendment. There are several different consistencies: coarse, medium and fine. The granules are treated so they are either water repellent or water absorbent.

When used with an open ended drip system, rockwool is easily irrigated with a nutrient solution controlled by a timer. The usual procedure in Europe is to apply a small amount of fertilizer several times a day. Enough excess

> Note: *Gardening: The Rockwool Book* is available at many garden centers or via the order blank in the back of this book. It is the best-selling book on growing with rockwool for the home gardener.

solution is applied to obtain a 10-25 percent leeching effect every day.

Do not let all of this control fool you. Even though rockwool holds 10-14 times as much water as soil and retains 20 percent air, it does not provide the buffering action available in soil. The pH of rockwool is about 7.8. Soaking the dry rockwool in an acidic fertilizer solution overnight is necessary to lower the pH of the slab. Once the pH of the rockwool has lowered, an acidic fertilizer solution (about 5.5 on the pH scale) is required to maintain the actual solution at a pH of 6.5 or lower. Errors made in the nutrient solution mix or with pH level, will be magnified. Be careful to monitor both the pH and nutrient level with a watchful eye.

There are some tricks to handling rockwool. Dry rockwool can be abrasive and act as an irritant to the skin. When handling dry rockwool, use gloves and goggles. Once the rockwool is thoroughly wet, it is easy and safe to work with; it creates no dust and does not irritate to the skin. Keep out of the reach of children and wash clothes thoroughly after prolonged use around rockwool as a safety precaution.

Rockwool stays so wet that algae grows on surfaces exposed to light. While this green slimy algae is unsightly, it does not compete with plants for nutrition. However, harmless fungus gnats could take up residence. Avoid the unsightly algae by covering the rockwool with plastic to exclude light.

Sterilizing

The medium must be sterilized before each new planting. Sterilizing is much easier than replacing the medium. For apartment dwellers, hydroponics provides an alternative to heavy, messy soil gardening. Instead of having to haul messy soil in and out of your home, the soilless medium is simply sterilized and reused. Soil can become expensive. The reason for sterilization is to prevent any bad micro-organisms from getting started in the garden.

Before sterilizing, the roots will have to be removed from the medium. An average tomato plant (four or five feet tall) will have a root mass about the size of a desk telephone. Roots can create a huge mass in larger bed systems. A few roots can remain in the system, but try to get at least 90 to 95 percent of them out. The system has less of a chance of clogging if few roots remain. A clogged system does not fill or drain properly.

The roots will tend to mat up near the bottom of the bed. It is easiest to remove them in one large mat. Some of the medium may be embedded in the roots. It is easier to get more medium than trying to pick it from between the roots.

There are many ways to sterilize the medium. The method used to sterilize most systems is very easy. First, remove the nutrient solution from the tank. Then, make up a solution of ordinary laundry bleach such as Clorox or Purex (calcium or sodium hypochlorite) or hydrochloric acid, the kind used in hot tubs and swimming pools.

Apply one cup of bleach per five gallons of water, flood the medium with the sterilizing solution for at least one half-hour, then flush. Use lots of fresh water to leach and flush the entire system: beds, connecting hoses and drains. Make sure all the toxic sterilizing chemicals are gone by flushing the entire system for at least one hour (two intervals of half an hour each) before replanting. The slabs may be removed from the system and flushed in the bathtub, outdoors or returned to the system for flushing.

The Hydroponic Nutrient Solution

To gain a more complete background on nutrients, etc., read Chapter Four, "Water and Fertilizer." Many of the basic principles that apply to soil also apply to the hydroponic medium.

A plastic covering prevents the growth of algae on rockwool slabs. The convenient square shape makes the slabs easy to stack and use for individual plants.

Its easy to maintain plants in this simple flood and drain garden.

Always use the highest quality, most complete fertilizer you can find. The fertilizers recommended in this book have worked well for hydroponic gardening. Regardless of the fertilizer you choose, make sure they are complete formulas. Hydroponic fertilizers should have

Gardening at School

Students at elementary schools, middle schools, high schools and colleges can all learn more about the plant kingdom, agriculture and horticulture by using HID lamps and hydroponics. Most students attend school in the fall, winter and spring. Unfortunately most plants are being harvested by the time students get settled in for their fall studies. During the winter months, much of the country is under a blanket of snow and it is too cold for plant growth. Sunlight is also limited both in intensity and duration. By the time most of the country warms enough in the spring to start a garden, the school year is over. A greenhouse could be constructed, but they are very expensive and require much planning and approval by the school district. And once they are set up, theyre is a limisted amount of sunligh A indoor garden set up in the classroom offers a solution to all of these limitations!

The HID lamp offers total control of the "sunlight". HID light is bright enough to grow all types of plants. This way the plants can grow to their portential before the school year is past. The light also allows students to conduct many experemients that require diferent levels of light or hours

This newly planted BABY BLOOMER by AMERICAN HYDROPONICS is an excelent choice for schools.

of light per day. For more information on possible experemients see chapter two of this book.
Hydroponic gardens offer the most precise control for students that want to conduct experemients. Many different experemients relating to pH, moisture, nutrient uptake, growing mediums, etc. are possible with the hydroponic garden.

If you are a student or are a parent with children in school, please discuss with with the appropriate faculty members the posssibilities in purchasing a HID lamp and hydroponic system for the school. Remember that plants are all around us, we eat them, they purify our air and water, they provide us with shelter, building materials and so many things that they are impossible to list here. Hands'on expereience as to how and why plants grow is essential for students to gain a well rounded education.

all of the necessary macro- and micronutrients.

Like soil, hydroponic gardens can be fertilized with organics or chemicals. An organic hydroponic garden is more work to maintain than one using prepared chemical fertilizers. Organic teas must be prepared in a tea bag to ensure that the pipes do not plug with residue and sludge. Cheap fertilizer (not recommended), like organic fertilizers, contains residues that do not dissolve, which could build up and require more frequent cleaning of the system.

Fertilizers should be chelated, to help nutrient uptake by roots. Chelated nutrients are more soluble and immediately available to the plant.

For fast-growing annuals, the nutrient solution should be changed at least every two (at the most three) weeks. Growth could slow and deficiencies result if the nutrient solution is not changed often. Changing the solution as often as every week would not hurt anything. Plants absorb nutrients at different rates and some of the elements are depleted before others. The best form of preventive maintenance is to change the solution often. Fertilizer is probably the least expensive necessity in a garden. If you skimp on fertilizer or try to save it, the garden may be stunted so badly it will not recover in time to produce a good crop and insects and disease could take hold.. The pH is also continually changing, due to its reaction to the nutrient uptake, another reason to change the nutrient solution frequently. The nutrients being used at different rates could create a salt (unused fertilizer) buildup. This problem is usually averted by using pure nutrients and flushing the soilless medium thoroughly with fresh, tepid water between nutrient solutions.

 Rule of Thumb: Change the nutrient solution every two weeks.

Hydroponics gives the means to supply the maximum nutrients a plant needs. It can also starve them to death or over-feed them rapidly. Remember most active hydroponic systems are designed for high-performance. If one thing malfunctions, - the electricity goes off, the pump breaks, the drain gets clogged with roots or there is a rapid fluctuation in the pH - it could cause severe problems with the garden. A mistake could kill or stunt plants so badly that they never fully recover.

PH

Most flowers and vegetables grow hydroponically within a pH range of 5.8 to 6.8, 6.3 is considered ideal. The pH in hydroponic gardens requires an extremely vigilant eye by the gardener. All of the nutrients are in solution. The pH of the nutrient solution changes easily. The roots use nutrients at different rates. The changes in the amounts of nutrients in the solution will alter the pH. If the pH is not within the acceptable hydroponic range (6 to 6.8), nutrients may not be absorbed to maximum capacity.

 Rule of Thumb: Check the pH every day or two to make sure it is near 6.3.

Do not use sodium hydroxide to raise pH. It is very caustic and difficult to handle. Potassium hydroxide is much easier and safer to use.

The Reservoir

Rule of Thumb: Check the level of the reservoir daily and replenish if necessary.

The reservoir should be as large as possible. Be prepared! Forgetting to replenish the nutrient solution could easily result in crop failure! Plants use much more water than nutrients. Water also evaporates from the system, especially in a dry atmosphere. Less evaporation occurs when the reservoir is covered. Expect a water loss of 5 to 25 percent per day, depending on climatic conditions and the size of plants. A 40 gallon reservoir could loose as much as 10 gallons per day! The concentration of elements in the solution increases when water is used. There is less water in the solution and nearly the same amount of nutrients. More sophisticated systems have a float valve that adds water as it is used from the reservoir. Most systems have a full line on the inside of the reservoir tank to show when the solution is low. Water should be added as soon as the solution level decreases, which could be as often as every day! The reservoir should contain at least 20 percent more nutrient solution than it takes to fill the beds to compensate for daily evaporation. The larger the volume of nutrient solution, the more buffering capacity and the easier it is to control.

It is a big job to empty and refill a hydroponic reservoir with 20 to 60 gallons of water. To make the task easier, the system should be able to pump the solution out of the reservoir. If the water must sit for a couple of days to let chlorine dissipate or to alter the pH before putting it into the tank, the system should be able to pump water back into the reservoir. Using the pump in the reservoir to change nutrient solution makes the task quick and painless. If you are unable to pump the used nutrient solution out of the reservoir, place the unit at such an altitude that it may be siphoned or flow by gravity into a drain or outdoor garden.

The used nutrient solution can pumped into the garden outdoors or down the nearest drain. Do not dump the nutrient solution into a septic tank. The fertilizer disrupts the chemical balance of a septic tank, causing it to overflow. Do not use this unbalanced nutrient solution on other indoor plants.

The Irrigation Cycle

The hydroponic irrigation or watering cycle depends on the same things as does the soil:

plant size, climatic conditions and the type of growing medium. If the particles in the growing medium are large, round and smooth and drain rapidly like pea gravel, the cycle will be often: two times daily. If using rockwool, more than 10 applications per day are possible.

Flood systems with pea gravel are generally flooded two or more times daily for 15 to 30 minutes. The water rises to within half an inch of the top of the medium and completely drains out of the medium at each watering. Top feed systems are usually cycled for about 30 minutes and watered two or more times daily depending on the medium.

During and soon after irrigation, the nutrient content of the bed and the reservoir are at the same concentration. As time passes between irrigation cycles, the nutrient concentration and the pH gradually change. If enough time passes between watering, the nutrient concentration may change so much that the plant is not able to absorb nutrients properly.

There are many irrigation regimens. As with soil, experimentation will probably tell you more than anything else. One gardener explained: "After a while you kind of get the feel for it". It took this hydroponic horticulturist nearly a year to master the irrigation cycle. If possible, try experiments on one or two plants at a time, instead of subjecting an entire bed or garden to an irrigation experiment.

The temperature of the nutrient solution should stay somewhere in the range of 65 to 75° F (18 to 24° C). If there is a problem keeping the room warm in winter, the nutrient solution can be heated instead of the room. To hear the nutrient solution, submerge a *grounded* aquarium heater or *grounded* heat cables. It may take a few days for the cables or heater to raise the temperature in a large volume of solution. Never place the heat cable in the soilless hydroponic medium. The heat from the cable will fry the roots when the medium dries out.

When air is cooler than water, the water evaporates into the air rapidly. The nutrient solution tank will need replenishment more often. The greater the temperature differential, the more humid the air. For more information, see "Relative Humidity", pages 116-118.

Replace the nutrient solution with water that is at least 60⁰ F (15⁰ C). Cold water shocks plants. The new water could take a few days to warm up, meanwhile all the plants suffer temperature stress! This stress slows the nutrient uptake rate and slows growth.

Never let the water temperature get higher than 85⁰ F (29⁰ C). If roots get too hot, they could be damaged. Submersible heaters of any kind must be *grounded* and constructed of materials (usually plastic) that give off no harmful residues. Aquarium heaters are safe and very popular.

Hydroponic Nutrient Disorders

When the hydroponic garden is on a regular maintenance schedule, nutrient problems are usually averted. Change the nutrient solution if you do not know the cause of the nutrient disorder. This method is the easiest and the most secure. If you can determine the exact cause of the disorder, add 10 to 20 percent more of the deficient ingredient for two weeks or until the disorder has disappeared.

Read "Nutrient Disorders," pages 92-94. Hydroponic gardens must be watched more closely than soil gardens. If an unstable pH causes a nutrient deficiency, novice gardeners may not notice the problem until it is too late. Treatment must be rapid and certain, but it will take a few days for plants to respond to the remedies. Foliar feed the sick plants for fast results. What if two or more elements are deficient at the same time? This may give plants the appearance of having no specific cause, just symptoms! When this sort of mind-bending problem occurs, change the nutrient solution immediately. Fresh nutrient solution supplies the missing elements. The plants do not have to be diagnosed, just treated.

 Rule of Thumb: If the garden has a nutrient disorder, change the nutrient solution and adjust the pH.

Overfertilization, once diagnosed, is easy to treat. Drain the nutrient solution, then flush with fresh tepid water. The number of times the system is flushed depends on the severity of the problem. Flush at least twice. Replace with properly mixed solution.

Nutrient disorders normally affect all plants of the same variety at the same time if they are receiving the same solution. Climatic and stress disorders - windburn, lack of light, temperature stress, fungi and insect damage - usually show up on the plants that are most affected. For example, plants that are next to a heat vent may show signs of heat scorch, while the rest of the garden looks healthy. Or a plant on the perimeter of the garden that receives less light will be small or leggy.

Building Your Own Hydroponic System

Building your own hydroponic system is easy, fun and rewarding. Several very important principles must be followed and safety precautions must be taken for the system to work properly. *No-leak* construction is imperative. Sealing all joints and using few or no seams are two basic codes of hydroponic garden construction. Seal seams with waterproof caulk or use fiberglass resin and material to ensure *no-leak* construction. Imagine how you would feel if you returned from vacation to find the hydroponic system flooded the afternoon you left. Drain holes or pipe connections must fit snugly, with no leaks. Teflon tape is a good anti-leak companion for threaded connections.

Many hydroponic systems using the fill-and-drain method must have elevated beds so the solution drains back into the reservoir.

Consider the added elevation when building and installing hydroponic units in rooms with limited ceiling space. The reservoir can be placed in a hole in the floor if ceiling space is limited.

A large covered reservoir is very convenient. The larger the container, the more solution and the more forgiving. The more solution available, the longer it takes to become depleted; the pH will fluctuate less and it will remain stable longer.

The size of the hydroponic container is important. The roots have to grow big enough to support a plant. In systems with large beds, the roots form a large mat of tangled roots. In smaller one-to three-gallon beds, roots could fill the container and grow out the bottom in two to six weeks. As with soil, the size of the hydroponic container dictates its buffering capacity.

Roots can clog and plug the drain. Place a small mesh screen (quarter-inch or less) made from a non-corrosive material, such as plastic, over the drain. The screen should be easy to remove and clean.

The frequency of watering depends on the soilless medium used. A fast-draining medium requires watering two or more times daily. Slow-draining vermiculite requires irrigation only once a day or less. Fill the bed so it is evenly moist. Drain it completely and rapidly so oxygen will be available to roots as soon as possible.

A simple flood system can be fabricated from a five-gallon plastic bucket filled with washed gravel that has a drain hole in the bottom. The hole is plugged with a cork. The nutrient solution, kept in another five-gallon bucket, is poured into the bed. After 20 to 30 minutes, the cork is removed and the nutrient solution drains back into the reservoir/bucket. This method is a little sloppy since the liquid is poured through the air (which also aerates it). This system provides an easy, inexpensive way for soil gardeners to get their hands wet with hydroponic gardening.

A basic hydroponic system is manufactured with a simple hose and a movable bucket.

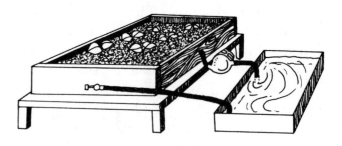

An external pump transfers the nutrient solution from the growing bed to the nutrient solution

Another manual, gravity-flow system has a reservoir/bucket attached to a bed/bucket with a flexible hose. The reservoir/bucket is raised above the bed/bucket so that the nutrient solution flows into it. After 15-30 minutes, the reservoir/bucket is lowered to let the solution flow back into the bed/bucket. This simple system could take a couple of hours to set up and may require a trip to the hardware store for

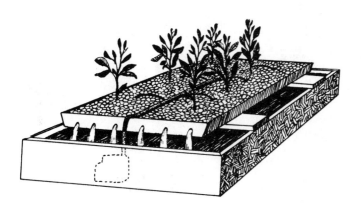

This hydroponic system moves the nutrient solution with a submergible pump (outlined).

some plastic fittings. Once set up, the system creates no mess and no fuss. Just be there daily to lift and lower the reservoir/bucket. Remember to pay close attention to the evaporation of the nutrient solution.

The next kind of active, recovery hydroponic system employs an aquarium pump and works on the flood and drain method. Air is pumped into a sealed container full of nutrient solution. The pressure created by the pump forces the solution into the hydroponic bed. The pump actually pumps air into the nutrient solution. After the solution is in the bed, the pump continues forcing air through the solution. It aerates the nutrient solution while it is in contact with the roots. This system is easily automated. An inexpensive timer can be attached to the pump so the system will operate automatically, keeping the solution in the bed for up to an hour. This system works great for people who will not be there every day to cycle the nutrients manually.

Note: Be careful to keep the pump from running dry.

Another active, recovery, flood system uses a submergible pump. This type of system is

able to recycle the nutrients several times daily at 20- to 30-minute cycles. This system is very popular among home gardeners and professionals. It is one of the most successful, because of its ease of operation and the control that may be exercised. The nutrient solution is cycled several times per day; maximum nutrient application and uptake are achieved. A timer can be attached to the pump, which automates the system. The pump should stay submerged to prevent air lock.

Getting Started

Starting seeds in the medium may not be very easy. Tiny seeds easily wash away, get too deep or dry out in coarse mediums. I prefer to plant seeds or cuttings in a peat pot or rockwool cube. The pot or cube is transplanted into the medium after the plant is two or three weeks old and roots are protruding from the sides. Cuttings transplant best into a hydroponic garden using a rockwool cube or peat pot. When cuttings are placed into the hydroponic medium, the rockwool cube will be able to hold the extra moisture it needs for the dry times between irrigation cycles.

Read "Transplanting" page 172-173. Transplanting is easy in hydroponics. Carefully remove the plant from the medium and place it in the new location. The younger the plant the better transplanting works. If the roots are allowed to grow too long, they will break when moved during transplanting. Shock will result if the roots are broken or jostled by clumsy hands. Gently return root ball to the medium. After transplanting, scoop up some of the nutrient solution or mix a B1 solution and pour it over the newly moved transplant. Next, cycle the nutrient solution through the system so it gets adequate moisture to let roots settle in.

It is okay to water a bed four to six times per day if necessary. Make sure the nutrient solution drains completely out after each irri-

gation. The maximum watering cycle should
be no longer than 30 minutes.

Chapter Six
Air

Fresh air is at the heart of all successful indoor gardens. In the great outdoors, air is abundant and almost always fresh. Indoor air pollution is much more common and can become more severe than outdoor pollution. For example, the level of carbon dioxide in the air over a field of rapidly growing vegetation could be only one-third of normal on a very still day. Soon the wind blows in fresh new air. Rains cleanse the air and plants of dust and pollutants. The ecosystem of the great outdoors is always in motion. When plants are growing in a small room, it is necessary to replicate the air of the great outdoors for best results. Since none of the natural elements to make carbon dioxide-rich, fresh air, you must take on the task!

Air is also used by the roots. Oxygen must be present along with water and nutrients for the roots to feed properly. If the soil is compacted or water-saturated, the roots have no air and suffocate. Air must be available to the roots!

Fresh air is still easy to find and inexpensive to maintain. An exhaust fan is the main tool used to maintain fresh air.

Air provides essential elements for plant growth. A plant uses carbon dioxide (CO_2) and oxygen (O_2) from the air. Oxygen is used for respiration, burning carbohydrates and other foods, which produces energy. Carbon dioxide must be present during photosynthesis. Without carbon dioxide a plant will die! Carbon dioxide uses light energy to combine with water, producing sugar. These sugars are used to fuel the growth and metabolism of the plant. Reduced levels of carbon dioxide, slows growth to a crawl. Oxygen is given off as a by-product of this process.

Plants and animals (remember people are animals too) complement one another. Plants give off oxygen as a by-product, making it available to people. People give off carbon dioxide as a by-product, making it available to plants. Animals inhale air, using carbon dioxide to carry on life processes and exhale oxygen as a by-product. Without plants, animals could not live and without animals, plants could not live as we know life today.

Air Movement

In order to have a good flow of air through the stomata, adequate air circulation and ventilation are necessary. Indoors, fresh air is one of

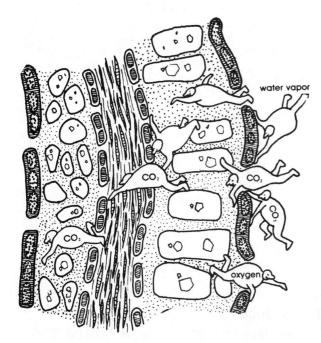

water vapor

CO_2

CO_2

CO_2

oxygen

Close up of the stomata shows the exchange of oxygen and CO_2.

the most commonly overlooked factors contributing to healthy plant growth. Fresh air is the least expensive element that can be made available to a plant. Experienced gardeners understand the importance of fresh air and take the time to set up a vent fan. Air movement is affected by three things: stomata, ventilation and circulation.

Stomata are microscopic pores on the leaf's underside similar to an animal's nostrils. Animals regulate the amount of oxygen inhaled and carbon dioxide exhaled through the nostrils via the lungs. In a plant, oxygen and carbon dioxide flows are regulated by the stomata. The larger the plant, the more stomata it has to take in carbon dioxide and release oxygen. The greater the volume of plants, the more carbon dioxide-rich air they need to keep them growing fast. Dirty, clogged stomata restrict the air flow. Stomata are easily clogged by dirt, polluted air or sprays that leave a filmy residue. Dirty clogged stomata are sealed off and unable

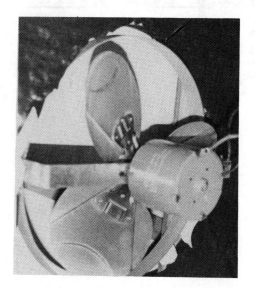

Vent fan is easily set in lower half of open window.

to function. In nature, stomata are cleaned by rain and wind. Indoors, the horticulturist must make rain with a sprayer and wind with a fan.

Rule of Thumb: Plants should be washed with clean, tepid water on both sides of the leaves at least once a month. See: "About Spraying," pages 154-157.

Circulation - If the air is totally still, plants tend to use all of the carbon dioxide next to the leaf. When this air is used and no new carbon dioxide-rich air is forced into its place, a dead air space forms around the leaf, stifling the stomata, slowing growth. Air also tends to stratify. The warm air stays near the ceiling and cooler air, close to the floor. All of these potential problems are avoided by opening a door or window and installing an oscillating fan. Air circulation is also important for insect and fungus prevention. Mold spores are present in all rooms. Fungal spores are less likely to land and grow when the air is stirred up by a fan.

Ventilation - 10-by-10-foot vegetable garden will use from 10 to 30 gallons of water per week. Where does all that water go? It transpires and evaporates into the air. Therefore, up to 30 gallons of water will be held in the air

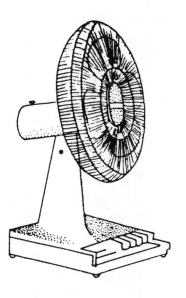

Many different vent fans and timers are available to the indoor grower.

An oscillating circulation fan will keep the air from stratifying in the garden room.

every week. If this moisture is left in a small room, plants suffer, leaves get limp, transpiration will slow and the stomata are stifled. This moisture must be replaced with dry air that lets the stomata function properly. A vent fan that pulls air out of the room will do the trick!

Successful indoor gardeners know that a vent fan is as important as water, light, heat and fertilizer.

In some cases fresh air is the most important growth inducing factor. All greenhouses have large ventilation fans. Grow rooms are very similar to greenhouses and their example should be followed. In most garden rooms there is a window or some easy-to-use opening in which to mount a vent fan. If no vent opening is available, one will have to be made.

When installing a vent fan, allow an adequate exchange of air, but prevent cold backdrafts. Use a dryer vent opening with a flap to prevent backdrafts. Use four-inch flexible dryer hose for smaller garden rooms and eight-inch galvanized heat duct pipe for large installations. Place one end of the hose outdoors. The other end of the hose is attached to the

vent fan. The vent fan is placed near the ceiling so that hot, humid air is vented. Check for leaks. Set up the fan. See: "Setting Up the Vent Fan," pages 124-126.

Greenhouse fans are equipped with baffles or flaps to prevent backdrafts. In cold or hot weather backdrafts could change the room temperature, stifle growth and encourage a menagerie of bad bugs and fungi. Vent flaps avoid this problem.

Vent fans are rated by the number of cubic feet of air per minute (CFM) they can replace or move. Buy a fan that will replace the volume (cubic feet) of the garden room in five minutes or less. The air pulled out is immediately replaced by fresh air that is drawn in through a fresh air opening in the room. If the garden room is sealed tightly to control moisture, an open window or air intake vent may be necessary to allow for enough inflow of new air.

Why use a vent fan? The reason is simple: efficiency. A vent fan is able to pull air out of a room many times more efficiently than a fan is able to push it out. A fan in the middle of a room that pushes the air out of a room is up against a tough physical principle. It is all a matter of pressure. The fan pushes air, increas-

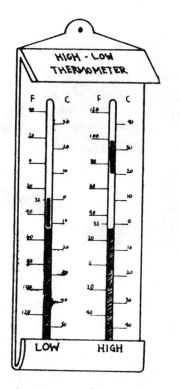

A maximum/minimum thermometer will measure the present temperature and tell you how cold it was last night.

ing the air pressure in the room. This pressure must increase substantially in order for a rapid exchange of air to take place. The vent fan, on the other hand, is able to change the pressure rapidly. It is much easier to lower the air pressure, causing new fresh air to rush in to fill the vacuum.

Temperature

Every garden room should be equipped with an accurate thermometer to measure the temperature. The mercury or liquid thermometer is usually more accurate than the spring or dial models. Thermometer are inexpensive and they supply important information. Make sure to get one. The ideal thermometer is a day-night or maximum-minimum type. Using this thermometer, the horticulturist is able to see how low the temperature drops at night and how high it reaches during

the day. This is very important for many reasons explained below.

Under normal conditions, the ideal temperature range for most indoor plant growth is 72 to 76° F (22 to 24° C). This temperature range changes with genus and species of plant. (see pages 195-197 for details.

At night, the temperature can usually drop 10 to 15° (1 to 2° C) with no noticeable effect on growth rate. The temperature should not drop more than 20° F (10° C) or excessive humidity and mold may become a problem. Daytime temperatures over 100° F (38° C) and below 60° F (15° C) seem to slow down growth in most plants. Maintaining the proper, constant temperature in the garden room promotes strong, even, healthy growth. Make sure plants are not too close to a heat source, such as a ballast or heat vent. It could dry them out, maybe even cause heat scorch.

Temperatures above 90° F (32° C) are not recommended. Increased temperatures speed chemical activity, causing excessive stress if ventilation is not increased. As explained in the following section on humidity, the greater the temperature, the more water the air is able to hold. This moist air stifles the stomata and slows rather than speeds growth. Other problems could result from the excess moisture, including: fungi and moisture condensation when the temperature drops at night.

Heat buildup indoors can become a problem in warm and hot weather. The ideal garden room is located underground in a basement with the insulating qualities of the earth. With the added heat of the HID and 100° (38° C) temperatures outdoors, a room can heat up really fast. In fact, you may choose to not grow indoors during hot weather. It is more work to grow indoors and so much easier to grow an outdoor garden if you have the space and sunshine. Several gardeners have lost their gardens to heatstroke during the Fourth of July weekend. This is the first big summer holiday and everybody in the city wants to get away to enjoy it. There are always some gardeners who forget to maintain good ventilation in the garden room while on vacation. In a room that is improperly set up, with no vent fan and no insulating walls, the summer temperatures may climb to 120° (48° C). There is no way a plant can live in this climate without incredible amounts of water and ventilation.

Winters are normally mild here in Portland, Oregon. Portland is located in USDA Zone 8. We can grow kiwis outside and garden under cover all winter. But one recent winter was exceptionally cold, catching residents off-guard. The cold caused the electricity to go out. The heat went off and pipes froze. Residents were driven from their homes until the electricity was restored a few days later. Unprepared gardeners returned home and their lovely gardens wilted, turning the deepest, most disgusting green only a freeze can bring. Broken pipes were spewing water everywhere. It is very important to keep the garden room above 35° F (2° C). If it drops far below 35° (2° C), the freeze will destroy the cells of warm-weather plants and foliage will die or not be able to grow very fast. Growth generally slows when the temperature is below 50° F (10° C), so do your best to keep the garden room warm.

A thermostat regulates the temperature in a room. It measures the temperature, then turns a heat or a cooling source on or off to keep the temperature within a specified range. A thermostat may be attached to an electric or combustion heater.

Thermostats operate either a heating or cooling device. A heating thermostat turns on a heater when the temperature *drops below* a trigger point. A cooling thermostat turns on a fan or cooler on when the temperature *climbs beyond* a point. The thermostat is attached to a vent fan in all but the coldest garden rooms. When it gets too hot, the thermostat turns the vent fan on, forcing the hot, stale air out of the room. The vent fan runs until the desired tem-

perature is reached, then the thermostat turns the fan off. The vent fan should be all the temperature control necessary. A refrigerated air conditioner can be installed if heat and humidity are a big problem. If excessive heat is a problem, but humidity is not a concern, an evaporative swamp cooler is the best value.

Thermostats are either single-stage or two-stage. The single-stage costs $30 to $40 and is able to keep the temperature the same both day and night. The two-stage thermostat is more expensive, ($50 or more), but can maintain different day and night temperatures. This is very convenient and can save you quite a bit of money, since the room temperature may drop 10 to 15° F at night with no effect on growth.

Uninsulated garden rooms and greenhouses experience broad changes in temperature. They require special considerations. First, it would probably be easiest to grow somewhere else, but if you have to use an attic or hot room, allow lots of ventilation. Make sure to enclose the room so that heating and cooling are easier and less expensive.

A .12 to .15 percent carbon dioxide enrichment requires temperature range from 75 to 85° F (24 to 30° C) to promote more rapid exchange of gases. Photosynthesis and chlorophyll synthesis are able to take place at a more rapid rate and plants grow faster. Remember, this extra 10 to 15° (6 to 9° C) increases water, nutrient and space consumption. Be prepared!

Seeds germinate faster and cuttings root quicker when the temperature range is from 75 to 85° F (24 to 30° C). Two easy ways to increase temperature when cloning include: using soil heating tape and building a (plastic) tent to cover young germinating seeds or cuttings. A plastic tent increases both temperature and humidity. Remove the tent cover as soon as the seeds sprout above the soil to allow for air circulation. Cuttings should remain covered throughout the entire rooting process. Always watch for signs of mold or rot when using a humidity tent with cuttings. Allowing little air circulation and ventilating cuttings under the tent daily helps prevent fungus. Misting the cuttings several times daily with a spray bottle is an alternative to a humidity tent.

The temperature in the garden room tends to stay the same, top to bottom, when the air is circulated with an oscillating fan. A 1000-watt HID lamp and ballast will provide enough heat in an enclosed garden room. A remote ballast placed on a shelf or a stand near the floor also helps break up air stratification by radiating heat upward. Cooler climates may be warm enough during the day when the outdoor temperature rises, but freeze at night. The lamp is adjusted to be on during the cold nights. This will warm the room both night and day.

Sometimes it is too cold for the lamp and ballast to maintain adequate room temperatures. Many garden rooms are equipped with a central heating and air conditioning vent. This vent is usually controlled by a central thermostat that regulates the entire home's heat. By adjusting the thermostat to 72^0 F (22^0 C) and opening all the internal doors in the home, the garden room can stay a cozy 72^0 (22^0 C). For some gardeners this is too expensive. Usually, keeping the thermostat between 60 and 65^0 (15 and 18^0 C), coupled with the heat from the HID system, is enough to sustain the desired temperature range. Other supplemental heat sources may work better than the above. Incandescent light bulbs and electric heaters are expensive, but provide instant heat. Incandescent bulbs also increase light intensity and add to the spectrum. Propane and natural gas heaters not only heat the air, but burn oxygen from the air, creating carbon dioxide as a by-product. This dual advantage makes their use even more economical.

There are several new kerosene heaters on the market that economically generate lots of heat. Look for a heater that burns its fuel completely and leaves no telltale odor in the room. Watch out for old kerosene heaters or inefficient fuel oil heaters of any type. They could

be dangerous! Diesel oil is a common type of indoor heat. Many furnaces use this dirty and polluting heat source. Wood stoves is not the cleanest, but work well as a heat source. A vent fan is extremely important to bring new fresh air into a room heated by a woodstove..

Insect populations and fungi are also affected by temperature. In general, the cooler it is, the slower the insects and fungus reproduce and develop. Temperature control is integrated into many insect and fungus control programs.

Humidity

Relative humidity is the ratio between the amount of moisture in the air and the greatest amount of moisture the air could hold at the same temperature. The hotter it is, the more moisture the air can hold the cooler it is, the less moisture the air can hold. When the temperature in a garden room drops, the humidity climbs and moisture condenses. For example, a 1000-cubic foot (10-by-10-by-10-foot) room will hold a maximum of about 14 ounces of water when the temperature is 70^0 (21^0 C) and relative humidity is at 100 percent. When the temperature is increased to 100^0 (38^0 C) the same room will hold a whopping 56 ounces of moisture at 100 percent relative humidity. That's four times as much moisture! When the temperature drops, the moisture condenses in the room. It has nowhere else to go.

Most plants grow best when the relative humidity range is from 40 to 60 percent. As with temperature, more or less constant humidity promotes healthy even growth.

Humidity affects the transpiration rate of the stomata. When high humidity exists, water evaporates slowly. The stomata close, transpiration slows and so does plant growth. Water evaporates quickly into drier air-causing stomata to open, increasing transpiration and growth.

The proper relative humidity level is essential for healthy tropical and subtropical plants.

Most flowering indoor plants require at least 50 percent relative humidity. Vegetables are just the opposite, they thrive in 50 percent or less, while indoor tropical gardens thrive in a relative humidity range of 65 to 70 percent.

Transpiration in arid conditions increases the flow of water and carbon dioxide out of the leaf's stomata. Transpiration will be rapid only if there is enough water available for roots. If water is inadequate, stomata will close to protect the plant from dehydration, causing growth to slow.

Relative humidity control is an integral part of insect and fungus prevention and control. High humidity (80 percent plus) can promote fungus and rot. Maintaining low (50 percent or less) humidity greatly reduces the chances of fungus formation. Some insects, for example, like humid conditions, others do not. Spider mites take much longer to reproduce in a humid room.

Relative humidity is measured with a hygrometer. This important instrument could save you and your garden much frustration and fungus. If you know the exact moisture content in the air, the humidity may be adjusted to a safe 50 percent level that encourages transpiration and discourages fungus growth.

There are two common types of hygrometers: the spring type, which is inexpensive (less than $10) and accurate to within 5 or 10 percent. This hygrometer is fine for most garden rooms, since the main concern is to keep the humidity near 50 percent. The other type of hygrometer, actually called a psychrometer, is a little more expensive ($30 to 50) but *very* accurate (See drawing page 118). This psychrometer uses a wet and dry bulb to measure relative humidity.

A humidistat is similar to a thermostat, but it regulates humidity instead of temperature. Humidistats are wonderful! Humidistats cost $30 to $60 and are worth their weight in flower blossoms. The more expensive models are the most accurate. The humidistat is wired in-line with the thermostat to the vent fan (See draw-

Relative humidity increases when the temperature drops at night. The more temperature variation, the greater the relative humidity variation. Supplemental heat or extra ventilation may be necessary at night if temperatures fluctuate more than 15^0 F (9^0 C).

Rule of Thumb: The moisture-holding capacity of air doubles with every 20^0 F (11^0 C) increase in temperature.

A 10-by-10-by-8-foot (800-cubic-foot) garden room can hold:

4 oz. of water at 32^0 F (0^0 C)

7 oz. of water at 50^0 F (10^0 C)

14 oz. of water at 70^0 F (22^0 C)

18 oz. of water at 80^0 F (27^0 C)

28 oz. of water at 90^0 F (32^0 C)

56 oz. of water at 100^0 F (38^0 C)

ing on page 119). Each can operate the fan independently. As soon as the humidity (or temperature) gets out of the acceptable range, the fan turns on to vent the humid (or hot) air outdoors.

 Rule of Thumb: A vent fan offers the best value to control humidity in most gardens.

The HID lamp and ballast radiate dry heat, which lowers humidity. Dry heat from the HID system and a vent fan are usually all the humidity control necessary. Other dry heat sources, such as a heat vent from the furnace or wood stove, work well to lower humidity. If using forced air from a furnace to lower humidity, make sure warm, dry air does not blow directly on plants. This dry air will dehydrate plants rapidly. One gardener sets out about 100 small silicon packets to absorb excess moisture in the

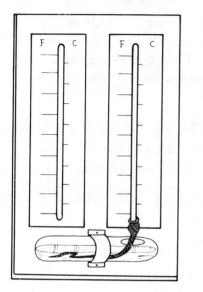

The drawing shows a very accurate psychrometer that measures relative humidity to within one percentage point.

small garden room. He then places the packets in a sunny window to dry them out before putting them back in the room.

Humidity is easily increased by misting the air with water or setting a bucket of water out to evaporate into the air. Draping a cheesecloth over the grill of a fan will buffer the breeze of a circulation fan over tender plants. This same principle can be used to make a simple but effective humidifier.

Simply place a wick between the cheesecloth and a container of water. The cloth wick draws water up into the cheesecloth. The fan will blow the moisture into the air. Humidifiers retail for $100 to $150. The humidifier are essentially a fan over a bucket of water controlled by a humidistat. The fan water evaporation into the air. A humidifier is usually not necessary unless there is an extreme problem with the room drying out. A dehumidifier removes moisture in a room. These units are a bit more complex, since the water must be condensed from the air. A dehumidifier can be

used anytime to help guard against fungus. Just set the dial at the desired percent humidity and presto, perfect humidity. They cost from $150 to $200, but are worth the money to gardeners with extreme humidity problems. The best price on dehumidifiers has been found at discount retail stores. Dehumidifiers can also be rented if needed for only a month or two. Young seedlings and rooting cuttings grow better when the humidity is between 70 and 80 percent. Under arid conditions, the underdeveloped root system is not able to supply water fast enough. High humidity prevents dehydration.

Carbon Dioxide Enrichment

Carbon dioxide (CO_2) is a colorless, odorless, non-flammable, non-toxic gas. The air we breathe contains .03 to .04 percent carbon dioxide. Plants use all of the available carbon dioxide in an enclosed garden room rapidly. Photosynthesis and growth slow to a crawl when the carbon dioxide level falls below .02 percent.

Carbon dioxide enrichment has been used in commercial greenhouses since the 1960's. It makes more carbon dioxide available to plants, stimulating growth. Indoor cultivation is similar greenhouse growing and the same principles can be applied to the indoor garden. Plants are able to use more carbon dioxide than the .03 to .04 percent that naturally occurs in the air. By increasing the amount of carbon dioxide to .10 to .15 percent (1000 to 1500 parts per million (ppm)), plants grow two to three times as fast, providing that light, water and nutrients are not limiting. Carbon dioxide enrichment has little or no effect on plants grown under fluorescent lights. The tubes do not supply enough light for the plant to process the extra available carbon dioxide. On the other hand, HID lamps supply ample light to process the enriched carbon dioxide air. In a garden room using an HID light source, carbon dioxide-enriched air, adequate water and nutrients, unbelievable results can be achieved. In fact, with this basic combination, plants grow much faster and more efficiently than outdoors under ideal conditions.

The demands of carbon dioxide-enriched plants are much greater than normal and plants require increased maintenance. They use nutrients, water and space about twice as fast as normal. A higher temperature range, from 75 to 85° F (24 to 30° C), will help stimulate more rapid chemical processes within the super plants. Properly maintained, they will grow so fast and take up so much space that flowering will have to be induced sooner than normal.

In fact, some people get frustrated using carbon dioxide. It causes plants to grow so fast, that unsuspecting gardeners are unable to keep up with them. With carbon dioxide-enriched air, plants that do not have the support of the other critical elements for life will not benefit from the carbon dioxide. The plant can be limited by just one of the critical factors. For example, plants use water and nutrients much faster. If water and nutrients are not adequately supplied, plants will not grow faster. They may even be stunted if not transplanted get it soon enough.

 Rule of Thumb: CO_2 enrichment requires more garden maintenance and moving up the garden calendar one to four weeks.

Increasing light intensity by adding another HID lamp helps speed growth, but might not be necessary. Use a light meter to see if plants really need more light. The extra lamp could make the garden grow too fast. More carbon dioxide does not require more hours of light per day. The photoperiod must remain the same as under normal conditions for healthy growth and flowering.

To be most effective, the carbon dioxide level must be kept near .10 to .15 percent every-

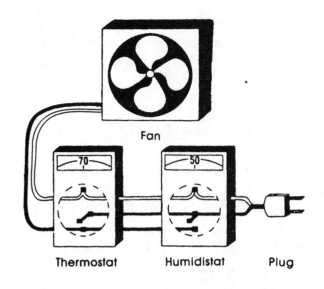

The simple diagram above shows how to wire a vent fan to a thermostat and a humidistat. The fan will vent the room when either the humidistat or thermostat activate.

where in the room. To accomplish even distribution of carbon dioxide, the garden room must be completely enclosed. Cracks in and around the walls over one-eighth-inch should be sealed off to prevent carbon dioxide from escaping. Enclosing the room makes it easier to control the carbon dioxide content of the air within. The room must also have a vent fan with flaps or a baffle. The vent fan will remove the stale air that will be replaced with carbon dioxide-enriched air. The flaps or baffle will help contain the carbon dioxide in the enclosed garden room and prevent cool backdrafts. Venting requirements will change with each type of carbon dioxide enrichment system. Venting is discussed in detail in the "Carbon Dioxide Generator" and "Compressed CO_2 Gas" sections below.

Some of the problems associated with keeping the number of carbon dioxide constant in the air are the amount of plants in the room and the rate at which these plants are growing. If the plants are growing rapidly and are tightly packed into a leaky room, the carbon dioxide level will be difficult to maintain. If the temperature climbs to 80 or 90° F (27 to 32° C), the carbon dioxide is diluted in the air and it must be increased. A room that is not tightly sealed could use as much as 50 percent more carbon dioxide.   •

Producing Carbon Dioxide

There are many ways to increase the carbon dioxide content of an enclosed garden room. Carbon dioxide is one of the by-products of combustion. Any hydrocarbon fuel can be burned to produce carbon dioxide, except for those containing sulfur dioxide and ethylene, which can be harmful to plants. (See "CO_2 Generators" below.) A by-product of fermentation and organic decomposition is CO_2 gas. The carbon dioxide level near the ground of a rain forest covered with decaying organic matter could be two to three times as high as normal. A by-product of decomposition is carbon dioxide. But bringing a compost pile indoors to cook down is not practical.

Dry ice is made from frozen carbon dioxide. The carbon dioxide is released when it comes in contact with the atmosphere. It can get expensive and can be a lot of trouble keeping a large room replenished with dry ice. There are lots of spin-offs to all of these principles and they all work in varying degrees. It is difficult to calculate how much carbon dioxide is released into the air by fermentation, decomposition or dry ice without using expensive equipment to measure it. Dry ice can get very expensive when used for a long time. Two pounds of dry ice will raise the carbon dioxide level in 10-by-10-foot garden room to about 2000 ppm. for 24 hours. One chagrined gardener remarked: "I can't believe that stuff melts so fast."

A decaying compost pile is out of the question indoors! Besides, a new compost pile would have to be moved twice a day to release enough carbon dioxide.

Fermentation is an acceptable way to produce carbon dioxide, but it is difficult to measure how much is produced. Here is a recipe for brewing carbon dioxide:

Use a one-gallon plastic milk jug or any gallon container to mix one cup of sugar and a packet of brewers yeast with about three quarts of warm water.

The concoction smells horrid, but produces an initial burst of carbon dioxide. Fermentation is one of the least expensive ways to produce carbon dioxide; it works best when used in a small growth chamber.

The carbon dioxide produced by fermentation is soon released in the enclosed chamber. The concoction is changed one to four times daily. Half of the solution is poured out, then 1 1/2 quarts of water and another cup of sugar are added. If the yeast does not continue to grow during the fermentation process, add another packet of yeast. The mix is similar to a sourdough starter mix. Try to keep it from dying out. As long as the yeast continues to grow, the mix can be used indefinitely to generate carbon dioxide. In fact, if a gardener were really into it, there could be several gallon containers and one would be changed every couple of hours. But the smell would soon gag a maggot!

CO_2 Generators

Commercial nurseries produce carbon dioxide with large generators. The generators produce carbon dioxide by using propane, butane or natural gas to burn oxygen out of the air in a chamber. The carbon dioxide-rich air is then circulated among the plants. Heat, carbon dioxide and water vapor are by-products of combustion. Each pound of fuel burned creates three pounds of carbon dioxide, 1 1/2 pounds of water and approximately 22,000 BTU's (British Thermal Units) of heat. Small, one lamp garden rooms can burn ethyl or methyl alcohol in a kerosene lamp. In a 10-by-

10-foot garden room, three ounces of fuel will produce about 2000 ppm of carbon dioxide in 24 hours.

Heat buildup makes large CO_2 generators impossible to use in the heat of summer. The CO_2 generators used in greenhouses are too large to be practical for the average garden room. Several companies manufacture small-scale CO_2 generators that are similar to the large commercial units. The leading company in the field is Green Air Products. The smaller CO_2 generators were designed for garden rooms of 1500 to 4000 cubic feet.

These CO_2 generators work very well for larger or cool garden rooms. The generators can create quite a bit of heat. Remember, each pound of gas burned will create about 22,000 BTU's and 1 1/2 pounds of water vapor. In a small room, the heat and moisture produced could make it impractical to use.

The CO_2 generators are of two basic designs. The first is normally hung from the ceiling. Carbon dioxide-rich air is produced and cascades over the plants. This model uses a pilot light with a flow meter and burner. The inside of the generator is similar to a gas stove burner with a pilot light enclosed, in a protective housing. For safety's sake, the generator must have a top covering the open flame at all times. The unit is equipped with a safety valve and a pilot light. It can be operated manually or placed on the same timer as the lamp to function automatically. An oscillating fan is placed near the floor to keep the carbon dioxide-rich air stirred up.

The second model is placed on the floor and has a fan on the side of the burner housing. The fan circulates the warm carbon dioxide-rich air among the plants. The generator has an electronic pilot light with a safety timer that is electronically controlled to relight safely if the flame blows out for any reason.

LP gas (propane) is readily available at gas stations the tanks are easy to move when full and very light when empty.

Propane is readily available. LP gas tanks

This carbon dioxide generator from Green Air Products will heat as well as produce carbon dioxide for the garden room.

are easy to acquire and painless to fill, unlike the heavy, awkward, compressed CO_2 tanks discussed below.

New propane tanks are normally filled with an inert gas to protect them from rust. Empty the inert gas out before filling a new tank for the first time. The inert gas does not mix well with propane, nor will it burn.

Some gardeners choose to manufacture their own CO_2 generator. To make a CO_2 generator, find a heater that burns clean and has a knob to control the exact flame produced. A blue flame is produced by propane or natural gas that is burning clean. A yellow flame has unburned gas (creating lethal carbon monoxide) and needs more oxygen to burn clean. Good examples of homemade CO_2 generators are propane heaters, stoves or lamps. In fact, even a Coleman lantern works quite well, but it must be started and stopped manually. One gardener uses unleaded or white gas rather than expensive Coleman fuel.

Unless your garden room is huge, you do not need to allow for carbon dioxide to be present in the air. This excess carbon dioxide will

Note: Never over-fill the propane tank! The gas expands and contracts with temperature change.

be compensated for by the carbon dioxide that leaks out the cracks in the walls and through open doors. The examples show how to figure out how much carbon dioxide to generate in a room. First, the total volume of the room is determined. Next the amount of fuel burned to produce the desired amount of carbon dioxide is calculated.

To find out how much carbon dioxide it will take to bring the garden room up to the optimum level, figure the total volume of the garden room, then divide by the optimum level of carbon dioxide.

Example:
Total Volume = L X W X H
Total Volume = 10' X 8' X 10'
Total Volume = 800 cubic feet

Optimum Level = .0015

Note: Carbon Dioxide is used by humans at low levels. Levels above .4 percent (4000 ppm) could be hazardous if inhaled for long. The carbon dioxide level is easy to control with the proper metering system. Besides being hazardous to people at high concentrations. Carbon dioxide can become toxic to plants at levels above .2 percent (2000 ppm).
A relatively small flame will alter the carbon dioxide level in an enclosed garden room. With the help of a vent fan, there is little chance of any carbon dioxide gas buildup. Apply a solution of 50 percent water and 50 percent concentrated dish soap to all connections to check for leaks. When the bubbles appear, gas is escaping. Never use a leaky system!

.0015 X 800 cubic feet = 1.2 cubic feet

It will take 1.2 cubic feet of carbon dioxide to bring the 800 cubic foot garden room up to the optimum level of 1,500 ppm.

Each pound of fuel (kerosene, propane or natural gas) burned produces approximately three pounds of carbon dioxide. One-third of a pound (5.3 ounces), produces about one pound of carbon dioxide. At 68^0 (20^0 C), one pound of carbon dioxide displaces 8.7 cubic feet.
Total amount of carbon dioxide needed / 8.7 X .33 = pounds of fuel.
1.2 / 8.7 X .33 = .045 pounds of fuel needed
.045 X 16 = **.72 ounce of fuel**

To measure the amount of fuel used, weigh the tank before it is turned on, use it for an hour, then weigh it again. The difference in weight is the amount of gas or fuel used.

It is easier and much less expensive to measure the amount of carbon dioxide produced rather than measuring the amount of carbon dioxide in the atmosphere of the garden room. There are no inexpensive measuring kits available to measure the atmospheric content of carbon dioxide.

Exact venting requirements are difficult to determine when using CO_2 generators. Since it is difficult to measure the exact amount of carbon dioxide present in the room, it is difficult to detect exactly how much to vent. The best way to figure out how much to vent a garden room would be to measure the amount of carbon dioxide present in the air, then vent the room accordingly. However, this practice is too expensive for most people. To vent a room using a CO_2 generator, wire a vent fan in line to a humidistat and thermostat (page 119). Set the humidistat at 50 percent relative humidity and the thermostat at 80^0 F (27^0 C). This will maintain the carbon dioxide close to the perfect level. If the vent fan is on all the time, come on more than once an hour for the carbon dioxide level to remain near the perfect level.

Compressed CO_2 gas generally works best in garden rooms smaller than 200 to 300 square feet. The carbon dioxide is injected into the room from the tank. It creates no heat and a meter controls the exact amount of carbon dioxide. A room could be any size and the exact amount of carbon dioxide could be injected. Carbon dioxide tanks reach a point of diminishing returns. That is, rooms over 1500 cubic feet allow more room for the heat produced by the CO_2 generator to dissipate. The CO_2 generator is also more cost-effective for larger rooms than compressed carbon dioxide. Some people do not want any kind of an unattended flame burning in their garden room. Use the carbon dioxide burner only if you feel comfortable with it.

The carbon dioxide emitter should disperse the carbon dioxide near the top of the room, so that the heavier-than-air carbon dioxide can cascade over the plants to be most effective.

When venting a carbon dioxide-enriched room, use a fan placed near the ceiling as far away as possible from the carbon dioxide source in the room. Carbon dioxide is heavier than air and less will escape when the room is vented.

Compressed CO_2

Compressed CO_2 gas is very safe, versatile and easy to control. Compressed CO_2 enrichment systems contain a combination regulator/flow meter, solenoid valve, short-range timer and tank of compressed CO_2 gas. There is a very good book on carbon dioxide systems, explaining in detail how each component of the system works. It is a *Manual on the Use of CO_2 With Metal Halide Grow-Lights*.

Compressed CO_2 is stored in metal cylinders or tanks under high pressure. Small cylinders contain 20 pounds and larger tanks contain 50 pounds. The gas is kept between 1,600 and 2,200 pounds of pressure per square inch (PSI). The carbon dioxide gas passes out of the tank into the flow meter/regulator where the pressure is reduced to 10 to 200 PSI. The solenoid valve opens and closes to let the carbon dioxide into the room. Most flow meter/regulators emit 10 to 50 cubic feet of carbon dioxide per hour. If the flow meter/regulator were set at 10 cubic feet per hour and left on for half an hour, five cubic feet of carbon dioxide would enter the room. The total amount of carbon dioxide needed to bring the level up to 1500 ppm for a 10-by-10-by-8-foot garden room is 1.2 cubic feet.

By altering the flow rate and time, the exact amount of carbon dioxide can be injected into the garden room.

For example:
Total amount of CO_2 needed / flow rate = time
1.2 / flow rate = time
1.2 / 10 = .12 hour
.12 hour X 60 minutes = **7.2 minutes**

If the flow meter is set at 10 cubic feet per hour, the timer will need to be on 7.2 minutes to bring the carbon dioxide level up to the optimum 1500 ppm.

A short-range timer measures short periods of time accurately. Inexpensive 24-hour timers do not measure increments of time less than one hour accurately. If the short-range timer is set to be on for 7.2 minutes every few hours, the carbon dioxide level of the room will go up to the optimum level, then taper off until the next burst of carbon dioxide is injected. It is a good idea to split the 7.2 minutes down into smaller increments so there is a regular supply of carbon dioxide in the room.

Vent the room using compressed CO_2 about 10 minutes before more carbon dioxide is injected into the room. Make sure the vent

A negative ion generator will keep garden rooms smelling fresh.

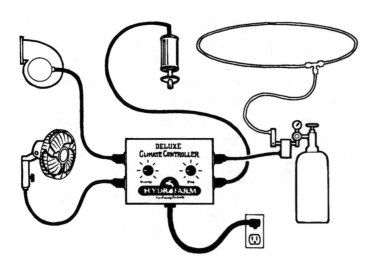

High tech carbon dioxide emitter developed by Hydrofarm delivers a constant level of carbon dioxide to the garden room.

fan is not on while the carbon dioxide is being injected into the room and for at least an hour afterward.

To vent the room with a ventilation fan, the carbon dioxide-enriched room should have the vent high in the room. The vent provides fresh, cool air without removing the carbon dioxide that is heavier than air.

Negative Ions

A deionizer or negative ion generator makes negative ions, which purify the air and remove odors and inhibit fungus. They produce a negative electrical charge or negative ions. The negative ions pour out into the air. They seek out and attach themselves to positively charged particles (pollutants, fungus spores and odors) in the air. When a negative ion attaches to a positive ion, a neutral ion is created.

Just after a rain storm, the air is packed with negative ions. The air feels still and smells

fresh. Negative ion generators create this same atmosphere in your garden room. Plants grown in such an environment are generally very healthy. The generator uses very little electricity and operates on a 110-volt electrical household outlet.

Visually check the negative ion generator filter every few days and make sure to keep it clean.

Setting Up the Vent Fan

Exhaust fans are rated by the amount of cubic feet of air they can displace or move in a minute (CFM).

 Rule of Thumb: Use a vent fan that is able to replace all of the air in the garden room in five minutes or less.

Step One: Calculate the total volume of the garden room. Length X width X height = total volume. A garden room 10-by-10-by-8-feet has a total volume of 800 cubic feet (10' X 10' X 8' = 800 cubic feet)

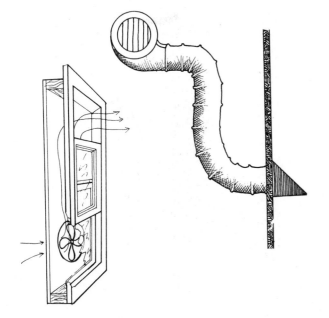

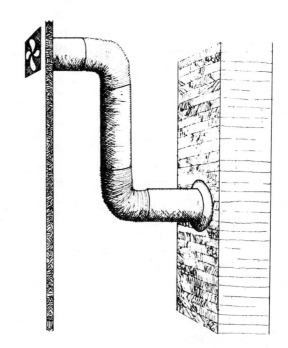

A wall fan built into an open window and a squirrel cage fan attached to a flexible four-inch plastic hose are two easy ways to vent the garden room.

A vent fan is easily vented out the chimney of a basement using 8-inch stove pipe.

Step Two: Find a vent fan that will remove the total volume of air from the room in five minutes or less. Buy a fan that can be mounted easily to the wall (8-inch fans are a favorite for larger rooms) or attached to the flexible 4-inch dryer hose. A high-speed squirrel-cage fan is necessary to maintain enough air flow through a 4-inch flexible duct.

Step Three: Place the fan high on a wall or near the ceiling of the garden room so that it vents off hot, humid air.

Step Four: If possible, cut a hole in the wall and secure the fan in place over the hole. However, most locations require special installation. See steps 5-9 below.

Step Five: Placing a fan in a window helps prevent backdrafts. Cut a quarter-inch piece of

plywood to fit the window sill. Cover the window with light-proof black paint or similar covering. Mount the fan in the top of the plywood to vent to the outside. Secure the plywood and fan in the window sill and open the window from the bottom.

Step Six: Another option that causes minimal backdraft is to use a 4-inch flexible clothes dryer hose. Vent the hose outdoors and attach a small squirrel-cage fan to the other end of the hose. Make sure there is a tight connection between the fan and the hose by using a large hose clamp. A dryer hose wall outlet with a flap will help decrease backdrafts.

Step Seven: Another option is to vent the air up the chimney. If using the chimney for a vent flue, first clean the excess ash and creosote from the inside. Hiring a chemney sweep is the easiest. Tie a chain to a rope. Lower the chain down the chimney, banging and knocking all debris inside to the bottom. There should be a door at the bottom of the chimney to remove the debris. This door can also be used as the vent hole.

Step Eight: The fan can be attached to a thermostat and humidistat to vent hot, humid air outside when necessary. Instructions are available with the thermostats to wire it to the vent fan. The diagram on page 96 shows how to wire a thermostat and humidistat to the same fan.

Step Nine: Attach the vent fan to a timer so that it runs for a specific length of time. This method is popular when used in conjunction with carbon dioxide enrichment. The fan is set to turn on and vent out used air just before new carbon dioxide-rich air is injected.

Chapter Seven
Insects and Fungi

Insects will creep into your garden, eat, reproduce and be merry. Insects live just about everywhere outdoors. Indoors, insects will live just about anywhere that you let them. Fungus is present in the air at all times. It can be introduced by an infected plant or blow in with air containing fungus spores. Fungus will settle down and grow if climatic conditions are right. Both fungus and insects can be prevented, but once an infestation has started, severe methods of control may be necessary to eradicate them.

Insect Prevention

Cleanliness is the key to insect and fungus prevention. The garden room should be totally enclosed so the environment can be easily controlled. Keep the floor clean. Keep all debris off soil surface. Do not use mulch. Insects and fungus like nice hideaway places such as dirty corners, old damp leaves and mulch. You, the horticulturist and your tools could be the transporters of many microscopic insects and fungi that could prove fatal to the garden. Thoroughly wash and disinfect all new plants that will be moved into the garden room. These plants are the potential carriers of devastating diseases.

This does not mean you and your tools have to be hospital-clean every time you enter the garden room. It does mean that normal and regular sanitary precautions must be taken. Wear clean clothes and use clean tools. Have a separate indoor set of tools to be used only in the garden room. Disinfect tools by dipping them in rubbing alcohol or wash with soap and water after use on a diseased plant. Insects and fungus love to ride indoors or from plant to plant on dirty tools.

Personal cleanliness is very important for insect and fungus prevention. Wash your hands before handling plants and after handling diseased plants. Do not walk around your buggy outdoor garden, then visit your indoor garden do it vice versa. Think before entering the indoor garden and possibly contaminating it. Did you walk across a lawn covered with rust (rust is a rust-colored fungus) or pet the dog that just came in from the garden outside? Did you just fondle your spider-mite-infested split-leaf philodendron in the living room?

Once you have grown an annual crop in a potting soil or soilless mix, throw it out. Some gardeners have used the same old potting soil more than once with acceptable results. Some

Integrated Pest Management

Integrated pest management (IPM) was developed for commercial pest control but the concept can be applied to even the smallest indoor garden and has gained popularity with home gardeners. IPM consists of the following:

* Identify the pest and use knowledge of its biology and natural enemies to control.

* Monitor pest populations using observation and traps.
* Discern the extent of injury to plants.

* Establish a tolerable threshold of injury.

* Use cultural, biological, and mechanical methods to control unacceptable pest populations with selected use of least toxic pesticides as a last resort.

* Keep records and evaluate the effects of each control strategy.

Pest controls include the following, simple techniques:

* Handpick or squash pests as soon as they are noticed.

* Spray insects with a jet of cold water.

* Use natural predators that consume pests.

* Use parasitic insects that kill particular pests by living on or in them.

* Use microbial organisms to make pests sick.

* Rotate crops.

* Use disease-resistant varieties.

Blasting insects off foliage with a fine jet of water is a simple and safe way to discourage many pest insects.

* Keep a clean and tidy garden.

* Destroy diseased plants.

* Maintain healthy, fertile soil that has abundant microbial life.

Patrol the garden looking for pests. You may find snails and slugs on leaves and cutworms at the base of plants. Simply handpick these undesirables and drop them in a jar of kerosene, soapy water, or strong salt water.

Blasting insects, especially aphids and mites, off foliage with a jet of water is a marvelous deterrent and pest control. The blasted bugs and mites have a difficult time returning for a comfortable meal. Most of these pests are comparatively stationary sap suckers, the blast of water knocks them to the ground where they starve, die of exposure, or get eaten by beneficial insects.

Washing insects off foliage also cleans plants of the fine layer of dust that builds up in dry weather. This layer inhibits plant transpiration and provides places for pests, such as spider mites, to hide.

All pesticides kill and are toxic! Just because a pesticide is botanical, organic or natural in origin does not mean that it is not toxic. In fact, pyrethrum is more toxic than malathion, however the pyrethrum's toxic life is shorter than most chemical pesticides.

The main benefit of using botanical insecticides is that the long-term toxicity is generally low. They do not accumulate in the environment, animals and wildlife the way many synthetic sprays do.

Plant disease- and insect-resistant varieties. With an increasing number of new varieties available, it is much easier to find ones that conform to your special climate conditions.

F^1 hybrids grow more vigorously than most open-pollinated varieties. This condition is known as hybrid vigor. An F^1 hybrid is the first-generation product of two different parents. Plants grown from the seeds of F^1 hybrids will be open-pollinated and will include reversions to the parent types.

The more vigorous a plant is, the less susceptible it will be to pests and diseases. Plants that are over- or under-fertilized are more susceptible to pest attack.
A roundup of pest and disease prevention tips includes the following:

*   Plant companion plants that repel or confuse pests with scents or tastes.

*   Disinfect contaminated tools.

*   Keep foliage dry. Do not let foliage go

into the night moist.

*   Select strong vigorous plants.

*   Grow varieties suited to your climate.

*   Purchase disease and pest resistant seeds and plants.

*   Do not crowd plants.

*   Identify pests and learn their life cycles.

*   Remove dead and diseased plant parts from the garden.

In conclusion, grow strong healthy plants that will resist diseases and pests. Never let the plants want for water or nutrients and keep an eye peeled for marauding pests.

of them place charcoal in the bottom of containers to absorb excess salts and maintain *sweet* soil. Used soil makes excellent outdoor garden soil. Used soil may harbor harmful insects and fungi that have developed an immunity to sprays. Starting with new potting soil will cost more initially, but will eliminate many potential problems.

Once potting soil is used it compacts easily and the texture is poor. Roots have trouble penetrating compacted soil and there is little room for oxygen, which restricts root respiration. Used potting soil is also depleted of valuable N-P-K nutrients as well as secondary and trace elements. A plant with a slow start in poor soil is a perfect target for disease.

Companion planting works to discourage insects. Most insects, with the exception of thrips, hate garlic. Garlic is readily available, takes up little room, transplants well and discourages insects. Garlic is one of the best companion plants for indoor gardens. When sowing seeds or transplanting, just plant a few cloves of garlic about a half-inch deep alongside. They sprout and grow in a week or two, driving insects away. Garlic will grow straight up, creating very little shade, and it has a compact root system attached to the bulb below the soil. When transplanting, move garlic along with the vegetable or flower. Garlic is very resilient, withstanding more shock during transplanting than most plants. Vegetables are usually harvested before the garlic matures. These garlic plants may be transplanted to companion other young plants through life. It is a good idea to dip the garlic transplant into an insecticide/ fungicide solution to prevent transferal of disease.

Marigolds also discourage insects, but not as well as garlic. Marigolds are much prettier than garlic, but they must be blooming to effectively discourage insects above the soil.

Keep plants healthy and growing fast at all times. Disease attacks sickly plants first. Strong plants tend to grow faster than insects can eat

or fungus can spread. With strong, healthy, fast-growing plants, a few insects or a little fungus does very little damage.

Forced-air circulation makes life miserable for insects and fungus. Insects hate wind they cannot hold on to the plants or fly very well in a windy environment. Fungus has little time to settle in a breezy room. Nor does fungus grow well on wind-dried soil, stems and leaves.

Ventilation will change the humidity of a room quickly. In fact, a vent fan attached to a humidistat is the most foolproof form of humidity control. One gardener was having a big problem with mold in his garden that did not have a vent fan. It was terrible! Upon entering the enclosed garden room, with the humidity near 100 percent, eyeglasses would steam up immediately. The room was so humid that roots were growing from the stems of plants. The gardener installed a vent fan, which drew the moist, stale air from the garden room, venting it outdoors. The mold problem disappeared.

Every indoor gardener should practice all of the preventative measures. It is much easier to prevent a disease from getting started than it is to wipe out an infestation. If insects or fungus multiply and are left unchecked, the entire garden could be infested in a few weeks.

Insect Control

Sometimes, even with all preventive measures taken, insects and fungus still sneak in and set up housekeeping. First they will establish themselves on a weak, susceptible plant, then launch an all-out assault on the rest of the garden. They will move out in all directions from the infested base, taking over more and more plants, until they have conquered the entire garden. This can happen in a matter of days. Bugs can lay thousands of eggs that grow into mature adults within a few weeks. For example, say you failed to take preventive measures or closely examine plants for insects and 100 microscopic munchers each laid 1,000 eggs, which grew into adults two weeks later. By the end of the month, there would be millions of insects attacking the infested garden.

Sprays essentially kill adults and all too often only some of them. Sprays should be applied soon after eggs hatch so young adult insects are caught in their weakest stage of life. Horticultural oil and insecticidal soap spray work well alone or as an additive to help kill larvae.

The availability of some sprays can be seasonal. Normally, the merchandise in the garden sections of stores changes to new and different products for the winter. The garden stock is sometimes kept in the storage room, but much of it is sold in a season-end sale. Excellent bargains on sprays and other garden products are available for the winter growing season at these season-end sales.

The products recommended in this book work well and are readily available. This does not mean they are the best or the only products to use. There are many local products that are just as good as the products mentioned here.

Insects

The indoor gardener has many options to control insects and fungi. Prevention is at the top of the list. There is a logical progression to insect and fungus control that is outlined in the chart below. Notice that it starts with cleanliness and progresses through the most basic elements.

 Rule of Thumb: Follow the logical progression for insect and fungi control.

Manual removal is just what the name implies: hand picking larger insects or smashing all insects in sight between the thumb and forefinger or between two sponges. Make sure not to infect other plants with filthy hands or sponges. (see IPM Side Bar)

Logical Progression of Insect Control
1. Prevention
  a. Keep the garden clean of debris. Wash tools in bleach solution regularly. Clean feet and wash hands before entering the indoor garden.
  b. Use new potting soil when planting.
  c. Maintain an indoor set of tools that is separate from your outdoor set of tools.
  d. Grow insect and disease resistant plants.
  e. Keep plants healthy.
  f. Remove sick plants.
  g. Control all of the climate factors to promote a healthy environment.
  h. Do not let animals frequent the garden room.
2. Manual removal
  a. Physically remove insects with your hands or smash them with sponges
3. Organic sprays
4. Natural predators

If you must use a spray, always use a natural one. Harsh chemicals are only a last resort, if used at all! With the development of environmental consciousness and technology, several new natural-based sprays have been developed. They offer unique qualities unknown to harsh chemical sprays. None-the-less, any spray always seems to slow plant growth down a little, even if it is natural. Spraying also envelops plants with the filmy residue of the spray. The stomata are clogged until the spray wears off or is washed off. Spray only when absolutely necessary. Please read "About Spraying" (pages 154-157).. Read all the labels on all sprays thoroughly before you use them and follow manufacturers directions. Use only contact sprays for edible plants. Systemic sprays can be used for ornamental plants. Do not use any sprays at all on young seedlings or tender cuttings. The spray could burn or kill the tender little plants.

Organic Pesticides

Botanical sprays are made from plants and other naturally occurring substances. Some botanical sprays are toxic to insects; others are just offensive and act as repellents.

Bacillus thuringiensis or BT

Bacillus thuringiensis, commonly referred to as BT, is the best known of several bacteria that have been discovered to attack the larval forms of insects. Other related microbial insecticides are *B. lentimorbus* and *B. sphaericus*.

Bt/H-14 sold under the trade names Vectobac and Gnatrol controls destructive soil nematodes. Destructive nematodes are difficult to see. They cause slow growth and slowly rotting roots.

Caterpillars and worms eat the bacteria that is applied to the surface of the foliage and within a short time their digestive system are poisoned. Cabbage loopers, cabbage worms, corn earworms, cutworms, gypsy moth larvae, hornworms and some nematodes are controlled. Bacterial insecticides containing one or more of the above-listed pathogens are sold as dormant spore dusts or liquids under many commercial names.

More than a half dozen different strains of BT are common today. *B. thuringiensis* var. *kurstaki* (BTK) is toxic to many moth and caterpillar larvae, including many of the species that feed on vegetables and ornamentals. *B. thuringiensis* var. *israelensis* (BTI) is effective against the larvae of mosquitoes, black flies and fungus gnats. *B. thuringiensis* var. *san diego* (BTSD) targets the larvae of Colorado potato beetles and elm beetle adults. *B. thuringiensis* var. *tenebrionis* (BTT) is lethal to Colorado potato beetle larvae. Other varieties are currently under development.

BT usually does not produce spores within insect bodies; several applications may have to be made to control an insect pest infestation.

All of these microbial bacteria are nontoxic to humans, animals and plants. Because these microbial insecticides are living creatures, they are extremely perishable. They must be kept within prescribed temperature ranges and applied according to directions. They are more effective when applied at certain stages of the target pests' lives. Be sure to read and follow instructions or get expert advice.

Diatomaceous Earth

Diatomaceous earth (DE) is the naturally occurring mined material that includes fossilized silica shell remains of the tiny one-celled or colonial creatures called diatoms. DE is fatal to most soft-bodied insects including aphids, slugs, and spider mites. DE also contains 14 trace minerals in a chelated (available) form.

DE is not registered as a pesticide or fungicide, so we can only make recommendations based on the research and observations of expert gardeners. Its effect on insects and other soft-bodied pests when they walk on it or it is dusted on them.

DE also will kill beneficial insects. It first abrades the waxy coating on pest shells or skin, allowing body fluids to leak out. If the pest ingests the razor-sharp diatomaceous earth, it acts similarly on the creature's gut.

Earthworms, animals, humans and birds however, can digest diatomaceous earth with no ill effects. Use a protective mask and goggles when handling this fine powder to guard against respiratory and eye irritations.

Mix 1 part DE with 3 to 5 parts water and a few drops of biodegradable dish soap to use as a spray. Apply this spray to infestations of pest insects.

Caution! Do not use swimming pool diatomaceous earth. Chemically treated and heated, it contains crystalline silica that is very hazardous if inhaled. The body is unable to dissolve the crystalline form of silica which causes chronic irritation.

Homemade Garden Pest Repellent Sprays

Many homemade spray preparations are outstanding pest repellents. A strong hot taste or smelly odor are the main principles behind most home-brewed pest-repellent potions. The sprays are normally made by mixing repellent plants with a little water in a blender. The resulting slurry concentrate should be strained through a nylon stocking or fine cheesecloth before being diluted with water for application, to keep it from clogging a sprayer.

Cooking or heating preparations generally destroys active ingredients. To draw out ingredients, mince plant and soak in mineral oil for a couple of days. Add this oil to the water including a little detergent or soap to emulsify (suspend) the oil droplets in water.

Biodegradable detergents and soaps are good wetting and sticking agents for these preparations. The soap dissolves best if a teaspoon of alcohol is also added to each quart of water.

Chrysanthemum, marigold, and nasturtium blossoms; pennyroyal, garlic, chive, onion, hot pepper, insect juice (target insects mixed in a blender), horseradish, mints, oregano, tomato, and tobacco residues all will repel many insects including aphids, caterpillars, mites, and whiteflies. Mixes that include tobacco may kill these pests if it is strong enough. These mixes can vary in proportions, but always filter the blended slurry before mixing with water for the final spray. One good recipe is 1 teaspoon of hot pepper or Tabasco sauce and 4 cloves of garlic blended with a quart of water. Grind this mix up in the blender and strain through a nylon stocking or cheese cloth before using in the sprayer.

A mix of one-eighth to one-quarter cup of hydrated lime mixed with a quart of water makes an effective insect spray, especially on tiny pests such as spider mites. Mix a non-detergent soap with the lime; the soap acts as both a sticking agent and insecticide. Lime can be caustic in large doses. Always try the spray

Mix homemade sprays in a blender and filter with cheesecloth before diluting in water for spray.

on a test plant and wait a few days to check for adverse effects to the plant before applying to similar plants.

Sprays that include chamomile plant parts are used to prevent damping-off and mildew. (See also fungicides)

Liquid laundry bleach usually is a compound called sodium hypochlorite that is a good fungicide. Usually sold as a five percent solution, it is an eye and skin irritant so wear gloves and goggles when using it. Mix 1 part bleach to 9 parts water and use this solution as a general disinfectant for greenhouse equipment, tools, and plant wounds. The bleach solution breaks down rapidly and therefore has little if any residual effect.

Another natural spray is made from chopped tomato leaves soaked in water. The water is used as a spray against white cabbage butterflies.

A spray made from pests ground up in a blender and emulsified in water will reputedly repel related pests.

agent when watering down peat moss, dry potting soil, or seedlings. Both soap and detergent reduce the surface tension of the water to give better penetration. Ivory or Castille soap can also be used as a spreader-sticker to mix with sprays. The soaps help the spray stick to the foliage better, which is important when using contact sprays. The soft soaps will only last for about one day before dissipating.

You will have to reapply these sprays after rain or above ground watering. In small concentrations, nicotine sulfate is not toxic to humans.

Nicotine (sulfate) and Tobacco Sprays

Nicotine is a non-persistent pesticide derived from tobacco. Although naturally derived, it is not usually recommended in organic programs because of its toxicity. It is toxic to most insects and humans if a concentrate is swallowed. This very poisonous compound affects the neuromuscular system, causing insects to go into convulsions and die. Many times nicotine is mixed with sulfur. One well-known brand on the market is Black Flag's Nicotine Sulfate.

Nicotine sulfate (tobacco juice mixed with sulfur) is an excellent insecticide on all plants except members of the nightshade family (eggplant, tomatoes, peppers and potatoes). You can purchase bottled nicotine sulfate or simply use tobacco diluted in water. Apply the nicotine as a spray to kill aphids.

There are far less toxic ways of coping with aphids such as knocking them down with a hard spray of water. It is wise to choose the most conservative means of pest control.

Horticultural Oil

Horticultural oil sprays are safe, non-poisonous and non-polluting insecticides. Similar to medicinal mineral oil, they kills slow moving and immobile sucking insects by smothering

Safer's™ Insecticidal Soap

Insecticidal Soaps

Insecticidal soaps are mild contact insecticides made from fatty acids of animals and plants. These soaps are safe for bees, animals, and humans. The soap controls soft-bodied insects such as aphids, mealybugs, spider mites, thrips, and whiteflies by penetrating and clogging body membranes.

Safer's Insecticidal Soap is a well-known commercial product. It is a potassium-salt based liquid concentrate that is toxic to insects but not to animals or humans. It is most effective when applied at the first appearance of insects pests.

Soft soaps such as Ivory liquid dish soap, Castille soap, and Murphy's Oil soap, are biodegradable and kill insects in a similar manner as insecticidal soap, but they are not as potent. Do not use detergent soaps as they may be caustic. Mix a few capfuls of one of these soaps to a quart of water to make a spray.

These soaps can also be used as a wetting

and suffocating them while the thin oily film remains invisible to humans. Oil spray control is useful in dealing with aphids, scale, spider mites, whiteflies, mealybugs, and thrips.

Modern horticultural oil sprays are petroleum products but are far lighter than the old forms and easier on the plants. They usually can be applied at any temperature without harming plants. To ensure the least possibility of leaf scorch from oil sprays, plants should be watered before applying oil sprays.

Oil sprays are widely used in greenhouses. They are not the same kinds of oils used in the car or sold at the hardware store. Do not use 3-in-1 oil or anything similar in place of horticultural petroleum oil. Horticultural oil is refined by removing most of the portion that is toxic to plants. Make sure it is a lightweight horticultural oil with a viscosity of 60 to 70. The lighter the oil, the less toxic it is to plants. Use oil sprays only during vegetative growth. This way, the residue has ample time to dissipate before harvest.

Mix two drops of oil spray (no more than a one-percent solution) per quart of water. More than a few drops could burn tender growing shoots and clog stomata. Repeat applications as needed, usually three applications, one every five to 10 days will do it. The first application will kill most of the adults and many eggs. Eggs hatch in about 10 days. The second spraying will kill the newly hatched eggs and the remaining adults. The third application will finish off any survivors.

Fish oil is an old product, but has recently been used as a dormant spray as well as a spreader sticker for fungicides and pesticides (do not use with copper sprays). When dry, fish oil constitutes a durable coating that is difficult to wash off. Make sure to clean you equipment after applying fish oil to prevent clogging.

Cruder oil, including petroleum distillates and diesel fuels, include sulfur compounds that are poisonous to plants. For that reason, these heavy oils are called "weed oils" and used only for weed control on roadways and railroad rights of way.

Sulfur

Sulfur, one of the oldest insecticides, remains a useful even today when there are countless sophisticated pest controls. One of the reasons for its continuing popularity is its low toxicity to humans. Sulfur dust, wettable sulfur and sulfur in large particles are the three main forms of sulfur.

Sulfur is also a good control for fungal diseases. Commercial products that add copper and oils to the sulfur are more potent than sulfur alone against plant diseases. For that reason, don't use that combination if you plan to apply oil sprays within a month. Avoid scorching foliage by never applying sulfur when temperatures are above 85 to 90°F.

Sulfur is a useful insecticide as well as a fungicide. It is toxic to insects and even more toxic to mites. When using indoors, use sulfur sparingly and at half the manufacturers suggested strength. It will burn foliage.

Botanical Pesticides

A number of naturally occurring substances derived from plants are popular pesticides among organic gardeners. Among them are the following.

Citrus Oils

Citrus oils, the byproducts of the fruit and juice industries that can be derived from tons of citrus peels and have insecticidal properties. They appear to be contact poisons and are recommended for use against fleas, aphids, and mites. They also will kill fruit flies, fire ants, flies, paper wasps, and crickets. They are comparatively new to the marketplace and show promise in controlling a wide range of garden

and agricultural pests.

Citrus oils, including limonene and linalool, are nontoxic to humans, although in high doses they could irritate skin eyes and mucous membranes. Some cats may be sensitive to applications of citrus oils for flea control.

Although very effective, citrus oils break down rapidly.

Garlic Oil

Garlic oil, long used as an insect repellent, is an effective control for some nematodes, larval mosquitoes, aphids, cabbage butterfly larvae, and Colorado potato beetle larvae. Unfortunately, it also will kill some of the natural controls for aphids which is why it should be used only when natural controls appear to be absent.

Neem

Neem oil, while relatively new to this country, has been used for many years as a botanical insecticide in Africa and southeast Asia where the neem tree (*Azadirachta indica*) is native. The neem tree, also a handsome ornamental shade tree, is grown in the southern part of our country.

Neem oil is extracted from the foliage and seeds of the tree and is an effective control for dozens of insect pests including, leafminers, mealybugs, whiteflies and caterpillars.

Neem oil acts as both a contact pesticide and a systemic. When bitter, strong-smelling neem oil is added to the soil, the essential ingredients become systemic, entering the plant's stems and foliage. Pests then either pass up the bitter, strong smelling plant parts, or eat them and die before maturing.

Neem oil has very low toxicity to mammals. The active ingredients break down rapidly in sunlight and within a few weeks in the soil.

Pyrethrum

Pyrethrum is an extremely powerful insecticide extracted from the flowers of the pyrethrum chrysanthemum (*Chrysanthemum coccineum* and *C. cinergrii folium*). A broad spectrum pesticide, pyrethrum is very toxic to most insects, including those that are beneficial. If applied as a spray, pyrethrum is a very effective control of flying insects. But if insects do not receive killing doses, they may revive. Pyrethrum is often combined with rotenone or ryania to ensure effectiveness. Use this non-selective insecticide to spot spray only heavily infested plants.

Pyrethrum refers to the plant and pyrethrin is the name of the active compound that is toxic to insects. Pyrethroids are synthetic materials that resemble the natural pyrethrin but are more toxic and more persistent.

Although pyrethrum is comparatively safe to use, repeated contact may cause allergic reactions or skin irritation in humans. It can toxic to cats in formulations that include more than .04 percent pyrethrum. Purchase as a dust or liquid.

Although this and other insecticides often are sold in aerosol formulations, aerosols do not target the pests as tightly as other forms of application. Too much is generally released in the air. Aerosol spray is very convenient, but can burn foliage if can is held closer than one foot from the plant. Some aerosols also contain piperonyl butoxide which is toxic to people. All forms of pyrethrum dissipate within a few hours in the presence of air and sunlight or HID light.

Quassia, Ryania and Sabadilla

Quassia, ryana and sabadilla are three different naturally occurring poisons that are derived from derivatives of different plants and act as a poison to numerous different pests. They are combined here because they often are sold in combination with one another in the same container.

Quassia is harmless to bees and ladybugs but kills other beneficial insects in the early stages of their lives. This spray is effective on most soft-bodied insects, including aphids, leaf miners, and some caterpillars. Most other insects are not affected.

Once the pests consume the dust, they stop feeding immediately. Ryana is slow acting and takes up to 24 hours or so to kill target insects. It is less harmful to beneficial insects and is considered harmless to humans and other warm-blooded animals. This insecticide is often mixed with rotenone and pyrethrum.

Rotenone

Rotenone is an extract of the roots of several plants including derris species, *Lonchocarpus*

species and *Tephrosia* species. The latter two also are used as fish poisons in South America and Africa. Applied as a spray (wettable powder) or dust, this non-selective contact insecticide is a stomach poison and slow-acting nerve poison to beetles, caterpillars, flies, mosquitoes, imported cabbageworms, thrips, weevils and beneficial insects.

Popular since the mid 1800's, rotenone does not harm plants and won't linger in the soil. The spray or dust residues break down in three to seven days in the presence of light and air. Use this spray only as a last resort and be careful not to let it wash into garden pools or streams as it is extremely toxic to fish. It is also toxic to birds and pigs.

Sabadilla breaks down rapidly sunlight. Although safer than rotenone, the dust may irritate eyes and nasal membranes if inhaled. Make sure to wear a mask and goggles when applying. It should be used conservatively and only when all else fails.

Pest Traps & Barriers

Black lights can be used to catch some egg-laying moths. Light and fan traps attract many insects, including beneficial insects, and their use may do more harm than good.

Pheromones, substances that attract insects by resembling their species' sex hormones, are available for some insect pests and can be good controls when used in combination with traps. When using sex-lure traps, place them away from sensitive plants so insects will be drawn away from them.

Traps
draw black light traps, Biolure trap, screen in a bucket of water,

A simple screen placed over a bucket or jar of sweetened water makes an excellent insect trap. Pour some water into a bucket and sweeten it with molasses or sugar and include some protein like powdered egg or yeast. Pests such as corn borers, cucumber beetles, cutworms,

When purchasing beneficial insects for release in the garden, the following rules-of-thumb are helpful:

Beneficial insects need to be released as soon as pests are seen. Most require several releases at 1-3-week intervals.

Insect pests are generally slow-moving and beneficial insects that prey on those pests are usually fast and agile.

During very hot or very cool weather, beneficial insect predators will be comparatively inactive and do little if any feeding.

The beneficial insects must have an ample supply of food in the garden or they will leave.

Trichogramma wasps, green lacewings, praying mantises, and lady beetles are the best known and most available predatory insects for bio-control in the garden.

tomato horn worms, cucumber beetles and more are attracted to this sweet trap.

Handpick: Drop pest insects in a jar of paint thinner, kerosene topped water or salt water.

Sticky Traps

Sticky traps such as flypaper or Tanglefoot™ are very effective. Sticky resins or other sticky materials can be smeared on attractive yellow or red objects to simulate ripe fruit. When the pests land on the "fruit" they are stuck forever! Tanglefoot™ can also be used as a barrier on plant stems and trunks.

These are particularly effective against white flies which can be tough pests in greenhouses and garden rooms.

You can make your own sticky trap cards by cutting them from bright yellow poster board or painting small boards with bright yel-

low enamel. Paint the yellow areas with a heavy grade automotive oil and place among or near infested plants. When the yellow areas are covered with bugs, just wash them off and repaint with oil.

Bug Bombs

Bug bombs are very strong insecticides that essentially exterminate everything living in the room They were developed to kill fleas and roaches. Bug bombs are used between crops to rid the garden room of all insects before introducing the next crop. Many manufacturers produce bug bombs under various brand names containing a wide variety of toxic chemicals.

Place the bug bomb in the empty room. Turn it on. Then leave the room. The chemicals are very toxic! Follow directions to the letter!

Beneficial Insects

Names like aphid wolf, assassin bug, dragonfly, mealybug destroyer and tiger beetle describe predatory insects, the tenacious flesh eaters of the garden. They are usually equipped with crushing or piercing jaws and are larger, stronger, and more agile than their prey. Predatory larvae must search out and devour insects for existence and many are more ferocious predators than their parents.

Parasites eat pest insects from the inside: Adults lay eggs in or on the host, the eggs hatch, the larva emerge and once inside the host, begin to feed. Some host insects die within 48 hours while others take several weeks. Most hosts get sick and quit eating within 24 hours of the parasite entering the body. Some parasites release a bacteria that kills the host.

Predators

The rate at which the predators keep the infestation in check is directly proportionate to

Homemade blacklight trap

Safer sticky traps

the amount of predators. The more predators, the sooner they will take care of any infestations. Predators breed faster than their victim. The predators are the crusading warriors in the never-ending battle of pest-free horticulture.

One of the best outlets in the country to buy predatory insects is from Natures Control, Medford Oregon. This supplier (Don Jackson) gives good advice and sends along specific instructions as well as a brochure about all the predators he offers. Another excellent supplier, AGS, 297 N. Barrington Road, Streamwood, IL 60107. Predators are shipped special delivery and may arrive after the daily mail delivery. The inside of a mailbox in the hot sun can reach 120º F (49º C) or the temperature can drop can be below freezing in winter. Check the mailbox regularly if ordering predators.

When any predator is introduced into the garden, there must be special precautions taken to ensure their well-being. Stop spraying all toxic chemicals and organic sprays at least two weeks before introducing the predators. Pyrethrum and Safer's Insecticidal Soap can be applied up to a few days before, providing any residue is washed off with water. Do not spray at all for 30 days after releasing predators.

Most of the predators that do well in the HID garden cannot fly. Bugs that can fly usually go straight for the lamp. The ladybug is a good example. If 500 ladybugs are released on Monday, by Friday, only a few die-hards will remain; the rest will have flown into the hot lamp and died. If using flying predators, release them when it is dark. They will last longer.

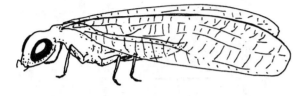

Lacewing

Predators are usually very small and must be introduced to each plant separately. This could take a little time and patience, so budget enough time. Predators also have specific climatic requirements. For best results, pay close attention note the predator's needs and maintain them.

Other beneficial insect predators to welcome to your garden are described below. Those in the list with a "star" by their name are available commercially; the rest are not.

Encarsia Formosa

The *encarsia formosa* is a parasite, about an eighth-inch long and much smaller than the whitefly. This small predator takes several weeks longer to eliminate and control the whitefly population. Once the parasite penetrates the whitefly, death is slow. The parasite feeds for some time on the host insect, then its eggs hatch inside the victim's body cavity. If you use them, set them out at the rate of two or more parasites per plant as soon as the first whitefly is detected. Repeat every two to four weeks until thrips are controlled.

Lacewings

Lacewings (Order Neuroptera) have beautiful, frail, lacy wings of green or brown that carry them in erratic flight patterns. Adults are

from 1/4 to 3/4 inch long and feed on honeydew, nectar, and pollen.

Larvae look like tiny alligators that grow up to 1/2 inch long. The predator consumes aphids, caterpillar eggs, mealybugs, mites, scale, and thrips so unmercifully that they are affectionately called aphid wolves or aphid lions.

The green lacewing is an important commercial pest control. Encourage egg-laying lacewing adults by interplanting blooming flowers among vegetables or set out a slurry of honey and water in the garden. This predator does not overwinter well in cool climates and the commercially available eggs may have to be reintroduced each spring.

Ladybugs

Ladybird beetles (Order Coleoptera, family Coccinellidae), are one of the best-known garden predators. There are numerous species. The most common one in this country is the convergent lady beetle (*Hippodamia convergens*) which orange with dark spots. Both the adult and their dark gray-colored larvae eat scores of aphids, scale, and insect eggs a day. The larvae dine on a greater assortment of insects than the adults including beetles, bugs, and weevils. They can wolf down over 30 aphids an hour.

A large bag of 5,000 ladybugs will usually cost just a few dollars more than a container of 1,000. After aphids show an increase in population, there will be enough food to sustain them.

Release several handfuls in the evening by gently setting them among garden plants in several locations. Store the remainder in the refrigerator where they will continue to hibernate for several weeks.

Mealybug Destroyer

Mealybug Destroyer (*Crytolaemus montrouzieri*) is a small black and orange member of the ladybird beetle family. The adults are

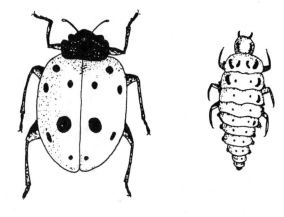

Adult Ladybird beetle (Ladybug) on left and larva on right

Praying mantis

called crypts. Both adults and larva attack mealybugs in all stages of life. They also feed on some stages of scale and aphids. The adult is 1/5-inch long and looks like a small dark-colored ladybug. The larvae resembles the mealybug. Like the ladybirds, these will be more effective in enclosed places. Outdoors they are more inclined to rove.

Praying Mantis

The European praying mantises (*Mantis religiosa*) and the native American mantises (*Stag momantis carolina*) grow up to 4 inches long. They are relentless predators that devour almost anything that cross their path including beneficial insects. For that reason, they currently are somewhat out of favor as biological controls.

Four-inch long predator kills their victims with a crushing chomp to the back of the neck with their powerful jaws. A mass of their eggs can be purchased on cards and set out in the garden in the spring to hatch. Occasionally, a trained eye will spot a mass of their eggs on a plant leaf in the autumn. To keep the eggs, prune off the entire twig and leaf containing the cluster. Store the twig containing the eggs in the refrigerator or a sheltered spot outdoors

in the garden so they will hatch out the following spring. Eggs live through a hard freeze. Do not leave them in a warm house for the winter or they will hatch out too soon. Large populations of insects will attract praying mantises to your garden. If they do not find enough food in your garden, they search for gardens that do.

Spiders

Spiders consume many garden pests including flying insects, even grasshoppers that are up to three times their size. When you see one of the many species of spiders in the garden, leave it alone. It will continue hunting day and night for garden insects.

Spiders may be frightening to some people but, despite their appearance, spiders are an asset in any garden. Many spiders build webs to snare their pray. Other spiders catch their prey on the run. They paralyze the prey with a bite, then dissolve and eat the innards of their victims.

Only two spiders present a threat to humans the black widow and the brown recluse; both are more often found in homes rather than gardens. A bite from the female black widow spider is painful but rarely fatal. The venom affects the nerves. The female is jet

Black widow spider - Note the red hourglass shape on the poisionus female's underside.

black, with a domed abdomen and has a red hourglass-shaped spot on her underside. The body is about _-inch long. Black widows are seldom found in the garden. They favor dark quiet locations with enough room to move around such as tool sheds, basements, water meter boxes, and garages.

The brown recluse spiders is shy and not aggressive. They hunt in a large area around their webs which are often in corners, and are occasionally found in bedding or clothing. They will bite when they get pushed or pinched.

These spiders have longer legs in relation to their 1/3-inch bodies than the black widows. There is a clear, distinctive violin-shaped mark on the top of the body just behind the head. The bite, if neglected, can cause an ulcerous wound and bad scar. In rare cases, the bite can cause kidney failure. If you are bitten, seek medical attention.

Pest Insects

Spider Mites

The spider mite is the most common insect found on flowers and vegetables indoors. These microscopic mites are found on the leaf's undersides, sucking away the plant's life-giving fluids. To the untrained eye, they are very difficult to spot. Most people notice the tell-tale yellowish-white spots (stippling) on the tops of the leaves first. More careful inspection will reveal tiny spider webs on the stems and under leaves. Webs may easily be seen when leaves are misted with water. The spider mites appear as tiny specks on leaf undersides. The naked eye has a hard time distinguishing the pests nonetheless, they can be seen. A magnifying glass or low power microscope helps to identify the yellow, white, two-spotted, brown or red mites and their light-colored eggs.

Control: has a logical progression. First make sure all preventative measures have been taken.

Note: The spider mite thrives in a dry - 70 to 80^0 F (21 to 27^0 C). It can reproduce in five days if the temperature is above 80^0 F (27^0 C).

In order to create a hostile environment for mites, lower the temperature to 60^0 (15^0 C) and spray the plants with a jet of water, making sure to spray under leaves. This will blast them off the leaves as well as increase humidity. Their reproductive cycle will be slowed and you will have a chance to kill them before they do much damage. If the leaves have been over 50 percent damaged, remove and throw away, making sure insects and eggs do not re-enter the garden. If mites have attacked only one or two plants, isolate the infected plants and treat them separately. Once a hostile environment has been established and leaves over 50 percent infected have been removed, you may select one or more of the following control methods:

Manual removal: Smash all mites in sight between your thumb and index finger or wash leaves individually with two sponges.

Homemade sprays work very well when there is not yet an infestation of mites. If these sprays have not eradicated the mites after four or five applications, switch to another, stronger spray.

Insecticidal soaps are wonderful products

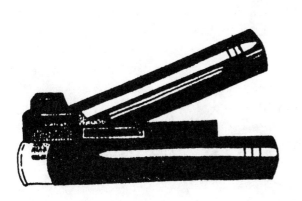

A 6X magnifying glass or a 30 X light scope will help identify tiny eggs and pests.

Mite eggs above look like translucent dots on the leaf underside. The bottom photo shows a close up of stripping caused by spider mites.

that control mites fairly well. Usually two or three heavy applications at intervals of five to 10 days will do the trick.

Pyrethrum (aerosol) is the best natural a miticide. Two or three applications at intervals of five to 10 days usually stops mites dead.

Predatory spider mites (*Phytoseiulus persimilis*) work very well. There are many things to consider when using the predators. First and foremost, predators only can eat about 20 eggs or five adults daily. This gives you an idea of how fast they can really control the spider mites, which are their only source of food. As soon as the predators' source of food is gone, they cannibalize one another or die of starvation. A general dosage of 20 predators per plant is a good place to start. You might even want to throw in a few more for good measure. Spider mites have a difficult time traveling from plant to plant, so setting them out on each plant is necessary. Temperature and humidity are the most important factors to maintain. Both must be at the proper level to give the predators the best possible chance of survival. There are two kinds of predators commonly used indoors: amblyseius californicus and phytoseiulus longipes.

When spider mites have infested a garden,

predatory mites can not eat them fast enough to solve the problem quickly. Predatory mites work best when there are only a few spider mites. The predators are introduced as soon as spider mites are seen and released every month thereafter. This gives predators a chance to keep up with mites. Getting started with predatory mites will cost about $30. Before releasing predators, rinse all plants thoroughly to ensure that all toxic spray residues from insecticides and fungicides are gone.

Whitefly

Whiteflies, also called leafhoppers, may cause white speckles (stipples) on the tops of leaves and hide underneath. The stipples are very similar to those made by spider mites. The easiest way to check for the little pests is to grab a limb and shake it. If there are any whiteflies, they will flutter from under leaves. An adult whitefly looks like a white moth about one millimeter long. They usually appear near

Aphids

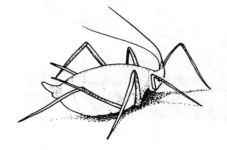

Whitefly

Aphid

the top of the weakest plant first. They will move downward on the plant or fly off to infest another plant.

Control: Take all preventive measures. Whiteflies are very difficult to remove manually they fly faster than the hand is able to squish them. Adults are attracted to the color yellow. To build a whitefly trap similar to flypaper, cover a bright yellow object with a sticky substance. Place the traps on the tops of the pots. The traps work very well, but are a mess to clean.

Whiteflies are easily eradicated with natural sprays. Before spraying, remove any leaves that have been over 50 percent damaged and cure with heat or burn.

Homemade sprays applied at intervals of two to 10 days work well.

Insecticidal soaps applied at intervals of five to 10 days.

Pyrethrum (aerosol) applied at intervals of two to 10 days does it.

The parasitic wasp, *encarsia formosa*, is the most effective whitefly predator. The small wasps attack only whiteflies. They do not sting people. As with all predators, all toxic sprays must be washed completely off before their introduction.

Aphids are most common indoors when they are plentiful outdoors. About the size of a pinhead, aphids are easily spotted with the naked eye. This insect may be green, yellow, black or pink and with or without wings. Aphids excrete a sticky honeydew and prefer to attack weak plants. They attack growing tips or buds first, sucking out fluids. Aphids love to hide on the leaves' undersides. An infestation of aphids can devastate a garden in a matter of days.

Control: Even though aphids may have wings, manual removal is easy and works well to kill them. They do not fly as well as whiteflies. Aphids bite into the plant, sucking out life-giving juices. When affixed to foliage, aphids are unable to move and easy to squish.

Homemade and Safer's sprays are very effective. Apply two or three times at intervals of five to 10 days, after manually removing as many aphids as possible.

Pyrethrum (aerosol) applied two to three times at intervals of two to 10 days eradicates them.

Lacewings are the most effective available predators for aphids. Release one to 20 lacewing per plant, depending on infestation level, as soon as aphids appear. Repeat every month. If possible, buy adult lacewing rather than larvae, which take several weeks to hatch and mature into adult aphid exterminators.

Ladybugs (ladybird beetles) also work very well to exterminate aphids. Adults are easily obtained at many retail nurseries during the summer months and mail order the rest of the year. The only drawback to ladybugs is their attraction to the HID lamp. Release about 20 lady bugs per plant. About half of them will go directly for the HID, hit the hot bulb and buzz. Within a few weeks, all the ladybugs will fall victim to the lamp, requiring frequent replenishment.

Ants

Ants come in a a wide variety of shapes and sizes. Ants seldom harm plants, but some ant species farm aphids and mealybugs, carrying them from plant to plant and protecting them from predators. Ants and their young feed on the sweet, sticky honeydew exuded by the aphids and mealybugs.

Controlling the aphids or mealybugs usually controls the ants. If the ants become an overwhelming problem, mix some sugar and borax soap in equal parts and deposit it in a covered coffee can with a window cut in it . The ants are attracted to the sweet mix and carry it back to the nest along with the borax. The borax will kill those ants it contacts. Diatomaceous earth or boric acid crystals sprinkled lightly along baseboards and in corners of cupboards and pantry closets are environmentally sound ways to get rid of most crawling insects.

Ants will not cross a line of bonemeal or pulverized charcoal. To keep ants from entering the house, sprinkle a little powdered cinnamon or squeeze some lemon juice around their points of entry.

A quick application of pyrethrum will kill ants most effectively. Pyrethrum is the best choice when ants have invaded the kitchen. Remember to cover or remove all food and eat-

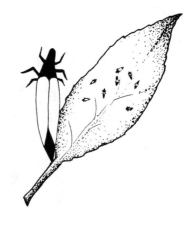

Thrip

ing utensils from the counter before spraying.

Discourage ants from climbing plants by smearing a three-inch ring of Tanglefoot^{TM} or other sticky material around the stems.

Thrips

Thrips are not very common indoors. These tiny, winged, fast-moving creatures rasp on the leaves and buds, then suck out the juices for food. They tend to feed inside flower buds or wrap up and distort leaves. Thrips are not hard to spot. Upon careful inspection, thrips appear as a herd of specks thundering across foliage.

Control: Preventive maintenance. Manual removal works if only a few thrips are present, but they are hard to catch.

Homemade sprays are very effective. Apply two to four times at intervals of five to 10 days.

Insecticidal soaps are very effective. Apply at intervals of two to 10 days.

Pyrethrum (aerosol) applied at intervals of two to 10 days does it.

Thrips have no readily available natural predators.

Mealy Bugs

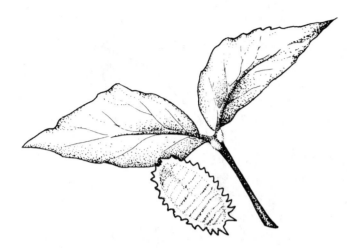

Mealy Bug

Mealy bugs are somewhat common. These oblong, waxy white insects, 2 to 7 millimeters long, move very little, mature slowly and live in colonies that are usually located at stem joints. Like aphids, mealy bugs excrete a sticky honeydew. Mealy bugs are easy to control, since they reproduce and move slowly.

Control: Preventive maintenance. Manual removal works very well for small populations. Pry them off by getting a fingernail underneath. Wet a Q-Tip with rubbing alcohol and touch them with it. The alcohol kills the mealy bugs quickly.

Homemade sprays work well, especially if they contain rubbing alcohol. Apply two or three times at intervals of five or 10 days.

Insecticidal soap applied at 5-10 day intervals kills mealy bugs in a day or two.

The ladybug (ladybird beetle) and the green lacewing are effective natural predators. Both work very efficiently and have no trouble eating mealy bugs faster than they can reproduce. If using these predators, manually remove all visible mealy bugs release five to 10 predators per plant, depending on need, as soon as the mealy bugs are noticed. Repeat releases at two week intervals. Within a month, there should be a noticeable reduction in mealy

Scale

bug population.

Many professionals prefer nicotine sulfate to control mealy bugs. Apply at intervals of five to 10 days. Do not use nicotine sulfite on tomatoes, peppers or eggplants. It will give them the fatal tobacco mosaic virus.

Scale

Scale is uncommon on many plants indoors. Scale looks and acts similar to mealy bugs, but is usually more round than oblong. Scale may be white, yellow, brown, gray or black. Their hard protective shell is 2 to 4 millimeters across and they rarely move. Check for mealy bugs around stem joints, where they live in colonies. Scale sometimes excretes a sticky honeydew.

Control: Preventive maintenance. Manual removal may be tedious, but is very effective. Wet a Q-Tip in rubbing alcohol and wash scale away. A small knife, fingernails or tweezers may also be necessary to scrape and pluck the tightly affixed scale from the plants.

Homemade sprays work well if they contain rubbing alcohol.

Insecticidal soaps work well to control scale. Apply at 10-day intervals.

scale. Apply at 10-day intervals.

Pyrethrum (aerosol) applied two or three times at intervals of 2 to 10 days does it.

Bees, Flies etc.

Bees and wasps may become a nuisance. They are not harmful to plants but hurt when they sting. They sneak into the garden room through vents or cracks, in search of flowering plants, a valuable commodity to bees and wasps in midwinter. Manual removal is out of the question! A circulation fan in the room is the best form of preventive maintenance. The artificial wind will impair their flight, causing them to seek a more hospitable garden. There are many aerosol sprays that kill bees and wasps. Wasp traps are also available. Sweet fly-paper is also a good alternative. Bees and wasps are attracted to the HID lamp. Many will fall victim to its outer envelope....BUZZ...POP!

Fruit flies and gnats can become a problem. They do no harm to the indoor garden, but are a nuisance to be around. If you are impatient and the chore of cleaning up insect bodies is not appealing, just about any indoor insect spray in the aerosol form will get rid of them.

Plant Diseases in General

Plant diseases are caused by bacteria, fungus, virus, other parasites or growth-inhibiting environmental conditions. Prevent diseases by avoiding conditions that cause them.

Many plant diseases are caused or encouraged by poor drainage, poor or imbalanced soil fertility, inadequate air circulation, insect damage and unsanitary conditions. For example, aphids that pierce and suck plant juices transmit viruses when they move from one plant to the next. The wounds aphids make begin to decay and become infected with airborne diseases.

Soil infertility and poor drainage are normally indicated by sickly plants that are prone to disease and insect attack. Throwing more fertilizers at the soil and trying to control pests on sickly plants may be more trouble than it is worth. In the case of poor soil, it is generally better to remove the sickly plants, change the soil and start over with new, healthy plants.

You, the gardener, may be responsible for spreading diseases by handling wet diseased plants and then touching uninfected plants. Smokers may unwittingly spread tobacco mosaic virus to their tomatoes.

Whenever possible, work in the garden when foliage is dry. Most bacteria and fungi need moisture to travel from one plant to another. Removing and destroying any diseased foliage and washing your hands afterward will go a long way to retain overall garden health.

Plant disease-resistant varieties. Look for new varieties that not only grow better in your climate but are much more resistant to disease. Years of careful breeding have given us all kinds of surprising plants.

Allow enough space between plants for air to circulate freely. Good air circulation prevents ever-present air-borne fungal spores from settling on foliage.

Plant diseases are more difficult to identify than insect attacks. They may start inside the plant or attack the roots and give little or no notice before killing plants. Many times by the time you notice a disease, it is too late to do anything about it. Other diseases such as gray mold or rust do show externally on foliage. They are much easier to identify and control.

Molds, yeasts, and mushrooms are all funguses. They reproduce by means of tiny spores which spread on the air. The best organic way to cope with fungal diseases in the garden is prevention by keeping the garden clean and using good cultural practices. If the disease is so severe that you decide to use a fungicide, identify the disease, choose the least toxic fungicide and use all appropriate safety precautions.

> **LOGICAL PROGRESSION OF FUNGUS CONTROL**
>
> 1. Prevention
>   a. cleanliness
>   b. low humidity
>   c. ventilation
> 2. Remove infected foliage and plants
> 3. Copper, lime, sulfur or potassium based sprays

Bacterial diseases are caused by primitive one-celled plants called bacteria. A disease caused by a bacterium will be more difficult to diagnose than one caused by a fungus.

Viruses, too small to be seen with a microscope, also cause plant diseases. They often are carried from plant to plant by other organisms, or by vectors such as insects, mites, or nematodes.

Bacterial and viral diseases are more difficult to control than those caused by fungi. Often the only solution is to destroy the infected plants and choose another species or a disease-resistant cultivar.

Some conditions that look like diseases are caused not by a fungus, bacterium, or virus but by the culture, the care you are providing. The classic example of a disease-mimicking condition is blossom end rot in tomatoes.

Fungus Prevention

Plant diseases are caused by bacteria, fungus, virus, other parasites or growth inhibiting environmental conditions.

Fungus is a very primitive plant. It is so primitive that it does not produce chlorophyll, the substance giving higher plants their green color. Fungi reproduce by spreading tiny microscopic spores rather than seeds. Many fungus spores are present in the air at all times. With proper conditions, spores will settle, take hold and start growing. Entire gardens have been wiped out in a matter of days by an uncontrolled outbreak of fungus. One garden room was close to a swamp filled with fungus spores. Unsterilized, soggy soil and humid, stagnant air provide the environment most fungi need to thrive. Although there are many different types of fungi, they are usually treated by the same methods.

Prevention is the first step and the true key to fungus control. In "Setting Up the Garden Room," I recommended you remove anything that might attract fungus or harbor mold, such as cloth curtains or clothes. Make sure the advice is followed as part of a preventive program. If the room is carpeted, make sure to cover it with white plastic visqueen. If mold should surface on the walls, spray it heavily with the fungicide used in the garden, wash down the wall with Pinesol (made from natural pine oil) or paint damp fungus covered walls with whitewash (page 66). Get all of the mold off when it is washed down. Repeat applications if the mold persists. The basic ingredients of mold and fungi control are cleanliness and climate control. Clean, well-ventilated garden rooms have little or no problem with fungi. Dingy, ill-kept gardens have fungus problems and yield sickly flowers and vegetables. If the garden is in a basement, the use of a flat white paint with a fungus-inhibiting agent is essential. One garden basement was carpeted with fungi. To combat fungus, the walls were whitewashed and lime was spread on the earth floor. The vent fan was turned on 24 hours a day and the room kept clean. There has been no trouble with mold in the room in more than a year.

There are many ways to lower humidity. Ventilation is the least expensive, easy and most often used. Remember, one of the by-products of burning a fossil fuel in CO_2 generators is water vapor. Dehumidifiers work exceptionally well, offering exact humidity control. They can be purchased or rented. Wood, coal, gas and electric heat all dehumidify the air.

Many garden rooms have a central heating vent. This vent may be opened to provide additional heat and lower humidity.

Fungus Control

Fungus is prevented by controlling all the factors, such as temperature and humidity, contributing to its growth. If prevention fails and fungus appears control measures must be taken. Remove dead leaves and alter soil, moisture and air conditions to prevent fungus from spreading. These methods work well in gardens that have only a few signs of fungus. Another method of treating fungus is to isolate the infected plant and treat it separately. Fungus can spread like wildfire. If it gets a good start, take all preventive measures, as well as spraying the entire garden with a fungicide. Spraying will be necessary if the fungus gets a good start and appears to be spreading, even though preventive measures have been taken.

need a good photo of a

Fungicides come in two basic categories: narrow-spectrum, specific against a few organisms and broad spectrum, effective against numerous fungi.

Fungistat inhibit, but do not destroy fungi. Fungistats are used by busy growers to keep fungi in check.

Growers must alternate broad- and narrow-spectrum fungicides to effectively fight gray mold (*botrytis*), alternating or mixing combats resistance to the fungicide.

Copper and sulfur sprays, can be used safely in light mixtures. Be careful when using these fungicides; they can severely damage young tender growth.

When using a fungicide, spray the garden or plant at least twice, 5 to 10 days apart, even if you cannot see the fungus during the second or third spraying. The fungus spores can be present on the recently infected foliage, but not visible.

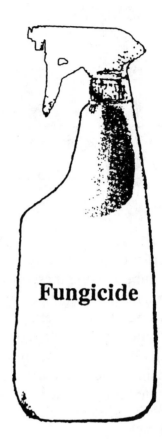

Fungicide

Damping-off

Damping-off is a soil-borne fungus that rots newly sprouted seedlings and occasionally attacks rooting cuttings at the soil line. The stem weakens, then grows dark at the soil line. Finally fluid circulation is cut, killing the seedling or cutting. Damping-off is normally caused by fungus already present in an unsterile rooting medium, overwatering, maintaining soggy soil or excessive humidity.

To prevent all three conditions, use fresh, sterile soil or soilless mix and clean pots. This will guard against harmful fungus in the soil. Careful daily scrutiny of soil will ensure that the proper amount of moisture is available to seeds, seedlings or cuttings. Many gardeners prefer to start seeds and root cuttings in fast-

Damping-off

draining, sterile, coarse sand, fine vermiculite or rockwool cubes. Using these mediums makes it almost impossible to overwater. Do not place a humidity tent over sprouted seedlings. A tent can lead to excessive humidity and damping-off. Cuttings are much less susceptible to damping-off and love a humidity tent to promote rooting. (See Chapter Four to learn more about seed and cutting water requirements).

Damping-off sets the stem at the soil line. It is usually caused by soggy soil.

Control damping-off in its early stages by watering with a fungicide such as a mild bleach solution (two to five drops per gallon). Dust seeds with diatomaceous earth to prevent this disease. Damping-off usually progresses rapidly and kills the young seedling in a matter of days. Overwatering is the biggest cause of damping-off and the key to prevention. An alternative to a humidity tent is to mist cuttings with water several times daily. This practice maintains leaf moisture and high humidity.

Soil-borne Fungus

Soil-borne fungus attacks the root system. It is usually seen on the soil surface first but can also be seen growing around the roots in the soil. Soil-borne fungus normally starts from using an unsterile planting medium and improper drainage. Poor drainage keeps roots too wet, making them susceptible to fungus and rot. Root rot and dry rot (common in bulbs) are soil borne diseases that are usually promoted by poor drainage and heavy, frequent watering, especially in the late afternoon and evening. The roots or bulbs turn brown and slimy. The foliage may discolor, wilt and even die. Aphids, nematodes and other insects act as vectors to these diseases.

Prevent root and bulb rots by supplying adequate drainage and water infrequently during the morning. Crop rotation helps prevent root rot because the disease that attacks one family of plants does not affect another.

Tomatoes and peppers may suffer from blossom-end rot. This disease causes the flower bud or fruit to turn a dark sickly color and drop. Blossom-end rot may occur after good growing conditions followed by drought during flowering and fruit formation. It can also be caused by overhead sprinkling and very humid conditions.

To prevent this type of fungus, a sterile planting medium and good drainage are essential. As explained in Chapter Three, good drainage is easily attained by having adequate drain holes and the proper soil texture.

Control soil-borne fungus by applying a biodegradable soap solution or mild bleach to the soil. Three or four applications are usually necessary. Mix at the rate of one teaspoon per gallon of water. Apply in a water solution. Make sure the soil is not overwatered and there is adequate drainage.

Downy and Powdery Mildew

Downy mildew or false mildew shows up on leaves, creating pale patches. Powdery mildew is a fine pale gray powdery coating on buds, growing shoots and leaves. Both downy and powdery mildews are fungi that attack a wide variety of plants. Both mildews cause foliage to yellow and an overall slowing in growth. Powdery mildew is limited to the surface of foliage. Downy mildew enters the plant's system growing outward and is fatal. Powdery mildew is at its worst when roots dry out and foliage is moist. It can be fatal.

Prevent both mildews by avoiding the conditions that they thrive in cool, damp and humid locations. Mulch the soil and keep foliage dry when watering to keep disease-causing conditions in check. If watering with sprinklers or hoses, be sure to allow time for the foliage to dry before night falls. Fungi like dark, moist places.

The best control is to look for disease-resistant plant varieties. Control downy and powdery mildew by spraying with Bordeaux mixture. If the condition is severe, remove the infected foliage and compost or destroy it. Many times a combination of both methods is necessary for control.

Foliar Fungus

Leaf and stem fungus, including leaf spot, attack foliage. They appear as dark spots just about anywhere on the foliage. These types of fungi are usually caused by using cold water when misting plants fungus-like spots are formed as a result of temperature stress (See "About Spraying," pages 154-157). The spots often develop into a fungus. Excessive humidity (over 60 percent) is the other leading cause of fungus.

Prevention of these types of fungi attacks is easy. Spray with tepid water; have a hygrometer to measure humidity; employ a vent fan to dissipate the excess moisture. Vast quantities of water are applied to actively growing plants. They transpire the water back into the air. If this moist air is allowed to remain in the tiny garden room, it will stifle growth. A vent fan will remove it rapidly. A hygrometer may be purchased for less than $10 at nurseries and garden centers. When humidity climbs above 60 percent, many fungi have the chance to start growing. The HID lamp and ballast emit dry heat. This heat, along with a vent fan, usually provide enough humidity control to prevent fungus in an enclosed garden room. During the winter or cooler months, dry heat from the HID system normally maintains humidity and 72^0 (22^0 C) temperatures while turned on. At night, when the HID is off, the temperature drops, causing moisture condensation, which raises humidity. Check the humidity, both day and night, to see if there is a substantial variation between them. If the humidity registers above 60 percent and fungus is a problem, turn on the vent fan at night. This will vent off all the moist air. If the temperature is a problem, use dry heat to raise the night time temperature 5^0 or 10^0 (3 to 6^0 C) below the daytime temperature. This will keep humidity more constant.

Control foliar fungus by removing all seriously damaged foliage, take all preventive measures, then spray with one of the recommended fungicides three or four times at intervals of three to five days.

Gray Mold Disease (*Botrytis*)

Gray mold, a form of botrytis, is one of the most common garden diseases. The appearance of gray mold signifies the advanced stages of many blights. The first signs of botrytis are motley brown splotches that progress to a furry gray mold. Botrytis prospers under cool, damp conditions.

Gray mold spores are always in the air. They can be present even in the cleanest of rooms. But, as long as the proper environment is maintained, they will not grow and reproduce. Gray mold occurs in two stages: non-germinated spores that live on foliage and germinated spores that grow and penetrate foliage tissue where the spores remain in a latent, inactive form until conditions promote disease outbreak. Gray mold loves to enter plant wounds and attack the weak plants. Spores seldom invade healthy growing tissue.

Plants can be infected with botrytis and have no outward sign at all. It is difficult to tell where the disease came from if there are new plants continually being introduced into the garden. Yellowing foliage defoliation, brown soft areas on dark-colored petals or white circular spots on white to tan flowers such as roses are tale tell signs. Spots will soon develop into the characteristic fuzzy gray mold during the reproductive stage when spores are released into the air.

Prevent gray mold with low humidity (50 percent or less). Remove any standing water, allow ample air circulation and especially ventilation. Humid geographic areas with an outside humidity over 70 percent present the biggest problem to fungus abatement. Bud mold may be triggered when dead foliage rots. When removing yellow leaves between dense buds, pluck the entire leaf so no foliage is left to rot. Avoid over-watering and over-fertilizing with nitrogen.

Control gray mold on the soil or walls by removing it manually. Use Pinesol to wash mold from walls and containers. Do not use harsh Pinesol on plants. You must use a vegetable fungicide on plants. If fungicide does not control botrytis, prune out and destroy affected tissue. This kind of fungus thrives when the garden room is dirty or stagnant water is present.

Blight

The term blight describes many plant diseases. Signs of blight include dark blotches on foliage, slow growth, sudden wilting and plant death. Most blights spread quickly through large areas of plants. Avoid blights by maintaining the proper nutrient balance in the soil and supply good drainage.

Rot

Rots are caused by various fungi and bacteria and can infect the fruit, flowers, roots, stems and trunks of many plants.

Root rot and dry rot (common in bulbs) are soil-borne diseases that are usually promoted by poor drainage and heavy, frequent watering, especially in the late afternoon and evening. The roots or bulbs turn brown and slimy. The foliage may discolor, wilt and even die. Aphids, nematodes and other insects are the vectors for these diseases.

Prevent root and bulb rots by supplying adequate drainage and water infrequently during the morning. Crop rotation helps prevent root rot because the specific disease that attacks one family of plants may not affect another.

Many rots can be avoided by planting resistant plant varieties, cutting out infected areas, keeping soil well drained, pruning to increase air circulation, starting cuttings in a sterilized planting medium and destroying affected plant parts.

Tomatoes may suffer from blossom-end rot. This is not a rot in the same sense as the others described in this section.

Sooty Mold

Sooty mold is a black surface fungus that grows on sticky honeydew excreted by aphids, mealy bugs, some scale and young whiteflies. This unsightly mold is not a big problem, but restricts flower bud and vegetable production.

The dark mold attacks many plants and is most common on citrus trees.

Control sooty mold by first controlling the insects that excrete honeydew. The mold will disappear once the honeydew is eliminated. In severe cases, use a horticultural oil spray to smother aphids and their eggs.

Viruses

Viruses are still a mystery. They act like living organisms in some instances and nonliving chemicals in other cases. We do know that viruses are spread by insect, mite, plant, animal and human vectors. Infected tools often carry viruses from one plant to another.

Typical symptoms of viral infection are sickly growth and low yields of flowers and fruits. In some cases, viral diseases can cause sudden wilt and death. Once a plant gets a virus, there's little you can do.

Mosaic is one of the most common forms of virus. It causes mottled yellow and green spots on blossoms and leaves. Leaf curl is another form of viral disease. Leaf curl causes leaves to curl up and stimulates excessive branching which inhibits the flow of fluids within the plant. Once affected with some viruses, virtually nothing can be done to save the plant. Remove and destroy affected plants. Replace with new, virus-resistant stock.

Tobacco mosaic is a common viral disease. This virus disease gets into the system of tomatoes and other members of the nightshade family (eggplants, peppers, potatoes and tobacco). The disease stops the flow of fluids within the stems. The tomatoes may appear healthy, but the leaves gradually grow smaller and if you break open a stem, it will be black and mushy inside. The only solution to this condition is to pull the plant and burn it to prevent the disease from spreading.

Tobacco mosaic virus is spread by insect vectors and by people. If you use tobacco, wash your hands before handling eggplants, peppers and tomatoes to prevent the possible spread of tobacco mosaic virus.

One of the most common viral diseases is cucumber mosaic virus which is transmitted by the striped cucumber beetle as it chews on the leaves of cucumber, melon, squash and pumpkin plants. The larvae also can transmit the disease as it feeds on plant roots. Control the virus by controlling the beetle.

Organic Fungicides

Fungicides that are listed here have low environmental impact and are recommended if needed in organic gardens. Many other commercially available fungicides are highly toxic and should be used with great care if at all in the home garden.

The less toxic pesticides often act more slowly on the target pests. This is one of the compromises you must be willing to make if you want to garden organically.

As with any garden chemical or compound, you should read instructions carefully and follow the recommendations for mixing, application and conditions under which the substance should be applied. Some of the naturally occurring fungicides, including copper and sulfur, have important restrictions as to the temperature range when applying.

If it is too hot when you apply copper- and sulfur-based sprays, these pesticides may burn the foliage, creating more damage than benefit. It's better to apply these fungicides during a period of cool weather. Copper-and sulfur-based pesticides are used as both insecticides and fungicides.

Bordeaux Mixture & Copper as Fungicides

Bordeaux mix combines copper, sulfur and lime in an effective fungicide. It was first used in French vineyards during the last half of the nineteenth century to discourage theft. Vintners soon discovered that the material, when painted on grape vines, eliminated powdery mildew, an introduced scourge of French vineyards at that time.

Variations of this fungicide use other materials in combination with copper sulfate. Wettable powders combine with water to make a sprayable solution. This fungicide coats foliage with a fine layer that remains active for several weeks.

Copper sulfate alone, also called bluestone,

is available for use as a fungicide. Bluestone is available is several forms: solid, wettable powder, dust or concentrated liquid.

Never apply Bordeaux mixture or any other pesticide including copper sulfate when the temperature is above 85º F. Applying these fungicides during a period of cool weather will be most effective.

Copper compounds are poisonous to fish and aquatic invertebrates. Copper compounds are moderately toxic to humans and irritating to skin and eyes. Therefore, these compounds should be treated with respect. Use mask, goggles and protective clothing to apply.

Diatomaceous Earth & Sphagnum Moss

Diatomaceous earth, a valuable multi-purpose substance is not just a good insecticide and barrier to soft-bodied pests, it also is a good control for damping-off. It's often applied as an alternative to the popular commercial product, Captan.

Milled sphagnum moss is another good deterrent to use to avoid damp-off. Use a sprinkling of milled sphagnum peatmoss on top of seed flats after you have planted the seeds. This should greatly reduce damp-off problems.

Fish Oil

Fish oil is a traditional substance that has long been used as both an insecticide and fungicide. More recently, it's being used as a dormant spray as well as a spreader sticker for fungicides and pesticides. Fish oil makes a hard coating that is difficult to wash off after it's dry. Clean equipment carefully and thoroughly after applying fish oil to prevent clogging. Never use fish oils with copper products.

Sulfur-Based Fungicides

Sulfur is useful as a fungicide, insecticide and miticide. By itself it has low toxicity for humans, but the dust should not be inhaled. Sulfur compounds are highly irritating to skin, eyes and mucous membranes. Use mask, goggles and protective clothing when applying. In considering its use, you should remember that it is toxic to beneficial insects and microorganisms as well as the undesirable ones.

It can be used as a dust or wettable powder to mix with water and a wetting agent to make a spray. It is effective against rust and will prevent mildew, scabs and several other fungal diseases. When heated, sulfur is very strong smelling and, in this form, has been used as a fumigant for centuries.

When sulfur is in a pesticide with copper and oils, the combination is very strong and should be used sparingly only in cool weather to avoid burning seedlings and succulent foliage.

About Spraying

Phytotoxicity is the injury to plants caused by sprays. Symptoms include burned leaves, slow growth or sudden wilt. If you are worried about a spray damaging foliage, spray a small portion of the garden and wait a few days to see if the plants wilt or look sick.

Use chemical sprays with extreme care if at all in enclosed areas; they are more concentrated indoors than outdoors in the open air. Always wear a mask.

A large one- or two-gallon sprayer costs from $15 to $30. Nurseries and garden stores carry these sprayers. Watch for spring and fall sales to get the best deal. The sprayers have an application wand and nozzle attached to a flexible hose, which makes it very easy to spray under leaves. Garden sprayers are also made of heavy duty materials and can take frequent use. Plastic rather than galvanized steel construction does not corrode or rust. Brass nozzle parts with rubber gaskets are easily cleaned with a paper clip or needle.

An electric fogger works well for large jobs. The fogger has an electric blower. The spray is metered out the nozzle under pressure. It produces a fine, penetrating fog of spray. The fogger works best with insecticidal soaps, pyrethrum and fungicides. Electric foggers are used to mist commercial greenhouse plants and are usually available through greenhouse suppliers.

Another favorite is a small, one- or two-quart spray bottle. The best bottle is found at a nursery. It will have a removable nozzle that can easily be taken apart and thoroughly cleaned if clogged. The new pump-up spray bottles are very convenient and deliver an adjustable spray. Homemade organic teas clog most sprayers. A straight pin should be handy to clear the nozzle hole. Buy a heavy-duty spray bottle that can take a lot of use. It takes about 3/4 quart of spray to cover a 10-by-10-foot garden. That is a lot of pumping for a very small plastic spray bottle!

Always wash the bottle and pump thoroughly before and after each use. Using the same bottle for fertilizers and insecticides is okay. However, for best results: Do not mix fertilizers and insecticides or fungicides together when applying. Mixing chemicals will lessen their effectiveness. Chemicals might also be incompatible, one inhibiting the other's effects.

Mix pesticides and fungicides just before using. Fertilizer solutions can be mixed and used for several weeks afterward. When finished spraying, empty the excess spray into the toilet. Spray residues have a tendency to build up in a partially clean bottle. Fresh water is the only liquid to leave in the spray bottle overnight.

Always spray early in the day. The moist spray needs a chance to be absorbed and dry out. If sprayed just a few hours before nightfall, moisture left overnight on foliage could cause fungus or water spots.

Always use tepid or room-temperature water. Water too hot or cold shocks plants and will cause water spots on leaves. Plants are able to absorb and process tepid water more rapidly.

Before spraying fungicides and pesticides, make sure the plants are well watered. With more water in the system, a plant suffers less shock from the spray. When foliar feeding the garden with a soluble fertilizer, just the opposite is true. Plants will absorb the soluble nutrients more rapidly when there is less moisture in the plant and soil. This is not a reason to let plants dry out!

When mixing, read the entire label and follow directions to the letter. Mix wettable powders and soluble crystals in a little hot water to make sure they get dissolved before adding the balance of the tepid water.

Novice gardeners who have never sprayed before may want to talk about the process over with their nurseryperson before starting.

Have an accurate measuring cup and spoon that are used only for the indoor garden. Keep them clean. If the spray is too heavy (easy to do when mixing small amounts) it will not kill any more insects any more dead; it will burn plants. Extreme precision should be exercised when mixing small quantities. A few drops could make the spray too potent and burn tender plants.

Spraying could promote mold, once flower buds form and growth becomes dense. The moisture could get trapped in dense foliage or flower. If this water is allowed to remain in the flower top a day or longer, the mold will find a new home.

Always rinse plants with tepid water one or two days after spraying. The water should actually drip from the leaves to have a cleansing effect. Misting plants heavily washes away all the stomata-clogging film and residue left from sprays. Fertilizer left on leaves is dissolved and absorbed by the rinse. Make sure both sides of the leaves are thoroughly rinsed.

Spray plants that have fragile foliage with wettable powders rather than liquid concentrates. Inert diluents used in many liquid concentrate wilts frail plants. A harmless visible white residue results from the powder spray,

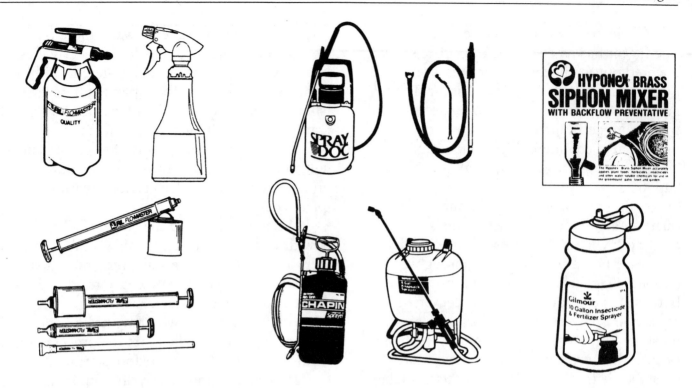

The small sprayers of the left are made for small jobs when the spray need to be very direct. These sprayers are suitable for most needs. The larger sprayers will hold from 1 1/2 to 3 gallons and are also very accutate. The siphon mixer and the hose-end sprayers are to spread fertilizers.

but not from the liquid concentrates. A wetting or spreader-sticker is often required with wettable powders and continuous agitation of the solution is necessary. This heavy, powdery film could require two or three rinses to wash it off foliage.

Always rinse vegetables several times with a fresh-water spray a week before harvesting.

Sprays are beneficial if not overdone. Every time a plant is sprayed with a fungicide or insecticide, the stomata are clogged and growth slows. Rinsing off spray helps, but if sprays are used over and over, the garden will be slow-growing.

Health conscious gardeners use insecticides and fungicides that are contact sprays that may be used on edible fruits and vegetables. Read the entire label to find the toxic or active life of the spray. Wait a few more days than the label recommends and thoroughly wash all vegetables before eating if you plan to use chemicals. Even ornamentals should be sprayed sparingly in the indoor environment.

Toxic sprays tend to linger much longer indoors. The toxic life or chemicals is normally twice as long indoors because sunlight and weathering breaks down many chemicals.

Organic or natural based sprays are also toxic and should be used sparingly. However, sprays such as pyrethrum and insecticidal soaps are not harmful to humans and animals. Most indoor gardeners prefer to use the natural sprays that are safe.

Use a respirator or face mask when spraying, especially if using an aerosol/fogger. Spray residues remain very concentrated in the enclosed garden room. This makes it easy for even the safest spray to be irritating if inhaled for long.

CAUTION! Raise HID lamp out of the way, so mist from spray will not touch the bulb. Temperature stress, resulting from the relatively cold water hitting the hot bulb, may cause it to implode. This could not only startle you, but could burn eyes and skin. If the bulb breaks, turn off the system immediately!

Applying Sprays and Powders

* Treat all pesticides with caution and respect. Remember they are poisons.

* Keep pesticides out of the reach of children.

* Always take protective measures when spraying any kind of pesticide. Wear a long-sleeved shirt, pants, hat, gloves, goggles and a respirator. Shower thoroughly after applying any toxic sprays. Wash your "spraying clothing" separately from your regular clothes.

* Only apply spray or dust to the target plant or ground around the plant that is infested with insect pests. Fungicides must be applied to the entire plant and adjacent plants.

* Spot spray whenever possible. Many pesticides kill beneficial insects.

* More expensive pressure sprayers costing over $10 are available that hold up to two quarts of spray.

* Use a small hand sprayer. Some of the best sprayers are inexpensive pump-and-squirt models that hold only one quart of solution.

* Buy a sprayer that has a nozzle that is easy to take apart and clean. Rebuilding kits are available for more expensive sprayers.

* Follow directions on the label regarding dilutions and rates of application as well as frequency. Do not concentrate or arbitrarily mix different materials.

* Dusters are very convenient. They are great to apply diatomaceous earth, lime, sulfur, or any other powder.

* Keep organic controls in their own containers that are well labeled.

* Always pour out excess spray and dispose of safely.

* Spray on calm, windless days in the morning or evening. Do not spray when the sun is shining on foliage.

* Do not spray open flowers, it could kill bees.

* Spray plants that have been watered. Spraying dry plants may stress them severely.

* If you must use aerosols, remember not to apply them too closely. The spray is close to freezing when it exits the nozzle. By the time the spray is a foot away from the nozzle, it has warmed to ambient temperature.

SECTION II
STAGES of GROWTH

The Seed and Seedling
Vegetative Growth
Transplanting
Bending and Pruning
Flowering
Container & Patio Gardens
Extending Seasons
Plant Selection Guide

Stages of Growth

Typically, an annual plant goes through three distinct stages of growth. The seedling stage lasts about a month. During this stage, the seed germinates or sprouts, establishes a root system, grows a stem and a few leaves. During vegetative growth, the plant produces much bushy green growth as well as a supporting root system. This stage may last from two months to over a year. The last stage of the life cycle comes when flowers form. If the flowers are pollinated, seeds will form.

Indoors when we create the entire climate: temperature, air humidity and flow, soil or growing medium conditions, nutrient availability and artificial light, we can control the entire life cycle of any plant. For example, tomatoes flower and set fruit when the temperature is between 55 and 85 degrees. Lettuce grows best when the temperature is below 80 degrees. Tropical plants such as peppers thrive in high humidity conditions. Poinsettias, Christmas cactus and chrysanthemums bloom when given 12 hours of light and 12 hours of darkness.

Chapter Eight
The Seed and Seedling

The genes within a seed dictate the plant's size, disease and pest resistance, root, stem, leaf and flower production, yield and many other variable growth traits. The genetic make-up of a seed is the single most important factor dictating how well the plant will grow under HID lamps.

A simple picture of a seed reveals an embryo, containing the genes and a supply of food, wrapped in a protective outer coating. Fresh, dry, mature seeds sprout quickly, while older seeds (one year or more) may take longer to sprout, if they sprout at all.

Seeds

Careful seed selection can make the difference between a successful garden and complete failure. Certain seed varieties are better adapted to growing under certain conditions than others. For example, the early-maturing, cold-tolerant Oregon Spring tomato grows in cool weather, setting flowers and fruit well before the larger beefsteak varieties. If you live in a cool region, with a short growing season, selecting Oregon Spring rather than a late-maturing beefsteak will make a fruitful harvest

almost certain. If you love broccoli but live in a warm climate, planting heat-tolerant 'Premium Crop' rather than 'Green Valiant' will prolong the harvest.

Many vegetable seed varieties available to-day are developed for modern agriculture. They are bred for qualities such as long shelf life, uniformity, disease resistance and the ability to withstand mechanical harvesting with little damage; taste is usually the last quality considered. Eating carefully selected varieties with superior taste, rather than tough vegetables that were developed for mechanized handling is one of gardenings rewards.

Open-pollinated seeds, also referred to as heirloom seed varieties, are the products of parents, selected at random by nature. You can produce these seeds yourself and save them to sow the following year; they will produce plants very similar to their parents. Some open-pollinated seeds are very popular today, such as the Kentucky Wonder pole bean. But since the advent of hybrids, many varieties have become difficult to find; some extinct. Several groups have been organized to preserve the heirloom varieties. *The Seed Savers Exchange, RR 3, Box 239, Decorah, IA 52101* is the largest

The introduction of hybrid or F_1 hybrid

A few mail order seed catalogs that are available.

seed has revolutionized modern agriculture and gardening. Hybrid seed is produced by crossing true breeding plants with desirable characteristics. The resulting seed is known as a F_1 hybrid. The F_1 hybrid has *hybrid vigor*, the ability to grow stronger and faster than the parents. The greater the vigor, the more obstacles, such as pests and diseases, it can overcome to produce a better plant. Hybrids are uniform in shape and size and harvesting time, but not identical. Even though the seeds are often more expensive, they are an excellent value. Carefully selecting hybrid seed for such qualities as taste, disease and pest resistance, cold and heat tolerance and conditions that prevail in your climate will help make your garden a success.

Today, modern seed production has largely replaced the older method of open field pollination, but such has disadvantages. The growing of one variety on a very large scale can be

dangerous, as should it be attacked by a pest or disease it can be wiped out. Diversity, that is growing more than one variety has definite advantages.

When selecting seed, you may notice some of them carry the label "All America Selection" or "AAS Winner." Seed varieties that were chosen as All America Selection winners have demonstrated superior growth and flavor in a wide variety of climates across America. Buying AAS varieties is recommended.

Some seed is treated with a fungicide to prevent such diseases as damping-off, a disease that causes seedlings to rot at the soil line. Typically, the fungicide is colored and some seed companies state in their catalog or on the seed packet that it is treated. Some seed is only available with a coating of fungicide. At least one major seed producer is using naturally occurring diatomaceous earth to protect seed.

The seed contains all the genetic characteristics of a plant. A seed is the result of sexual propagation, having genes from both male and female parents. Many plants contain both the male and female genes in the same flower. Flowers that contain both the male and female flower parts are called hermaphrodites. Male and female flower parts of other plants are found on distinct male and female plants. Plants that are male or female are called dioceous.

Plant seeds need only water, heat and air to germinate. They sprout without light in a wide range of temperatures. Most seeds, properly watered, will normally germinate in 2 to 10 days, in temperatures from 70 to 90° F (21 to 32° C). The warmer it is, the faster germination takes place. Germination temperatures above 90° F (32° C) are not advised. When the seed germinates, the outside protective shell splits and a tiny white sprout pops out. This sprout is the tap root. The seed leaves emerge from the shell as they push upward in search of light.

Starting seedlings with fluorescent lights.

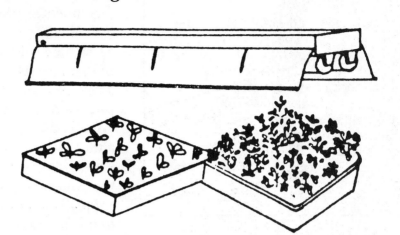

After sowing seed, place the container in a sunny, south-facing window. If there is not enough light the seedlings can become lanky and spindly. Set them under a fluorescent gro-light so they have the light needed for good balanced growth if this happens. (See Fluorescent Lamps, page 37).

A cold frame is a perfect place to transfer 1-2-week-old plants in cold weather and less hardy seedlings until the weather warms. Cold frames generally stay 10° to 15° F. warmer than the daytime temperature and 5 to 10 degrees warmer at night.

Fertilize the little seedlings with fish emulsion or any soluble, complete fertilizer. Be sparing with the fertilizer, applying it quarter strength because the little plants have a small root system.

There are many ways to germinate seeds. In a warm location (70 to 90° F, 21 to 32° C) place large seeds such as pumpkin, cucumber, beans, etc. in a moist paper towel or cheesecloth, making sure they are in darkness. Keep the cloth moist, letting excess water drain away freely. The cloth will retain enough moisture to germinate the seed in a few days.

The seed contains an adequate food supply for germination, but watering with a mild mix of liquid fertilizer will hasten growth. In a humid climate, water with a mild bleach or fungicide solution (two to five drops per gallon) to prevent fungus. Once the seeds have sprouted and the white sprout is visible, plant them. Take care not to expose the tender rootlet to prolonged, intense light or wind. Plant the germinated seed in a quarter-inch to half-inch of fine planting medium with the white sprout tip (the root) pointing down.

Another popular germination and planting method is to sow the seed in a shallow planter, one- to five-gallon pot, peat pellet or rockwool cube. The planting medium is then maintained evenly moist. If the seedling is to be transplanted from the shallow planter, use a spoon to contain the frail root ball. Peat pellets or rockwool cubes may be transplanted in 2 to 3 weeks or when the roots show through the sides. Do not forget to fertilize them if they begin to yellow.

One gardener sows the seeds in a nursery flat and places it on top of the warm refrigerator. n the drawer of her heated waterbed. As soon as the seeds sprout, they are moved into the garden room.

Remember, seeds have no roots and need little water, just enough to keep the seed coat moist to enable the roots and shoots to break out of the sheath or seed coat. Compacted soil with a crusty surface is almost impossible for most tender shoots to penetrate. Placing a piece of newspaper, burlap, a thin layer of peat moss or fine mulch over the seed bed helps retain moisture evenly and keeps soil from forming a crust. Remove the paper or burlap as soon as the seed germinates.

A moisture tent can be constructed over the seedling container. Just put plastic bag over the seeded soil. This will maintain high humidity and temperature. Usually the seeds need only one initial watering when this method is used. Remove the bag as soon as the first sprout appears; leaving it on will lead to damping-off or other fungus problems.

It is not necessary, but the planted seeds may be placed under the HID lamp while germinating. The lamp will add dry heat and the soil will require more watering. Placing heat tape under or in soil will expedite germination without drying the soil out as fast.

Hardening-off:

Seedlings grown indoors or at a nursery have not always been exposed to the harsh elements outdoors. They must be hardened-off, that is, gradually introduced to their new outdoor environment. To harden-off seedlings that you have raised in a cold-frame, greenhouse or window sill, place them outdoors in a shady or protective location. Expose them to the sunshine for a couple of hours. Increase the amount of sunshine gradually over the course of a few days and then plant.

Growing Seedlings

Raising your own seedlings is no more difficult than germinating seed outdoors in the garden, but provides the option of picking the varieties that perform the best in your climate. If grown properly, they produce transplants that will perform well for you.

Start seed indoors in shallow nursery flats, egg cartons, peat pellets, cell blocks or any small clean containers. Use bagged potting soil or fine sifted organic soil from your garden. Seedlings have a small, root system and must be watered regularly, especially in a heated environment.

The biggest problem most people have with germinating seeds is overwatering. The soil must be uniformly moist. A shallow flat or planter with a heat pad underneath may require daily watering, while a deep, one-gallon pot will need watering every 3 to 7 days. When the surface is dry a quarter-inch deep it is time to water. Remember there are few roots to absorb the water early in life and they are very delicate.

It is a good idea to plant more seeds than are expected to mature for harvest. This is the best way to ensure success and a full garden room. When plants are small, they take up very little room. The HID lamp uses the same amount of electricity to grow 10 small plants as it does to grow 100. As the plants mature, the small and sick may easily be weeded out. Strong, healthy plants are transplanted to larger containers or given to friends.

When the seed sprouts, the first leaves that appear are called cotyledon or seed leaves. The seed leaves spread out as the stem elongates. In a few days, the first true leaves will appear. The plant is now in the seedling stage, which will last about three more weeks. During this time, a root system grows rapidly and green growth is slow. Water is critical. The new root system is very small and requires a small but constant supply of water. Too much water will drown the roots and may cause root rot or damping-off. Lack of water will cause the infant root system to dry up. As the seedlings mature, some will grow faster, be stronger and appear generally more healthy. Others will sprout slowly, be weak and leggy. If many seeds were planted, the sick and weak can be thinned out and the strong kept. This thinning process should take place around the third to fifth week of growth. Seedlings may also be transplanted easily without any damage.

Seedlings

Transplanted seedlings get a head start on directly-seeded crops and they mature earlier. A healthy seedling is predictable and virtually guarantees uniformity in plantings.

Tomato, cucumber, pepper and squash seedlings are some of the most commonly purchased. Also, you can purchase seedling starts of several different varieties. The reason being that most gardeners do not need many plants of these and it is economical.

Buying Seedlings

Purchasing vegetable starts at a tip top retail nursery takes little skill.

Purchasing from some outlets can be somewhat risky if the staff are not familiar with the care of seedlings.

Buy seedlings that are kept in good growing conditions. Do not buy seedlings that are kept in a sunny location. The small amount of soil around the roots in small plastic pots/packs can heat up, "cooking" the roots. The temperature is more constant in a shade house, which also protects the tender plants from other climate extremes. The root system is the most important part of the seedling. Select plants that good color and are of uniform size.

The best seedlings to transplant have a root system that holds the soil together and have just begun to reach the outside of the soil in the small container.

If only rootbound plants are available, soak the soil with water before planting. Remove any matted roots, then gently separate the remaining roots just before planting so that they will penetrate the soil better and not be so inclined to "bunch-up."

You may prefer to buy seedlings with root systems that are not fully developed and hold them at home in a partially shady location a week or two before transplanting. This way you can watch their progress as they gradually get used to their new environment.

Pull plants apart gently when transplanting from flats. Take care not to squeeze roots and crush tender root hairs.

Chapter Nine
Vegetative Growth

After anyseedling is established, it enters the vegetative growth stage. When chlorophyll production is in full swing, the plant will produce as much vegetative or green, leafy growth as light carbon dioxide, nutrients and water will permit. Properly maintained, many flowers and vegetables will grow from half an inch to two inches a day. If the plant is stunted now, it could take weeks to resume normal growth. A strong, unrestricted root system is essential to supply much-needed water and nutrients.

Rule of Thumb: Unrestricted vegetative growth is the key to a healthy garden andharvest.

During vegetative growth, the plant's nutrient and water intake changes. Transpiration is carried on at a more rapid rate, requiring more water. High levels of nitrogen are needed; phosphorus and potassium are used at much faster rates. The larger a plant grows, the more water it uses and the faster the soil dries out. A larger root system is able to take in more water and nutrients. Strong lateral branches are produced. They will soon be filled with flower buds. The more vegetative growth, the more flowers and fruit produced.

Eighteen hours of light is conducive to vegetative growth after that a point of diminishing returns is reached and the light loses effectiveness. Many annual plants will remain in the vegetative growth stage more than a year as long as the 18-hour photoperiod is maintained.

Starting Cuttings

Taking cuttings or cuttings is one of the most efficient and productive means of plant propagation known today. Almost all flowers and vegetables can be reproduced or propagated sexually or asexually. Seeds are the product of sexual propagation, cuttings are the result of asexual or vegetative propagation. Taking cuttings is simply cutting some growing branch tips and rooting them. Many people have taken cuttings from a house plant such as a philodendron, ivy or coleus and rooted them in water or sand. The rooted cutting is then placed in rich potting soil.

Identical cuttings will vary if they are grown in different climates. If the climate is poor for growth, the plant will develop poorly and be stunted. If the garden room is well cared for and has a perfect climate, strong,

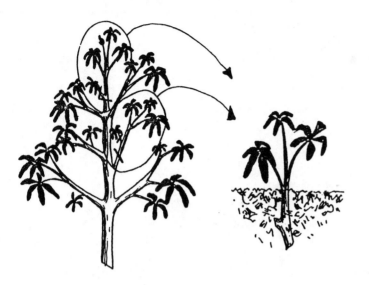

A single branch of a parent plant can be cut into several pieces. Each piece of the branch can be rooted and will turn into a plant just like the parent.

healthy flowers and vegetables are prodiced.

Vegetative propagation yields an exact genetic replica of the parent plant. These cuttings will all have the characteristics of the favorite parent. Fast, squat, bushy growth is at the same rate and lends itself to easy maintenance.

Light intensity is much greater, since the cuttings do not have a chance to get too tall. Remember, the closer the light is to the entire plant and garden, the faster they grow. Lower branches, heavily shaded by upper branches and leaves, will grow slowly and spindly.

Because a cutting of any age is larger than a plant grown from seed, the root system is small and compact, making cuttings well suited for containers. By the time the root system is inhibited by the container, it is time for harvest. A five- or six-month old plant, grown from seed, is easily pot-bound and stunted. This compounds any insect or nutrient disorder.

The stronger a plant and the faster it grows, the less chance it has of being affected by dis-

eases or insects. A spider mite infestation, developed in the fifth or sixth month of a sexually propagated (seed) crop, may have to suffer through many applications until the infestation is arrested. The garden room cannot be totally cleaned and fumigated until the plants have completed flowering or producing vegetables and been harvested.

All plants may be removed for a couple of days in order to fumigate the room or paint it with antiseptic whitewash. The plants are sick to begin with and moving injures them. When returned to the garden room, they will take a long time to resume normal growth. On the other hand, cuttings are not in the garden room as long the infestations have less time to launch an all-out attack or build an immunity to sprays.

Healthy cuttings taken from a proven, disease-resistant parent is the route to a bountiful harvest. An insect infestation that gets out of hand among small cuttings is easily stopped. The small cuttings are removed with little or no damage the garden room is then fumigated.

Experiments are more easily controlled with cuttings. Since cuttings are all the same, different stimuli (fertilizer, light, bending, etc.) introduced on selected groups of cuttings and a true comparative analysis may be made.

Cuttings have some negative points. The parent plant will produce cuttings just like itself. If the parent is not disease-resistant or produces poorly, cuttings also share these weaknesses. An insect or fungus infestation, left unchecked, could wipe out an entire cutting crop.

Taking cuttings from three or four different parents will help ensure a healthy garden. Clean garden rooms rarely have insect or disease problems. Infestations are also promoted by continued use of an ineffective spray used to kill insects or fungi.

Taking cuttings is simple and easy. A consistent 100 percent survival rate may be achieved by following the simple procedures outlined in this book. The parent plant can be grown from seed or propagated by cutting. It should be at least two months old and possess all the characteristics you find desirable.

Cuttings can be taken from just about any plant, regardless of age or growth stage. Cuttings taken in the vegetative stage root quickly and grow fast. Cuttings taken from flowering plants may root a little slower.

Taking cuttings is the most traumatic experience plants experience. Cuttings go through an incredible change when growing branch tips are cut from the parent plant. Their entire chemistry changes. The stem that once grew green leaves must now grow roots in order to survive. Sprays should be avoided now, as they compound cutting stress.

Research has found that plants tend to root much better when the stems have a high carbohydrate and low nitrogen concentration. Leaching the soil with copious quantities of water washes out nutrients including nitrogen. Heavy leaching could keep soil too soggy. An alternative to leaching the soil would be to leach the leaves themselves by reverse foliar-feeding. To reverse foliar feed, fill the sprayer with clean, tepid water and mist plants heavily every morning for a week. This washes the soluble nitrogen out of foliage rapidly. The parent plant's growth slows as the nitrogen is used, giving carbohydrates a chance to accumulate. Carbohydrate content is usually highest in lower, older mature branches. A rigid branch that will fold over easily when bent, rather than bend, is a good sign of high carbohydrate content. Older branches low on the plant give the best results. While rooting, cuttings require a minimum of nitrogen and increased levels of phosphorus to promote root growth.

There are several products available that stimulate root growth. They are available in a liquid or powder form. Professionals prefer the liquid type (root-inducing hormones) for penetration and consistency. The powder types are avoided because they adhere inconsistently to the stem and yield a lower survival rate.

In order for a cutting to grow roots from the stem, it must change from producing stem cells, to producing undifferentiated cells and finally producing root cells. The rooting hormone promotes the rooting process by stimulating undifferentiated growth. Substances that are known to stimulate this type of growth are: napthalenaecetic acid (NAA), indolebutyric acid (IBA) and 2,4-dichlorophenoxyacetic acid (2,3 DPA). The following products have been used successfully as rooting hormones. Many of these commercial rooting hormones have one or all of the above ingredients and a fungicide to help prevent damping-off.

Dip-N-Grow
Hormex
Rootone - F

Note: Some of these products are not recommended for use with edible plants. Read the label carefully before deciding to use a product.

Cuttings root faster if the soil is a few degrees warmer than normal. The soil heat promotes faster chemical activity, spurring growth. For best results, the rooting cuttings' soil should be kept at 70 to 80° F (21 to 27° C). The cuttings will transpire less if the air is about 5° (3° C) cooler than the soil. Misting cuttings with water is a good way to cool foliage and lower transpiration. This helps the cuttings retain moisture that the roots do not yet supply.

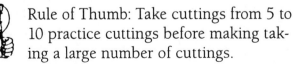 Rule of Thumb: Take cuttings from 5 to 10 practice cuttings before making taking a large number of cuttings.

Taking Cuttings: Step-by-Step

A cutting from a geranium is being taken.

Next, the cutting is dipped into diluted Hormex, a liquid root hormone and placed in a small rockwool cubes. Roots emerge in about two weeks.

Step One: Choose a parent at least two months old and 24 inches tall. Leach the soil daily with at least 2-gallons of water per 1 gallon of soil (make sure drainage is good) or wash down leaves with a misting of warm water (reverse) foliar feeding every morning. Start seven days before taking cuttings and leach every morning to wash out nitrogen.

Step Two: Choose some of the older lower branch tips for cuttings. With a sharp, clean blade, make a 45-degree cut across firm, healthy branches about an eighth- to a quarter-inch in diameter and two to eight inches in length. It is very important to keep from smashing the end of the stem when making the cut. Trim off two or three sets of leaves and buds so the stem can fit in soil. There should be at least two sets of leaves above the soil line and one or two sets of trimmed nodes below ground. When cutting, make the slice halfway between the sets of nodes. Getting too close to nodes could cause one of the remaining nodes to have mutated

growth. Place the cut end in a glass of fresh, tepid water. This is will keep an air bubble from lodging in the tiny hole in the center of the stem, blocking the transpiration stream. If this hole is blocked, the new cutting will die within 24 hours. Leave the cuttings in the water overnight in subdued or no light.

Step Three: If possible, use peat pots or rock-wool cubes, because they make maintenance easier and facilitate transplanting. Fill small containers or nursery flats with coarse, washed sand, fine vermiculite, soilless mix or, if nothing else is available, potting soil. Line the containers up and saturate them with tepid water. Use a pencil or chopstick to make a hole in the rooting medium a little larger than the stem. The hole should stop at least half an inch from the bottom of the container to allow for root growth.

Step Four: Use a root hormone. Professional nurserypeople prefer a liquid root hormone. Mix it just before using. There will be dilutions for hardwood and softwood cuttings in the mixing instructions. Use the formula for the softwood cuttings. Swirl each cutting in the hormone solution for 10 to 20 seconds. Place the cutting in the hole. Pack rooting medium gently around the stem. Powder root hormones require no mixing. Just roll the moistened stem in the powder. When planting, take special care to keep a solid layer of hormone powder around the stem while gently packing soil into place.

Step Five: Lightly water with a mild solution of B^1, until the surface is evenly moist. Water as needed.

Step Six: Cuttings root best with 18 hours of fluorescent light (some gardeners swear by 24 hours). If no fluorescent lamp is available, place the cuttings three to four feet under the halide and shade them with a cloth or screen. The shade will cut light intensity and prevent shock.

Step Seven: Place a tent over rooting cuttings to keep humidity near 80 percent. Construct the tent out of plastic bags, plastic film or glass. Remember to leave a breeze-way in the container so the little cuttings can breathe. An alternative to the humidity tent is to mist the rooting cuttings with tepid water several times daily. Either method helps retain moisture, since there are no roots to supply the leaves with water.

Step Eight: The humidity tent will maintain the temperature at about 70 to 80° F (21 to 27° C). However, some plants may fall victim to damping-off if there is not an ample supply of fresh, circulating air. If more heat is needed, just moving the flat up off the floor will raise the temperature a few degrees. If the container does not raise it enough, place a heat pad, heat cable or incandescent light bulb below rooting cuttings.

The photograph above shows small nodes emerging from the stem of a miniature rose that has been rooting for only ten days. Below, is a bed of carnation cuttings rooting under fluorescents.

Step Nine: Some cuttings may wilt for a few days or the leaves may rot if touch moist soil. Remove rotten leaves. Cuttings should look normal by the end of a week. If cuttings are badly wilted at the end of a week, they probably won't live or are so stunted they will never catch up to the others.

Step Ten: In one to four weeks, the cuttings should be rooted. The tips of leaves will turn yellow and roots start growing out drain holes and cuttings will start upward vertical growth. To check for root growth in flats or pots, carefully remove a cutting to see if it has good root development. Roots will show through the bottom and sides of peat pots and root cubes.

Transplanting

To transplant a four-inch rockwool cube, simply place it on top of the larger slab.

When a plant has outgrown its container, it must be transplanted into a larger pot to ensure that the roots have room for continued rapid outward growth. Inhibiting the root system will stunt plants. Some of the signs are slow, sickly growth and leggyness. Branches develop with more distance between them on the main stem. It will take a long time for the plant to resume normal growth.

Transplant into the same type of soil, so there is no new soil for the roots to get used to. For cuttings rooted in vermiculite or sand, just shake away as much of the medium as possible (without damaging roots) before setting the root ball into the new soil. Novice and lazy gardeners may want to start seeds or cuttings in root cubes or peat pots. They are very easy to transplant. Just set the cube or peat pot in the soil and backfill with soil.

Next to taking cuttings, transplanting is the most traumatic experience a plant can live through. Transplanting requires special attention and manual dexterity. Tiny root hairs are very delicate and may easily be destroyed by light, air or clumsy hands. Roots grow in darkness, where their environment is rigid and secure. When roots are taken out of contact with the soil, they soon dry up and die.

Transplanting should disturb the root system as little as possible. Vitamin B^1 is recommended to help ease transplant shock. Plants need time to get settled-in and re-establish a solid flow of fluids from the roots through the plant. They will require low levels of nitrogen and potassium, but use large quantities of phosphorus. When Up-Start is applied properly and roots are disturbed little, there will be no signs of transplant shock or wilt.

After transplanting give new transplants filtered or less intense light for a couple of days. If there is a fluorescent lamp handy, place transplants under it for a couple of days before moving them under the HID.

Transplant late in the day so transplants will have all night to recover. The secrets to successful transplanting are manual dexterity, vitamin B^1 and lots of water. Water helps the soil pack around roots and keeps them from drying out. Roots need to be in constant contact with the soil so they can supply water and food to the plant. Transplants will be a little shocked no matter what is done. Think about the plant. It has changed soil and will need to settle in. During this time of settling in, photosynthesis and chlorophyll production are at a low, as is water and nutrient absorption through the roots. It needs subdued light to keep foliage growing at the same rate as roots are able to supply water and nutrients.

Plants should be as healthy as possible before suffering the trauma of transplanting. None-the-less, transplanting a sick, root-bound plant to a large container has cured more than one ailing plant.

Transplanting Step-by-Step

In this example, we will transplant a one-month-old cutting started in a four-inch container of vermiculite into a six gallon pot.

Step One: Water the four-inch cutting with half strength vitamin B[1], one or two days before transplanting.

Step Two: Fill the six-gallon container with rich potting soil or soilless mix to within two inches of the top.

Step Three: Water soil until saturated.

Step Four: Gently roll the four-inch pot between hands to break sand away from the sides of pot. Place your hand over top of container with stem between fingers turn it upside down and let root ball slip out of pot into your hand. Take special care at this point to keep the root ball in one integral piece.

Step Five: Carefully place root ball in a prepared hole in the six-gallon container. Make sure all roots are growing down.

Step Six: Backfill around the root ball. Gently, but firmly pack soil around the root ball.

Step Seven: Water with a dilute vitamin B[1] solution, making sure soil is completely saturated, but not soggy.

Step Eight: Place new transplants on the perimeter of the garden or under a screen, so light remains subdued for a couple of days. The transplants should be able to take full light within a day or two.

Step Nine: The new, rich potting soil will supply enough nutrients for about a month. After that, supplemental fertilization will

This pothos will have much more room to grow in its new container.

probably be necessary. Soilless mixes require balanced N-P-K fertilization a week or less after transplanting.

Step Ten: See the chart on "Minimum Container Size" in Chapter Three, page 77.

Bending and Pruning

Bending and pruning alter the basic growth pattern of a plant. The alteration affects physical shape, liquid flow and growth hormones. Pruning strongly affects the plant, while bending has more subdued affects.

When a branch is pruned off, two branches will grow from the nodes just below the cut. This does not mean the plant will grow twice as much. A plant can grow only so fast. A quick branch amputation is not going to make it grow faster or add any more foliage. In fact, an indoor garden is already being pushed to the limit and trimming or cutting it will slow growth for a few days. Think about pruning

Pinching back the growing tip of this coleus will force growth on lower branches and make it more bushy.

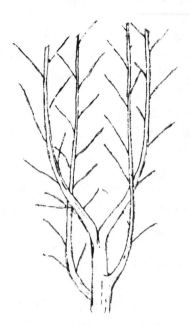

This tomato has been pruned to four main branches.

before hacking away! Any time a plant is pruned, valuable foliage is being removed.

Pruning will make a plant grow bushier. The lower branches will develop more rapidly when the terminal bud is removed. Removing the terminal bud alters the concentration of growth-inhibiting hormones. These hormones (auxins) prevent the lateral buds from growing very fast. The further a branch is from hormones at the plant tip, the less effect the auxins have.

Always use clean instruments when pruning. A single-edged razor blade, a sharp pair of pruners or a pair of scissors, all work well. Do not use indoor pruners on anything but the indoor garden. If using pruners outdoors, they will have everything from aphids to dog dung on them. If using outdoor clippers, dip the blades into rubbing alcohol to sterilize them before use.

Pinching back branches will diffuse floral hormones, making the plant bushier. Pruning the plant when it is one or two months old and again a month later will make it bushier.

Continual pruning will keep it in a solid hedge-like shape. Some gardeners prune plants into ornamental shapes.

Another pruning technique removes all but four main branches. This method is commonly used with tomatoes. The central growing tip is removed and the four branches are left intact. This concentrates the floral/fruit hormones in the four main branches.

Note: Only complete branches are pruned leaves are left alone!

The idea behind this principle is that if there are fewer branches, they will be stronger, bearing more and heavier fruit. The seedling or cutting is generally 1- to 3-months old when the four main branches are selected. The branches selected are usually the strongest.

Pruning all the branches is not advised. It shocks the plant too much. Pruning the tall branches that get in the way and rob light from the rest of the garden works well. However, if taking cuttings from a parent, you may want to sacrifice its well-being for more cuttings. Remember, if it is pruned down to stubby branches, it could take it a month to resume normal growth.

Pruning too much over a period of time may alter the hormonal balance so much that the plant produces spindly growth. If a plant must be pruned heavily for cuttings, it is usually best to prune it right down to a few leafy growing tips on the trunk or main stem and let it grow back from there.

All leaves are to be left alone! Somehow a rumor started about how removing large shade leaves would supply more light to smaller growing tips, making them grow faster. This is bad gardening! A plant needs all the leaves it can get to produce the maximum amount of chlorophyll. Removing leaves slows chlorophyll production and stunts growth. Removing the leaves stresses the plant. Stress inhibits growth especially during vegetative growth. Only leaves that are clearly dead, insect- or fungus-infected, should be removed. Leaf removal is not pruning, it is hacking up a normally healthy plant.

Pruning or trimming off lower branches that have spindly, sickly growth, is acceptable. When pruning, cut off the entire branch. Pruning the lower branches has a minimal effect on floral hormone concentration.

Chapter Ten
Flowering

In order for a plant to complete its annual life-cycle successfully, it must first flower. Dioecious plants are either male (pollen producing) or female (ovule producing). Hermaphrodite plants are bisexual, with both male and female flowers on the same plant.

One of the many tiny grains of pollen from the male (staminate) flower pod lands on a pistil of the female (pistilate) flower. Each calyx harbors an ovule and a set of pistils. Actual fertilization takes place when the grain of male pollen slides down the pistil and unites with the female ovule, deep within the calyx. Once fertilization takes place, pistils turn brown and a seed will form within the calyx or seed bract. Seeds are the result of this sexual propagation and contain genetic characteristics of both parents.

Long-day plants

In nature, annual plants' life cycle comes to an end in the fall, after the long, hot, days of summer. The long nights and short days of autumn signal short-day plants to start the flowering stage. Growth patterns and chemistry change: Stems elongate, flower formation is rapid at first, then slows. All this causes new nutrient needs. Attention is now focused on flower production, rather than on vegetative growth. Production of chlorophyll, requiring much nitrogen, slows. Phosphorus uptake increases to promote floral formation. Light needs change as well. During autumn, in most climates, the sun takes on a slightly reddish appearance, emitting a light that is a more red than white. Growth and floral hormones are stimulated by this red or harvest sun.

The harvest sun phenomenon is not fully understood. However, experiments have proved that by increasing the amount of red light during flowering, floral hormones are stimulated and flower yield increases substantially.

Indoors, flowering may be induced in short-day plants just as it is in nature, by shortening the photoperiod from 18 to 12 hours. Once the days are changed to 12 hours, flowers should be clearly visible within one to three weeks. In fact, some gardeners have two garden rooms: a vegetative garden room with one metal halide that supplies 18 hours of light. The other room for growing short-day plants that has both a halide and HP sodium that is on for 12 hours a day.

Using this combination of rooms and

Chrysanthemums are short-day plants that bloom under 12 hours of light and 12 hours of total darkness.

lamps, the electricity bill remains relatively low and the horticulturist has the luxury of having both summer and fall every day of the year!

The additional stimulation of a red or harvest sun may be simulated by an HP sodium lamp (the phosphor-coated halide also emits a little more red than the clear halide). The HP sodium may increase flower production 20 to 50 percent over a halide.

The harvest sun is simulated one of three ways: (1) Adding an HP sodium lamp to a garden room already containing a metal halide. This more than doubles the available light, especially in the red end of the spectrum. The halide maintains blues in the spectrum necessary for continued chlorophyll production. (2) Replacing the halide with an HP sodium. This increases the reds, but cuts the blues. A result of this practice has been more yellowing of vegetative leaves, due to lack of chlorophyll production and more stem elongation than if the halide were present. (3) Adding or changing to

a phosphor-coated halide. Not only are these halides easier on the eyes, their coating makes them produce a little bit more red in their spectrum, thus promoting flowering.

Water needs of a flowering plant are somewhat less than in the vegetative stage. Adequate water during flowering is important to carry on the plant's chemistry. Withholding water to stress a plant will actually stunt growth and the yield will be less.

Hermaphrodites

A hermaphrodite is a plant that has both male and female flowers on the same plant. The majority of plants fall into this category.

Indoors, the outdoor environment is manufactured and the normal life cycle of any plant can be altered. Creating summer in December, taking cuttings, prolonging the life cycle and leaching the soil - all the wonderful things we are able to do indoors, mixes up even the strongest plant somewhat. When this stress is coupled with weak seeds, the outcome is uncertain. High humidity, over-pruning and old age seem to promote hermaphrodites more than other environmental factors. In short, if a plant starts to go sour and you do not know the reason why, it could be because it was stressed too much.

Seed Crops

Seed crops are harvested when the seeds are mature. Often seeds may actually split open their containing calyx or seed pod. The flower grows many ready, receptive calyxes until pollination occurs. Seeds are normally mature within six to eight weeks. Watch out for fungus that might attack the weakening flower and cache of ripe seeds.

When seeds are mature, remove them from the pods and store them in a cool, dry place. The seeds are viable and ready for planting as soon as they are harvested, but they may grow sickly plants. Let the seeds dry out a few months before planting. Dry seeds will produce much healthier plants and the germination rate will be higher.

Back Issue and Subscription Order Form

the GrowingEDGE

Single *GrowingEDGE* back issues are $7.00 U.S. and Canada ($10 overseas). Four or more are $5 ($7.50 overseas). Prices include shipping and handling. Please indicate desired quantity.

___ **Vol. 1 #1** — Out of Print

___ **Vol. 1 #2** Basil Production for the Small Grower / Propagation in Rockwool / Biological Pest Control / The Fine Art of Micropropagation / Hydroponic Nutrient Solutions / Phytofarms of America / Toxins in the Garden / Environmental Dynamics: Part II / Wine-Red Strophalia

___ **Vol. 1 #3** Bananas: Grown in Oregon / In-Store Hydroponics in Houston / Pest Management for Hydroponics / Bioponics: Part I / Hydroponics for the Home Hobbyist / Quebec's Hydroponic Tomatoes / Shiitake Mushrooms

___ **Vol. 1 #4** Build Your Own Hydroponic System! / Plant Selection for Hydroponics / Water Should Taste Good to Plants! / Basil Production: An Update / Mid-South Greenhouse / Look Out Holland, Here Comes B.C.! / Grow Your Own Mushrooms Indoors / Softwood Cloning for Beginners

___ **Vol. 2 #1** Aero-Hydroponics / A Computer in Your Garden / Hydroponic or Organic? / Deep Water NFT / The Earth as Greenhouse / The Sip of Life: Cutting Survival / Optimizing High Pressure Sodiums / Growing Oyster Mushrooms Indoors

___ **Vol. 2 #2** Low-Tech, High-Performance Hydro / Allelopathy: Bio-Weapon of the Future / Bioponics: Part II / Recycling Nature's Gifts / Brooklyn Botanic Garden / NASA's Ames Research Center / SLUG: Garden for the Environment / (Very) Basic Hydroponics

___ **Vol. 2 #3** Rockwool: Cube and Slab Gardens / Foliar Feeding: Fast Food for Plants / Hydroponic Herbs at Home / Artificial Lighting in Horticulture / Bioponics: Part III / Desert Botanical Gardens / Assault on Eden! / Shiitake Growing Indoors / Computer Control Systems

___ **Vol. 2 #4** Thigmomorphogenesis / Hydroponic/Aquaculture Food Systems / Bioponics - Part IV / Drip Irrigation: The Basics / A 'Sound' Diet for Plants / New Efficiency for Home Lighting

___ **Vol. 3 #1** The Origin of Botanical Species / New World Fruits / Hardy Kiwi for Every Climate / The Garden Hacker / Plant Plane Hydroponics / The Struggle for Sunlight / Sununu Effect vs the Greenhouse Effect

___ **Vol. 3 #2** Carbon Dioxide Enrichment / White Owl Waterfarm / Subirrigation Systems indoors / Subirrigation on the Cheap / Nitrogen Fixing Plants / The Domesticated Citrus

___ **Vol. 3 #3** Growing Bananas indoors / Hydroponics for the Rest of Us / The Garden Hacker: Part III / Planetary Healing with Biology / Nature's Pharmacy: Medicinal Plants / Clean Air Update / Water Wise Garden

___ **Vol. 3 #4** Bedroom Garden / Goldfish Production / Designing With Nature / Gardening at the South Pole / Small Scale Solutions / Cloning / The Garden Hacker: Part IV / The $50 Greenhouse

___ **Vol. 4 #1** Hydroponics — A Global Perspective / Iceland — Land of Fire, Ice and Flowers / Paradise Found — Indoor Palms / Pest Control for Greenhouse Growers / Seeding Diversity, Reaping a Future / Sokol's Gourmet Sprouting Co. / Understanding Plant Names

___ **Vol. 4 #2** Hydroponics—Dynamic Sustainable Agriculture / Coffee, Tea or Hot Chocolate - Hot Drinks You Can Grow / Biological Alchemy and the Living Machine / A Moment of Hope by John Todd / Bioponics: Part V - Enzymes for Hereditary Potential / Mutation Breeding: Part I - Bypassing the Birds and the Bees / High-Tech Nursery / The Role of Gases in Nutrient Solutions / An Orchard of Lettuce Trees / Demystifying Plant Propagation / Hydroponic Solutions for Beginners

___ **Vol. 4 #3** The Lives of a Plant: Part 1/ Seeds - Embryonic Plants / The Orchid Environment - An Artificial Alternative / A Down-to-Earth Space Garden / Mutation Breeding: Part II / Healing a Wounded Planet / The Fruit/Herb Dryer / More Oxygen for your NFT

___ **Vol. 4 #4** Hydro-Organics—Organic Hydroponic Solutions / Bioponic Greenhouse / A Microbial Culture Chemostat / Organic Nutrient Extractor / System Earth—Urban Hot Spots / Rain Gutter Hydroponic System / The Lives of a Plant: Part 2 / Site Selection for Beginners / The Search for the Perfect Seedless Grape / The Fabric of Plant Diversity

___ **Vol. 5 #1** Hydroponics in Schools / Leaf Analysis / Mist Propagation and Fog Systems / Oxygen Intensive Water Culture / Basic Backyard Breeding / Pesticides in Our Communities / Winterize Indoor Plants / Systems for Beginners

___ **Vol. 5 #2** Building a Better Tomato / Computerize Your Garden / Gardening on Ice / Agriculture for the Millennium-Part I / Wheelchair Garden / More Green from Your Garden / Genius of Simplicity

___ **Vol. 5 #3** Soliva Greenhouse / Lemon Substitutes / Computer Control Systems / Non-circulating Hydroponic System / Check Your Nutrient IQ / Best Compost Pile Ever / Treating Horticultural Soils With Microwaves / Biological Controls for Specialty Collections / Agriculture for the Millennium

___ **Vol. 5 #4** Under the Dome: Biodome de Montreal / An Introduction to Herb Mint / Frankenfood / Biological Systems for Glasshouse Horticulture / Lighting for Beginners Part I-The Meaning of Light / Biological Controls for Specialty Collections Part II

___ **Vol. 6 #1** Cultivating Passiflora / Commercial Hydroponics / Mushrooms / Water Gardening / Visit to an Experimental Beijing Market / Lighting for Beginners - Part II

___ **Vol. 6 #2** Windowsill Herb Garden / Fatal Attraction: the Fascinating World of Carnivorous Plants / A Taste of Things to Come / Tissue Culture / Hydroponics: Beyond the Basics / Greenhouse Growing Southern Style / Fruit Cocktail Planting / The Methane Greenhouse

___ **Vol. 6 #3** E=MC² A Lesson in Plant Growth / Port-O-Pict: Growing Edibles in Containers / Zero Gravity Gardening / Garden of the Future / Sweet or Fiery: Peppers are Hot! / What's in Your Soil? / Biological Revival / Greenhouse Covering...Uncovered

___ **Vol. 6 #4** Hydroponics: Making Waves in the Classroom/ The Rice Paddy Kid / In Praise of Prairie Plants / A World Ahead...The Leaders in Hydroponic Technology / Wildlife Habitat Gardens / Cherry Cheaters / Biological Revival Part II / Gardening in Cyberspace

---

The Growing Edge — please send me:

☐ Back issues (checked above) .... $ _____

☐ 1 year subscription (4 issues, U.S. only) $17.95
   ☐ check here if renewal

☐ 2 year subscription (8 issues, U.S. only) $34.00

☐ First Class 1 year subscription (U.S. & Canada) $24.95
   (Sent First Class in a protective envelope)
   ☐ check here if renewal

☐ Overseas subscription (1 year, 4 issues) $45.00
   (Sent Air mail in a protective envelope)
   ☐ check here if renewal

Total Cost (U.S. funds only) .... $ _____

Please send order to:

Name _____

Address _____

City _____

State/Province _____

County _____ Zip or Postal Code _____

I have enclosed payment: Personal check, money order (U.S. funds. Personal checks will delay delivery), or bill my charge card: VISA, MASTERCARD, DISCOVER OR AMERICAN EXPRESS.

No. _____ _____ _____ _____ Exp. Date: _____ /_____

Telephone number (charge card orders): _____

Cardholder Name _____

Signature _____

NEW MOON Charge card orders 1-800-888-6785 (U.S. only)
Please send form and payment to:
NEW MOON PUBLISHING
P.O. Box 1027 · Corvallis, OR 97339
PUBLISHING ☎ (503) 757-8477 · ✠ (503) 757-0028

GVP-GI

Chapter Eleven: Extending Growing Seasons

About Extending Growing Seasons

The easiest and most economical ways to extend growing seasons are to add warmth and shelter to protect plants from cold weather and high winds. Modern materials have greatly expanded the products available for protecting plants from early and late cold during spring and fall. These new products, in addition to traditional ones, such as cloches and improvised ones allow gardeners to grow vegetables earlier and longer than the weather would suggest.

In addition, these products make it possible to be able to grow desirable plants in a zone that is one or more zones farther north than the plants would grow if unprotected.

You can also lengthen the growing season by finding the mini-environments of your property where the soil warms up and stays warm longer. Some mini-environments occur because of orientation to the sun plus protection from wind. Other warm sites occur near buildings that are not very weather-tight. Still others occur next to brick, stone and mortar walls and fences which, by holding heat, buffer the surrounding climate and help prevent the very damaging freeze-thaw cycles so common in the Midwest and other parts of the country.

Dark walls will absorb and hold more heat than light-colored walls, another factor that may affect nearby growing conditions. Dark soil absorbs more heat than light-colored soil which is another factor to take into account when trying to extend growing seasons for useful and ornamental plants.

A body of water such as a lake, pond, or small creek will also moderate the air temperature. If your garden is near water, the winter temperature will be higher and the summer temperature warmer than the more distant surrounding area.

If untimely hard frosts threaten tender plants, an old-fashioned trick to avoid plant injury is to turn sprinklers or misters on the plants. This will work for tender trees and shrubs as well as smaller plants. One year, we saw tuberous begonias that were covered with thick ice after being sprinkled to avoid frost damage. When the sun came out, they were beautiful in a strange and sparkling way. When the ice melted, the plants were as healthy as before the frost hit.

Low spots will be colder than sites with a higher elevation. Cold air sinks. That's why an ideal site for an orchard is a slope. Cold air flows down the slope providing good air circu-

Spun fiber such as Reemay™ will protect plants from cold weather and the elements while letting air circulate freely.

lation to the orchard trees while avoiding the frosty air that flows down to the lower area below them.

In a pinch, if you have a cold-sensitive shrub, small tree, or smaller plant outdoors when early or late frost threatens, put a sheet or blanket over the plant and rig a low-wattage electric light bulb under the covering. Make sure the bulb is not near the fabric which might catch on fire. The bulb under the cover will keep the temperature 10 to 15° above the ambient temperature in the rest of the garden.

Dark plastic mulches, which also shade weeds and prevent moisture loss, are an inexpensive way to increase the temperature of the soil 5 to 15° on sunny days. As plants grow, the leaves shade the dark soil, gradually stopping the warming affect. Clear plastic is more efficient in warming the soil than black!

Placing dark rocks strategically is a simple way to moderate temperature in small areas of the garden. You can create your own mini-environments with these rocks which will absorb and hold heat over a long period, slowly releasing it in its own immediate vicinity.

In the Northwest where the winters are

cloudy, you need to use maximize what light is available. Greenhouses need to be glass or very clear plastic to transmit light well. Southern climates with more light, can use less expensive plastic or double-walled greenhouses that do not transmit as much light.

Cool weather plants need the opposite kind of shelter. You must protect them from too much heat and sun in order to extend their growing season. If you shade these plants, including lettuce and cabbage family members, from afternoon sun when the hot season arrives, you can extend their harvest time and keep them from bolting. Thick organic mulches help hold moisture and keep the soil cool.

Covers, Tunnels & Cloches

Covering plants with row tunnels, covers and cloches will protect them from extreme cold and freezes. They make it easy to plant earlier in the spring and have harvests far into the fall.

Spun fiber coverings, including the brands Agronet and Reemay, will protect plants from late and early frosts if set over young plants and anchored around the perimeter with soil or rocks. Plants will support the light spun-fiber row covers and no superstructure is needed.

When using flexible row covers, you may need to buy the large staples that are available for securing row covers and plastic mulches in place. Or you can make your own from old coat hangers by cutting off the two curved ends. Staples that are one-inch-wide and four to six inches long are handy.

Row covers can be made of clear corrugated fiberglass that is bent into an arch and secured in the garden. The size of this kind of row cover is limited only by the size of the fiberglass panels.

There are commercial row covers that combine polypropylene with hoops to make season extenders that will protect garden crops down to temperatures as low as 25° F. These come in sizes large enough to use on dwarf fruit trees and mature tomato vines. They also come in smaller sizes for pepper plants, eggplants and rose bushes.

Cloches made of plastic, glass, or wet-strength waxed paper protect individual plants. Plastic milk jugs with the bottoms cut out make the simplest of cloches. And who does not remember rose fanciers who used Mason jars to protect small rose cuttings that they started in their garden beds.

There are commercial cloches in all sizes. Typical are the cone-shaped caps made of rigid transparent plastic or wet-strength waxed paper that are easy to use and will stack conveniently.

The water-filled teepee known as Wall O' Water is a season extender for protecting plants from cold at night and shielding them from excess heat during the day. They are ideal for extending the season for individual plants and, although most often used during spring months, also have potential for extending the fall season. Each water teepee holds three gallons of water and will last from three to five years if given proper care.

During the day, the water absorbs the heat of the sun and moderates the temperature inside the teepee. When night falls and the air becomes colder than the water in the teepee, the water slowly releases its heat. If the water begins to freeze, it will release more heat. These teepees will protect plants down to 10° F. Each one can release as much as 900,000 calories, according to the product literature.

Cold Frames

A cold frame is a rectangular plastic- or glass-topped container about 3' by 4' that is placed on the ground to protect plants from climate extremes. The heat inside is provided by from the sunlight. A cold frame will slow soil-moisture evaporation, warm both soil and air and also protect plants from pests.

The Wall-O-Water™ is the most efficient way to keep small plants protected from freezing weather.

A cold frame will extend the spring season by six weeks to two months. If you plant tomatoes in a cold frame two months earlier than recommended, you will have fresh fruit two months to six weeks earlier than everyone else. This big a jump on the growing season may be possible in mild climates such as the Pacific Northwest, but not in more rigorous climates such as the Upper Midwest.

Open a cold frame or simple greenhouse during the heat of the day to provide cooling and air circulation. Fancier cold frames have wax-filled vents that operate automatically. When the heat rises in the frame, the wax expands, opening the vent. When the temperature cools, the wax contracts closing the vent.

Cold frames come in many forms, the simplest of which is old window sashes laid over a rectangle of straw bales. This simple cold frame is as effective as more expensive ones.

Half or three-quarter-inch galvanized metal conduit pipe bent into an arc makes a great superstructure for a cold frame. Many local hardware stores or electrical supply companies will bend the pipe for you or loan you the pipe

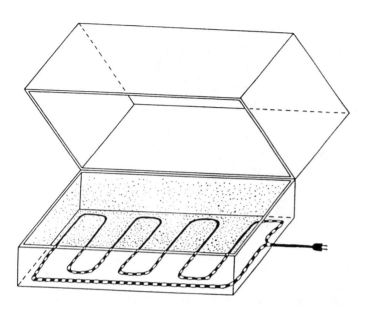

An inexpensive heating cable warms this hotbed.

bender for a day to bend it yourself. Half-inch schedule 40 PVC irrigation pipe also works well and can simply be bent by hand.

A piece of plastic is simply stretched over the dome-shaped conduit or PVC pipe. It is held in place with clamps so that it can be easily removed on warm days or completely covered at night. The ends are easy to open to form a breezy tunnel on medium warm days.

PolyWeave, made of 8-mil polyethelene reinforced with woven nylon mesh is a typical new plastic fabric. It transmits up to 90 percent of sunlight, can be sewn or taped and has a life span of up to five years.

Hotbeds

Hotbeds are cold frames that are heated and have insulation. As such, they also can be made of anything appropriate. They, too, can be simple like the straw bales and window sashes mentioned above or they can be made more elegantly. Either way, they will work fine in the garden to extend growing seasons at both ends,

spring and fall.

Convert your cold frame into a hotbed by placing heating cable or heating mats, available in most garden centers and hardware stores, on the soil below. Over the cable or mat put a two-inch layer of soil, newspaper or a two-inch thick piece of Styrofoam to distribute the heat evenly to the bottoms of the containers and flats.

Most heating cables or mats come with a built-in thermostat that is set at 72° F. As with all electrical equipment, read and follow the directions in order to use the heating cable or mat safely. Heating cables or mats will not heat the entire hotbed volume well, but will maintain the bottom heat needed for strong seedling growth.

You can also provide heat in a hotbed by digging a 2-foot deep pit the length and width of the frames that will be placed on the soil surface. Fill the pit with a blend of straw and fresh manure to within 6 inches of the surface. Then put down a layer of straw and 1-2 inches of topsoil. Place the hotbed frame over the area and you are ready to plant or put your seedling flats inside.

Greenhouses

A multipurpose solar greenhouse attached to the home can be used to grow plants and will also help heat and humidify the home. It is a nice place for afternoon tea or happy hour and a bright and cheery spot for a winter picnic.

Conventional greenhouses do not retain heat well. As a result, at night or on cloudy days, they are expensive to heat. To solve this problem, one grower in Portland, Oregon, heats his greenhouse with compost. He stacks organic matter up on the sides of the greenhouse to a height of about five feet, both inside and out. As the piles decompose they give off heat which keeps the greenhouse warm. This also might be

Greenhouses will allow you to garden all year long. They will also allow you to start plants much earlier in the season.

a good solution for a home greenhouse on a large property.

Greenhouses are made of many materials and can function in any climatic conditions, if you're willing to foot the bill. The most economical way to use a greenhouse is as a kind of large cold frame. Use it mostly to extend the growing seasons and its utilities won't amount to much. But, if you live in a cold climate and want to grow exotic tropicals, be prepared for high heating bills. In sunny regions, solar heat can help reduce heating costs.

Solar grow frames hold their heat by using insulation. Solar (or any kind of greenhouse) also benefits from insulation and, in larger units, heat-retaining materials such as drums filled with water to serve as thermal mass.

Commercial growers use greenhouses in hot climates to shade plants and keep them cooler than the ambient air. Shade cloth and whitewash are the two classic ways to shade greenhouses in the summer. The home greenhouse can be shaded in summer in those same ways, or you can plant deciduous trees which

will provide shade in the summer and allow the sun through their branches in cold months.

If you plan to add a greenhouse room onto your home, consult with experts and talk to someone who already has this kind of an addition. Double- or even triple-glazed coverings on greenhouses, although expensive, will be effective in cutting utility costs.

Before laying out time, money and energy to build a greenhouse, analyze the project carefully on paper. List what you want to use the greenhouse for. Be very specific and figure in the square footage that you would need. Study the possible sites for a greenhouse and list the pluses and minuses of each. Then and only then, you are ready to begin discussing the project with an expert or developing plans to do it yourself.

It may be that you want a simple freestanding work area with a potting bench where you can start plants from seed and grow them into transplants. If that is the case, you could probably get away with having a temporary plastic cover like a tent over the area during the late winter and early spring months. This, combined with heating cables and a heater in case of unseasonable freezes, might be all you need.

Protection From The Elements

Windbreaks protect plants from heat and water loss. They also can increase the average temperature from 1 to 5° on the downwind side of the windbreak.

Traditional windbreaks in the prairies and plains where prevailing winds are strong and quite constant, are poplars and other fast-growing deciduous trees combined with tall evergreens such as Norway spruce. The evergreens are staggered along the windward side of the windbreak, with the deciduous trees arranged in random rows on the lee side.

Windbreaks for homes and home gardens need not be on such a heroic scale. They can include smaller trees and shrubs. They can also function as sound and sight barriers. Irregular rows of tall plants also can protect outdoor living areas from summer sun, often a very important function.

The best windbreaking hedges are not orchard trees and bushes, but woody plants chosen for their foliage and growth pattern as wind buffers. The flowers and fruit of edibles are damaged by high winds. There are a few exceptions, such as carob, mulberry, olive and nut trees.

Arbors, Shade, & Lath Houses

Arbors, shade houses and lath houses are excellent ways to protect people and plants from too much heat and sun. A shade structure can be used over both the patio and garden beds, especially when the vegetable varieties are chosen for their ornamental appeal and arranged in an artistic way.

Arbors and pergolas, ornamental structures built to support plants and create pathways and sitting areas in the garden, are classic solutions to providing shade in an attractive way. They are ideal for grape vines.

Arbors and pergolas are well-suited for climbing roses and clematis. And, they are also interesting challenges for growing the vining vegetables the squashes, cucumbers, beans and peas. Once the vines are growing well, use the shade inside or on the north side for growing shade-loving plants. Leaf lettuce will do better in the shade during the hot months and it also makes a beautiful border plant.

Shade houses are created by attaching shade cloth to a frame. They may be used for a picnic area or also provide protection for potted plants during the intense heat of summer. Shade cloth is a synthetic material available in a range of sun-blocking ability. Homeowners and gardeners are just beginning to discover the many uses for shade cloth. It can be found in any horticultural supply store.

A lath house built from thin, narrow strips of wood can provide 25 percent shade, 50 percent shade, or even more, depending on how close you place the laths. Lath houses can be simple, stark structures to fulfill a practical function only or they can be built with aesthetics in mind so that they are handsome as well as utilitarian.

Chapter Twelve:
Plant Selection Guide

African violets, begonias and impatiens flower constantly under lights. Begonias of all types, ferns, oxalis, geraniums, annuals, small shrubs and trees such as jasmine, gardenia, crape myrtle, dwarf lantana and dwarf pomegranate, citrus and figs all grow well under HID's.

Cacti and succulents - jade, miniature crassulas, Christmas, Easter and Thanksgiving cactus etc. - are probably the easiest to care for under lights. They require a minimum of care and infrequent watering, but lots of light.

African Violets, parent plants and cuttings of this short-day plant are given 18 hours of light a day at a level of 6,000 mWm^2. Flowering is induced with a short 12 to 14-hour photoperiod.

Azalea cuttings propagated under a light level of 6,000 mWm^2, 18 hours a day grow fast and uniform. Flowers are effectively forced by supplying 3,000 mWms^2 for 16 hours a day.

Begonias: Supplemental lighting promotes cuttings to form on the varieties Rieger, Elatior and Lorraine when natural light is lacking. A light level of 6,000 mWm^2 is the norm. Use 6,000 mWm^2 18 hours a day to nurture young seedlings and to speed flowering. Rooting is stimulated in begonia cuttings by artificial light.

Bromeliads: A light level of 6,000 mWm^2 18 hours a day is used to promote stronger growth and the development of seedlings and young plants. On larger bromeliads, supplemental lighting is normally used to help stimulate floral formation.

A light level of 4,500 mWm^2 for 24 hours a day is used to stimulate flowering. Many times other flower-inducing means are combined with lighting to hasten blooming.

Cacti: In winter when the days are short, cacti greatly benefit from intense supplemental light. A lighting level of 9,000 mWm^2 for 18 hours a day will produce phenomenal results in seedlings, cuttings and adult cacti. Some varieties of cactus respond more favorably to 24 hours of light.

Calceolaria Early flowering is achieved by applying supplemental lighting (3,000 mWm^2) for 24 hours a day from bud induction until flowering. Maintain the temperature between 60 and 65 degrees for maximum productivity.

Carnations, like chrysanthemums, are propagated very successfully by using a parent plant and supplemental light. In fact, side shoots from cut flowers make excellent cuttings. Cuttings are taken and given 16 hours of

This cyclamen has been blooming for more than three months and continues to bloom.

light (6,000 mWm²). Excessive flowering may occur if more than 16 hours of light per day is permitted. The carnation is a long-day plant, it is possible to light it 24 hours a day to grow more and more profuse flowers. However, after 18 hours of light a day, the extra light produces a minimum of growth.

Chrysanthemums are one of the most responsive flowers to supplemental light in all stages of life. In winter parent plants are given 9,000 mWm², 20 hours a day. Given lighting during the first month of vegetative growth increases bud count and foliage production. Being a short-day plant, the chrysanthemum requires 20 hours of light a day during the first month of vegetative growth and 12 hours of light (4,500 mWm² and 12 hours of uninterrupted darkness to flower properly.

Cucumber seedlings grow exceptionally well under HID lights. Give young seedlings a light level of 4500 mWm² for the first 10 days of growth for 24 hours a day. After this, shorten the photoperiod to 16 hours per day and increase the light level to 6000 mWm².

Cyclamen seedlings given supplemental lighting (6,000 mWm²) have more uniform growth and less damping off. The young plants are given 18 hours of light a day.

Geraniums and pelargoniums propagated by seed or from cuttings greatly benefit from supplemental light. Parent plants are given 18 hours of light at a level of 6,000 mWm² to increase cutting production. The cuttings are given less light but for the same 18 hours a day. Geraniums are a short-day plant and flower with shorter days or colder temperatures.

F1 hybrid seed-propagated geraniums can be given 24 hours of light a day at a level of 6,000 mWm² from the beginning of life. These F1 hybrids do not need short days for flower induction.

Gloxinas are given a light level of 6000 mWm² 18 hours a day to enhance growth and development of seedlings and young plants. Give potted gloxinas a light level of 4500 mWm² to promote large healthy flowers.

Kalanchoe parent plants are given 18 hours of light a day to prevent flowering of this long-day plant. Normally propagated vegetatively, cuttings are given 18 to 24 hours of light at a level of 6,000 mWm². Flowering is induced by giving the plants an equal 12 hours of light and 12 hours of darkness.

Lettuce is lighted at a level of 6000 mWm² during its entire life. If given a higher level of light, lettuce might bolt.

Orchids: The blooms and overall growth of many varieties of orchids are greatly enhanced by supplemental lighting during the winter. See: special section below on light requirements of orchids.

Roses love light. Miniature roses grow incredibly well under HID light. Levels of 6,000 mWm², 24 hours per day will greatly increase flower yield, size and quality. Supplemental carbon dioxide really boost growth of these super-productive roses.

Snapdragons are a favorite fall and early spring flower. There are two genetically different types of snapdragons short-day, referred to as Group I or II or "winter flowering," and long-day, referred to as Group III or IV or "summer flowering." When setting this plant out for early spring blooms, give seedlings supplementary lighting at a level of 9,000 mWm^2 so that a day length of 16 hours is reached. This will speed flowering by about four weeks. In fact, even better results can be achieved by giving long-day plants 24 hours of light (4,500 mWm^2) throughout their life. Short day snapdragons should receive short 12 hour days after they are about two months old for maximum blooming potential.

Tomatoes, peppers and eggplants flourish under HID light. The more light these plants are given the bigger they grow and the more fruit they produce. Give these plants 9000 mWm^2 as soon the first true leaves appear and maintain the light level throughout their entire life.

Orchid Culture Under Lights

Light requirements for orchids fall into three categories.

High: 3000 foot-candles or more, which is equivalent to the amount of light available to plants growing in the middle of a sunny field.

Medium: 1500-3000 foot-candles, which is similar to the amount of light received by lightly shaded plants.

Low: under 1500 foot-candles, for plants that grow deep beneath the canopy of the forest.

Temperature requirements are divided into three groups:

Warm: (70 to 75° F, 21 to 24° C) day, (60 to 65° F, 15 to 18° C) night similar to the climate of a seacoast or swampy lowland.

Medium: (65 to 70° F, 18 to 21° C) day, (55 to 60° F, 13 to 15° C) night similar to rolling forests and fields.

Cool: (60 to 65° F, 15 to 18° C) day, (50 to 55°, 10 to 13° C) night similar to high moun-

Transplanted on the same day, the small stone plant (lithops) on the left was in a dim corner of the garden room. The large stone plant on the right received intense halide light.

tainous regions.

Orchids can be referred to as being high light, cool-air plants. The Cymbidium is a good example of this type of orchid. The Phalaenopsis genus is a low-light, warm-air orchid.

All plants may be divided into two groups: species and hybrid. Hybridization often eliminates many of the natural limitations imposed by the original climatic requirements of an orchid. For example, if you breed a high-light, warm-air species with a medium-light, medium-temperature species, the result is a hybrid that grows well in either category.

Back Issue and Subscription Order Form

the GrowingEDGE

Single *GrowingEDGE* back issues are $7.00 U.S. and Canada ($10 overseas). Four or more are $5 ($7.50 overseas). Prices include shipping and handling. Please indicate desired quantity.

___ **Vol. 1 #1** — Out of Print

___ **Vol. 1 #2** Basil Production for the Small Grower / Propagation in Rockwool / Biological Pest Control / The Fine Art of Micropropagation / Hydroponic Nutrient Solutions / Phytofarms of America / Toxins in the Garden / Environmental Dynamics: Part II / Wine-Red Stropharia

___ **Vol. 1 #3** Bananas: Grown in Oregon / In-Store Hydroponics in Houston / Pest Management for Hydroponics / Bioponics: Part I / Hydroponics for the Home Hobbyist / Quebec's Hydroponic Tomatoes / Shiitake Mushrooms

___ **Vol. 1 #4** Build Your Own Hydroponic System! / Plant Selection for Hydroponics / Water Should Taste Good to Plants! / Basil Production: An Update / Mid-South Greenhouse / Look Out Holland, Here Comes B.C.! / Grow Your Own Mushrooms Indoors / Softwood Cloning for Beginners

___ **Vol. 2 #1** Aero-Hydroponics / A Computer in Your Garden / Hydroponic or Organic? / Deep Water NFT / The Earth as Greenhouse / The Slot of Life: Cutting Survival / Optimizing High Pressure Sodiums / Growing Oyster Mushrooms Indoors

___ **Vol. 2 #2** Low-Tech, High-Performance Hydro / Allelopathy: Bio-Weapon of the Future / Bioponics: Part II / Recycling Nature's Gifts / Brooklyn Botanic Garden / NASA's Ames Research Center / SLUG: Garden for the Environment / (Very) Basic Hydroponics

___ **Vol. 2 #3** Rockwool: Cube and Slab Gardens / Foliar Feeding: Fast Food for Plants / Hydroponic Herbs at Home / Artificial Lighting in Horticulture / Bioponics: Part III / Desert Botanical Gardens / Assault on Eden! / Shiitake Growing Indoors / Computer Control Systems

___ **Vol. 2 #4** Thigmomorphogenesis / Hydroponic/Aquaculture Food Systems / Bioponics - Part IV / Drip Irrigation: The Basics / A 'Sound' Diet for Plants / New Efficiency for Home Lighting

___ **Vol. 3 #1** The Origin of Botanical Species / New World Fruits / Hardy Kiwi for Every Climate / The Garden Hacker / Plant Plane Hydroponics / The Struggle for Sunlight / Sununu Effect vs the Greenhouse Effect

___ **Vol. 3 #2** Carbon Dioxide Enrichment / White Owl Waterfarm / Subirrigation Systems Indoors / Subirrigation on the Cheap / Nitrogen Fixing Plants / The Domesticated Citrus

___ **Vol. 3 #3** Growing Bananas Indoors / Hydroponics for the Rest of Us / The Garden Hacker: Part III / Planetary Healing with Biology / Nature's Pharmacy: Medicinal Plants / Clean Air Update / Water Wise Garden

___ **Vol. 3 #4** Bedroom Garden / Goldfish Production / Designing With Nature / Gardening at the South Pole / Small Scale Solutions / Cloning / The Garden Hacker: Part IV / The $50 Greenhouse

___ **Vol. 4 #1** Hydroponics — A Global Perspective / Iceland — Land of Fire, Ice and Flowers / Paradise Found — Indoor Palms / Pest Control for Greenhouse Growers / Seeding Diversity, Reaping a Future / Sokol's Gourmet Sprouting Co. / Understanding Plant Names

___ **Vol. 4 #2** Hydroponics—Dynamic Sustainable Agriculture / Coffee, Tea or Hot Chocolate - Hot Drinks You Can Grow / Biological Alchemy and the Living Machine / A Moment of Hope by John Todd / Bioponics: Part V - Enzymes for Hereditary Potential / Mutation Breeding: Part I - Bypassing the Birds and the Bees / High-Tech Nursery / The Role of Gases in Nutrient Solutions / An Orchard of Lettuce Trees / Demystifying Plant Propagation / Hydroponic Solutions for Beginners

___ **Vol. 4 #3** The Lives of a Plant: Part 1/ Seeds - Embryonic Plants / The Orchid Environment - An Artificial Alternative / A Down-to-Earth Space Garden / Mutation Breeding: Part II / Healing a Wounded Planet / The Fruit/Herb Dryer / More Oxygen for your NFT

___ **Vol. 4 #4** Hydro-Organics—Organic Hydroponic Solutions / Bioponic Greenhouse / A Microbial Culture Chemostat / Organic Nutrient Extractor / System Earth—Urban Hot Spots / Rain Gutter Hydroponic System / The Lives of a Plant: Part 2 / Site Selection for Beginners / The Search for the Perfect Seedless Grape / The Fabric of Plant Diversity

___ **Vol. 5 #1** Hydroponics in Schools / Leaf Analysis / Mist Propagation and Fog Systems / Oxygen Intensive Water Culture / Basic Backyard Breeding / Pesticides in Our Communities / Winterize Indoor Plants / Systems for Beginners

___ **Vol. 5 #2** Building a Better Tomato / Computerize Your Garden / Gardening on Ice / Agriculture for the Millennium-Part I / Wheelchair Garden / More Green from Your Garden / Genius of Simplicity

___ **Vol. 5 #3** Soliva Greenhouse / Lemon Substitutes / Computer Control Systems / Non-circulating Hydroponic System / Check Your Nutrient IQ / Best Compost Pile Ever / Treating Horticultural Soils With Microwaves / Biological Controls for Specialty Collections / Agriculture for the Millennium

___ **Vol. 5 #4** Under the Dome: Biodome de Montreal / An Introduction to Herb Mint / Frankenfood / Biological Systems for Glasshouse Horticulture / Lighting for Beginners Part I-The Meaning of Light / Biological Controls for Specialty Collections Part II

___ **Vol. 6 #1** Cultivating Passiflora / Commercial Hydroponics / Mushrooms / Water Gardening / Visit to an Experimental Beijing Market / Lighting for Beginners - Part II

___ **Vol. 6 #2** Windowsill Herb Garden / Fatal Attraction: the Fascinating World of Carnivorous Plants / A Taste of Things to Come / Tissue Culture / Hydroponics: Beyond the Basics / Greenhouse Growing Southern Style / Fruit Cocktail Planting / The Methane Greenhouse

___ **Vol. 6 #3** E=MC² A Lesson in Plant Growth / Port-O-Plot: Growing Edibles in Containers / Zero Gravity Gardening / Garden of the Future / Sweet or Fiery...Peppers are Hot! / What's in Your Soil? / Biological Revival / Greenhouse Covering...Uncovered

___ **Vol. 6 #4** Hydroponics: Making Waves in the Classroom/ The Rice Paddy Kid / In Praise of Prairie Plants / A World Ahead...The Leaders in Hydroponic Technology / Wildlife Habitat Gardens / Cherry Cheaters / Biological Revival Part II / Gardening in Cyberspace

---

The Growing Edge — please send me:

☐ Back issues (checked above) .... $ _____

☐ 1 year subscription (4 issues, U.S. only) $17.95
  ☐ check here if renewal

☐ 2 year subscription (8 issues, U.S. only) $34.00

☐ First Class 1 year subscription (U.S. & Canada) $24.95
  (Sent First Class in a protective envelope)
  ☐ check here if renewal

☐ Overseas subscription (1 year, 4 issues) $45.00
  (Sent Air mail in a protective envelope)
  ☐ check here if renewal

Total Cost (U.S. funds only) .... $ _____

Please send order to:

Name _____

Address _____

City _____

State/Province _____

County _____ Zip or Postal Code _____

I have enclosed payment: Personal check, money order (U.S. funds. Personal checks will delay delivery), or bill my charge card: VISA, MASTERCARD, DISCOVER OR AMERICAN EXPRESS.

No. _____ _____ _____ _____ Exp. Date: _____ / _____

Telephone number (charge card orders): _____

Cardholder Name _____

Signature _____

NEW MOON Charge card orders 1-800-888-6785 (U.S. only)
Please send form and payment to:
NEW MOON PUBLISHING
P.O. Box 1027 • Corvallis, OR 97339
PUBLISHING ☎ (503) 757-8477 • (503) 757-0028

Glossary

This Glossary contains many very simple and some not so simple words in the context of their usage in this book. Many examples are given to promote good indoor horticultural practices.

Alternating Current (AC) - an electric current that reverses its direction at regularly occurring intervals. Homes have AC.

Acid - a sour substance: An acid or sour soil has a low pH.

Adobe - heavy clay soil, not suitable for container gardening

Aeration - supplying soil and roots with air or oxygen. Aeroponics - growing plants by misting roots suspended in air

Aggregate - medium, usually gravel, that is all nearly the same size and used for the inert hydroponic medium.

Alkaline - refers to soil with a high pH: Any pH over 7 is considered alkaline.

All-purpose (General-purpose) fertilizer - A balanced blend of N-P-K: all purpose fertilizer is used by most growers in the vegetative growth stage.

Amendment - changing soil texture by adding organic or mineral substances

Ampere (amp) - the unit used to measure the strength of an electric current: A 20-amp circuit is overloaded when drawing more than 17 amps.

Annual- a plant that normally completes its entire life cycle in one year or less: Marigolds and tomatoes are examples of annual plants.

Arc - luminous discharge of electricity (light) between two electrodes.

Arc tube- container for luminous gases also houses the arc.

Auxin - classification of plant hormones: Auxins are responsible for foliage and root elongation.

Bacteria - very small, one-celled organisms that have no chlorophyll.

Beneficial insect - a good insect that eats bad flower and vegetable-munching insects.

Biodegradable - able to decompose or break down through natural bacterial action: Substances made of organic matter are biodegradable.

Bleach- Ordinary laundry bleach is used in a mild water solution as a soil fungicide.

Bolt - term used to describe a plant that has run to seed prematurely.

Bonsai - a very short or dwarfed plant.

Breaker box - electrical circuit box having on/off switches rather than fuses.

Breathe - Roots draw in or breathe oxygen, stomata draw in or breathe carbon dioxide.

Bud blight - a withering condition that attacks flower buds.

Buffering - the ability of a substance to reduce shock and cushion against pH fluctuations. Many fertilizers contain buffering agents.

Bulb - 1. the outer glass envelope or jacket that protects the arc tube of an HID lamp 2. clove or bulb of garlic.

Calyx - the pod harboring female ovule and two protruding pistils, seed pod.

Carbon dioxide (CO_2) - a colorless, odorless, tasteless gas in the air necessary for plant life.

Carbohydrate - neutral compound of carbon, hydrogen and oxygen. Sugar, starch and cellulose are carbohydrates.

Caustic - capable of destroying, killing or eating away by chemical activity

Cell - the base structural unit that plants are made of: Cells contain a nucleus, membrane and chloroplasts.

Cellulose - a complex carbohydrate that stiffens a plant: Tough stems contain stiff cellulose

CFM - Cubic feet per minute.

Chelate - combining nutrients in an atomic ring that is easy for plants to absorb.

Chlorophyll- the green photosynthetic matter of plants: Chlorophyll is found in the chloroplasts of a cell.

Chlorine - chemical used to purify water.

Chloroplast - containing chlorophyll Chlorosis - the condition of a sick plant with yellowing leaves due to inadequate formation of chlorophyll Chlorosis is caused by a nutrient deficiency, usually iron or imbalanced pH.

Circuit - a circular route traveled by electricity.

Clay - soil made of very fine organic and mineral particles: Clay is not suitable for container gardening.

Climate - the average condition of the weather in a garden room or outdoors.

Color spectrum - the band of colors (measured in nm) emitted by a light source.

Color tracer - a coloring agent that is added to many commercial fertilizers so the horticulturist knows there is fertilizer in the solution. Peters has a blue color tracer.

Compaction - soil condition that results from tightly packed soil: Compacted soil allows for only marginal aeration and root penetration.

Companion planting - planting garlic, marigolds, etc. along with other plants to discourage insect infestations.

Compost- a mixture of decayed organic matter, high in nutrients Compost must be at least one year old. When too young, decomposition uses nitrogen after sufficient decomposition, compost releases nitrogen.

Core - the transformer in the ballast is referred to as a core.

Cotyledon - seed leaves, first leaves that appear on a plant.

Cross-pollinate - pollinate two plants having different ancestry.

Cubic foot - volume measurement in feet: Width times length times height equals cubic feet.

Cutting - 1. growing tip cut from a parent plant for asexual propagation 2. clone

Damping-off- fungus disease that attacks young seedlings and cuttings causing stem to rot at base: Overwatering is the main cause of damping-off.

Direct Current (DC) - an electric current that flows in only one direction

Deplete - exhaust soil of nutrients, making in infertile: Once a soil is used it is depleted

Desiccate - cause to dry up. Safer's Insecticidal Soap desiccates its victims.

Detergent - liquid soap concentrate used as a: 1. wetting agent for sprays and water 2. pesticide. Note: Detergent must be totally organic to be safe for plants.

Dioecious - having distinct male and female flowers.

Dome - the part of the HID outer bulb opposite the neck and threads.

Dome support - the spring-like brackets that mount the arc tube within the outer envelope.

Drainage - way to empty soil of excess water: with good drainage, water passes through soil evenly, promoting plant growth with bad drainage water stands in soil, drowning roots.

Dripline - a line around a plant directly under its outermost branch tips: Roots seldom grow beyond the drip-line.

Drip system a very efficient watering system that employs a main hose with small water emitters. Water is metered out of the emitters, one drop at a time.

Dry ice a cold, white substance formed when carbon dioxide is compressed and cooled: Dry ice changes into CO_2 gas at room temperatures.

Dry well - drain hole, filled with rocks.

Electrode - a conductor used to establish electrical arc or contact with non-metallic part of circuit.

Elongate - grow in length.

Envelope - outer protective bulb or jacket of a lamp.

Equinox - the point at which the sun crosses the equator and day and night are each 12 hours long: The equinox occurs twice a year.

Extension cord - extra electrical cord that must be 14-gauge or larger (i.e. 12- or 10-gauge).

Feed - fertilize.

Female- pistilate, ovule, seed-producing.

Fertilizer burn - overfertilization: First leaf tips burn (turn brown) then leaves curl.

Fixture - electrical fitting used to hold electric components.

Flat - shallow (three-inch) deep container, often 18 by 24 inches with good drainage, used to start seedlings or cuttings.

Flat white - very reflective, whitest white paint available.

Fluorescent lamp - electric lamp using a tube coated with fluorescent material, which has low lumen and heat output: A fluorescent lamp is excellent for rooting cuttings.

Foliage - the leaves or more generally, the green part of a plant

Foliar feeding - misting fertilizer solution which is absorbed by the foliage.

Fritted - fused or embedded in glass. Fritted trace elements (FTE) are long-lasting and do not leach out easily.

Fungicide - a product that destroys or inhibits fungus.

Fungistat - a product that inhibits fungus keeping it in check.

Fungus - a lower plant lacking chlorophyll which may attack green plants: Mold, rust, mildew, mushrooms and bacteria are fungi.

Fuse - electrical safety device consisting of a metal that MELTS and interrupts the circuit when circuit is overloaded.

Fuse box- box containing fuses that control electric circuits.

GPM - Gallons per minute

General purpose fertilizer - See: ALL-PURPOSE FERTILIZER.

Gene - part of a chromosome that influences the development and potency of a plant: Genes are inherited through sexual propagation.

Genetic make-up - the genes inherited from parent plants: Genetic make-up is the most important factor dictating vigor and potency.

Halide - binary compound of a (halogens) with an electropositive element(s).

Halogen - any of the elements fluorine, chlorine, bromine, iodine and astatine existing in a free state: Halogens are in the arc tube of a halide lamp.

Hermaphrodite - one plant having both male and female flowers: The breeding of hermaphrodite is hard to control.

Hertz (Hz) - a unit of a frequency that cycles one time each second: A home with a 60 hertz AC current cycles 60 times per second.

HID - High Intensity Discharge.

Honeydew- a sticky, honey-like substance secreted onto foliage by aphids, scale and mealy bugs.

Hood - reflective cover of a HID lamp: A large, white HOOD is very reflective.

HOR - The abbreviation stamped on some HID bulbs meaning they may be burned in a horizontal position.

Horizontal - parallel to the horizon, ground or floor.

Hormone - chemical substance that controls the growth and development of a plant. Root-inducing hormones help cuttings root.

Hose bib - water outlet containing an on/off valve.

Humidity (relative) - ratio between the amount of moisture in the air and the greatest amount of moisture the air could hold at the same temperature.

Humus - dark, fertile, partially decomposed plant or animal matter: Humus forms the organic portion of the soil.

Hybrid - an offspring from two plants of different breeds, variety or genetic make-up.

Hydrated lime - instantly soluble lime, used to raise or lower pH.

Hydrogen light, colorless, odorless gas: Hydrogen combines with OXYGEN to form water.

Hygrometer - instrument for measuring relative humidity in the atmosphere: A hygrometer will save time, frustration and money.

Inbred - (true breed) offspring of plants of the same breed or ancestry.

Inert - chemically non-reactive: Inert growing mediums make it easy to control the chemistry of the nutrient solution.

Intensity - the magnitude of light energy per unit: Intensity diminishes the farther away from the source.

Jacket - protective outer bulb or envelope of lamp.

Jiffy 7 pellet - compressed peat moss wrapped in an expandable plastic casing: When moistened, a Jiffy 7 pellet expands into a small pot that is used to start seeds or cuttings.

Kilowatt-hour - measure of electricity used per hour: A 1000-watt HID uses one kilowatt per hour. Lacewing insect that preys on

Leach - dissolve or wash out soluble components of soil by heavy watering.

Leader - See MERISTEM.

Leaf curl - leaf malformation due to overwatering, over fertilization, lack of magnesium, insect or fungus damage or negative tropism.

Leaflet - small immature leaf.

Leggy - abnormally tall, with sparse foliage: Leggyness of a plant is usually caused by lack of light.

Life cycle - a series of growth stages through which plant must pass in its natural lifetime: The stages for an annual plant are seed, seedling, vegetative and floral.

Light mover - a device that moves a lamp back and forth across the ceiling of a garden room to provide more even distribution of light.

Lime - used in the form of DOLOMITE or HYDRATED LIME to raise and stabilize soil pH.

Litmus paper - chemically sensitive paper used for testing pH.

Loam - organic soil mixture of crumbly clay, silt and sand.

Lumen - measurement of light output: One lumen is equal to the amount of light emitted by one candle that falls on one square foot of surface located one foot away from one candle.

Macro-nutrient - one or all of the primary nutrients N-P-k or the secondary nutrients magnesium and calcium.

Mean - average throughout life: HID's are rated in mean lumens.

Meristem - tip of plant growth, branch tip.

Micro- nutrients- also referred to as TRACE ELEMENTS, including S, Fe, Mn, B, Mb, An and Cu.

Millimeter - thousandth of a meter approximately 04. inch.

Moisture meter - a fantastic electronic device that measures the exact moisture content of soil at any given point.

Monochromatic - producing only one color: LP sodium lamps are monochromatic.

Mulch - a protective covering of organic compost, old leaves, etc.: Indoors, mulch keeps soil too moist and possible fungus could result.

Nanometer - 000001. meter, nm is used as a scale to measure electromagnetic wave lengths of light: Color and light spectrums are expressed in nanometers (nm).

Necrosis - localized death of a plant part.

Neck - tubular glass end of the HID bulb, attached to the threads.

Nutrient - plant food, essential elements N-P-K, secondary and trace elements fundamental to plant life.

Ohm's Power Law - a law that expresses the strength of an electric current: Volts times Amperes equals watts.

Organic - made of, derived from or related to living organisms.

Outbred - see hybrid.

Overload - load to excess: A 20-amp circuit drawing 17 amps is overloaded.

Ovule - a plant's egg found within the calyx, it contains all the female genes When fertilized, an ovule will grow into a seed.

Oxygen - tasteless, colorless element, necessary in soil to sustain plant life.

Parasite - organism that lives on or in another host organism: Fungus is a parasite.

Peat - partially decomposed vegetation (usually moss) with slow decay due to extreme moisture and cold.

Perennial - a plant, such as a tree or shrub, that completes its life cycle over several years.

pH - a scale from 1 to 14 that measures the acid-to-alkaline balance a growing medium (or anything): In general plants grow best in a range of 6 to 6.8 pH.

pH tester - electronic instrument or chemical used to find where soil or water is on the pH scale.

Phosphor coating - internal bulb coating that diffuses light and is responsible for various color outputs.

Photoperiod - the relationship between the length of light and dark in a 24-hour period.

Photosynthesis - the building of chemical compounds (carbohydrates) from light energy, water and carbon dioxide.

Phototropism - the specific movement of a plant part toward a light source.

Pigment - The substance in paint or anything that absorbs light, producing (reflecting) the same color as the pigment.

Pollen - fine, yellow, dust-like microspores containing male genes.

Pod seed - a dry calyx containing a mature or maturing seed.

Pot-bound - bound, stifled or inhibited from normal growth, by the confines of a container: Root system become pot-bound.

Power surge - interruption or change in flow of electricity.

Primary nutrients- N-P-K.

Propagate - 1. Sexual - produce a seed by breeding different male and a female flowers 2. Asexual - to produce a plant by taking cuttings.

Prune - alter the shape and growth pattern of a plant by cutting stems and shoots.

PVC pipe - plastic (polyvinyl chloride) pipe that is easy to work with, readily available and used to pipe water into a garden room or make a watering wand.

Pyrethrum - natural insecticide made from the blossoms of various chrysanthemums: Raids' Pyrethrum is the most effective natural spider mite exterminator.

Rejuvenate - Restore youth: A mature plant, having completed its life cycle (flowering), may be stimulated by a new 18 hour photoperiod, to rejuvenate or produce new vegetative growth.

Root-bound - see POT BOUND.

Salt - crystalline compound that results from improper pH or toxic buildup of fertilizer. Salt will burn plants, preventing them from absorbing nutrients.

Secondary nutrients - calcium (Ca) and magnesium (Mg).

Short circuit - condition that results when wires cross and for m. a circuit. A short circuit will blow fuses.

Socket - threaded, wired holder for a bulb.

Soluble - able to be dissolved in water.

Spore - seed-like offspring of a fungus.

Sprout - 1. a recently germinated seed 2. small new growth of leaf or stem.

Square feet (sq. ft.) - length (in feet) times width equals square feet.

Staminate - male, pollen-producing.

Starch - complex carbohydrate: Starch is manufactured and stored food.

Sterilize - make sterile (super-clean) by removing dirt, germs and bacteria.

Stroboscopic effect - a quick pulsating or flashing of a lamp.

Stress - a physical or chemical factor that causes extra exertion by plants: A stressed plant will not grow as well as a non-stressed plant.

Stomata - small mouth-like or nose-like openings (pores) on leaf underside, responsible for transpiration and many other life functions: The millions of stomata, must be kept very clean to function properly.

Sugar - food product of a plant.

Super-bloom - a common name for fertilizer

high in phosphorus that promotes flower formation and growth

Synthesis - production of a substance, such as chlorophyll, by uniting light energy and elements or chemical compounds.

Sump - reservoir or receptacle that serves as a drain or holder for hydroponic nutrient solutions.

Tap root - the main or primary root that grows from the seed: Lateral roots will branch off the tap root.

Teflon tape - tape that is extremely useful to help seal all kinds of pipe joints. I like Teflon tape better than putty.

Tepid - warm 70 to 80° F (21 to 27° C). Always use tepid water around plants to facilitate chemical processes and ease shock.

Terminal bud - bud at the growing end of the main stem.

Thin - cull or weed out weak, slow growing seedlings.

Toxic life - the amount of time a pesticide or fungicide remains active or live.

Transformer - a devise in the ballast that transforms electric current from one voltage to another.

Transpire - give off water vapor and by products via the stomata.

Trellis - frame of small boards (lattice) that trains or supports plants.

True breed - see INBRED.

Tungsten - a heavy, hard metal with a high melting point which conducts electricity well: Tungsten is used for a filament in tungsten halogen lamps.

Ultraviolet - light with very short wave lengths, out of the visible spectrum.

Variety - strain, phenotype (see strain).

Vent - opening such as a window or door that allows the circulation of fresh air.

Ventilation - circulation of fresh air, fundamental to healthy indoor garden. An exhaust fan creates excellent ventilation.

Vertical - up and down perpendicular to the horizontal.

Wetting agent - compound that reduces the droplet size and lowers the surface tension of the water, making it wetter. Liquid concentrate dish soap is a good wetting agent if it is biodegradable.

Wick - part of a passive hydroponic system using a wick suspended in the nutrient solution, the nutrients pass up the wick and are absorbed by the medium and roots.

Index

Notes

Notes

Notes

Notes

Notes

Notes

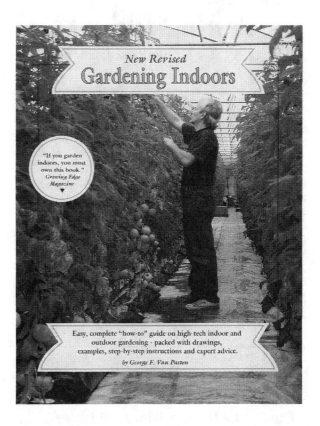